General Studies for Technicians

Hutchinson TEC texts

Learning by Objectives
A Teachers' Guide
A. D. Carroll, J. E. Duggan and R. Etchells

Engineering Drawing and Communication
First Level
P. Collier and R. Wilson

Physical Science
First Level
A. D. Carroll, J. E. Duggan and R. Etchells

Workshop Processes and Materials
First Level
P. Collier and B. Parkinson

Electronics
Second Level
G. Billups and M. T. Sampson

Engineering Drawing
Second Level
P. Collier and R. Wilson

Engineering Science
Second Level
D. Tipler, A. D. Carroll and R. Etchells

Mathematics
Second Level
G. W. Allan and A. Hill

Site Surveying and Levelling
Second Level
J. Pettet

Control of Manufacture
Third Level
W. Bolton

Electronics
Third Level
G. Billups and M. T. Sampson

Communication Skills
P. Panton

General Studies for Technicians
P. Denham, H. Bamforth and J. Derbyshire

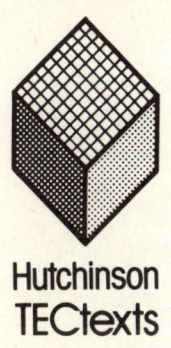

Hutchinson
TECtexts

General Studies for Technicians

P. Denham, H. Bamforth &
J. Derbyshire

Hutchinson
London Melbourne Sydney Auckland Johannesburg

Hutchinson & Co. (Publishers) Ltd
An imprint of the Hutchinson Publishing Group
17–21 Conway Street, London W1P 6JD

Hutchinson Group (Australia) Pty Ltd
30–32 Cremorne Street, Richmond South, Victoria 3121
PO Box 151, Broadway, New South Wales 2007

Hutchinson Group (NZ) Ltd
32–34 View Road, PO Box 40–086, Glenfield, Auckland 10

Hutchinson Group (SA) (Pty) Ltd
PO Box 337, Bergvlei 2012, South Africa

First published 1982
Reprinted with amendments 1983

Set in VIP Times by
D. P. Media Limited, Hitchin, Hertfordshire

Printed and bound in Great Britain by
Anchor Brendon Ltd, Tiptree, Essex

British Library Cataloguing in Publication Data
Denham, Paul
    General studies for technicians.
    1. Education, Humanistic
    I. Title II. Derbyshire, John
    III. Bamforth, Howard
    001'.02462   LT310

ISBN 0 09 145061 6

Contents

Acknowledgements

The authors and publisher are grateful to the following for their permission to reproduce textual material or illustrations:
Posy Simmonds, by permission of A. D. Peters & Co. Ltd., page 20; *Motorcycling: Begging for Credit* by Neil Millen, pages 80–2; HMSO: *How to put things right*, Office of Fair Trading, by permission of the Controller of HMSO, page 83; The Daimler-Benz Museum, page 89; BBC Hulton Picture Library, pages 90 and 108; The Council of the Institution of Mechanical Engineers: *Engineering Heritage, Volume II*, page 96; Dover Publications, Inc., page 97; Sean Sprague, Third World Photographs, page 107; Pluto Press: *The Hazards of Work* by Patrick Kinnersly, page 127; Les Gibbard, page 155; Bob R. W. Ruggles, page 157; *Womens Voice: Their law to keep their order*, page 165; Express Newspapers, page 177; Sidgwick & Jackson: *The Third World War: August 1985* by General Sir John Hackett and others, page 192.

Every effort has been made to reach copyright holders, but the publisher would be grateful to hear from any source whose copyright they may unwittingly have infringed.

The authors are especially grateful to all those who have provided inspiration and material for this book and, in particular, would like to thank their colleagues at Stockport College of Technology; David Lynch of Stoke-on-Trent Technical College, who was there at the beginning; and Diane Denham, without whose patience, encouragement and innumerable cups of coffee it would not have been written.

Introduction

'Let me explain,' the principal said patiently, '. . . the 1944 Education Act laid down that all apprentices should be released from their places of employment to attend day-release classes at technical college. . . . The courses they attend . . . are craft-orientated with the exception of one hour, one obligatory hour of liberal studies. Now the difficulty with liberal studies is that no one knows what it means.'

'Liberal studies means,' said Mrs Chatterway, '. . . providing socially deprived adolescents with a firm grounding in liberal attitudes and culturally extending topics. . . .'

'It means teaching them to read and write,' said a company director. 'It's no good having workers who can't read instructions.'

'It means whatever anyone chooses it to mean,' said the principal hastily. 'Now if you are faced with the problem of having to find lecturers who are prepared to spend their lives going into classrooms filled with gasfitters or plasterers or printers who see no good reason for being there, and keeping them occupied with a subject that does not, strictly speaking, exist, you cannot afford to pick and choose the sort of staff you employ.'

Tom Sharpe, *Wilt* (Pan 1978)

We do not entirely agree with any of these points of view, but they neatly sum up the central problem of *general studies for technicians*.

Most authorities – across the entire spectrum of education, government and industry – now accept that an unbalanced programme of technical training, designed solely to meet the immediate demands of industry, is unlikely to produce individuals who can competently and readily adapt to the changing conditions of modern life. But what kind of *general education* should technicians receive, and what do the students themselves want?

Over recent years traditional ideas about 'liberal studies' have been challenged and revised. A powerful force in this process has been the introduction of Technician Education Council (TEC) courses which incorporate a unit of general and communication studies. The aim of this subject is to offer an opportunity for study which both complements the vocational content of the student's programme and seeks to broaden his or her perspective. TEC recommends that the general and communication studies element should:

Comprise at least 15 per cent of the total course

Provide an educational experience that will be satisfying to the student

Be concerned (in approximately equal proportions) with the student's personal, social and vocational development

Thus, general and communication studies is *not* English, history, sociology, drama or philosophy (though it may contain elements of these and other subjects). *Nor* is it intended primarily to make you a 'better' engineer or electrician or chemist or surveyor, but obviously it is concerned with students who are engineers, electricians, etc. The technician's occupational 'role' as an employee is only part of a much wider network of personal and social relationships.

We see the aims of general studies as the development of your confidence and ability, in a wide range of situations, to:

Communicate and express yourself effectively

Think clearly and grasp new ideas

Use your own judgement to make the best decisions

Carry out independent research

Play the greatest possible part in organizing your activities

Co-operate with others to achieve your common aims

Enjoy mature and satisfying relationships

The purpose of this book is to assist and encourage you to investigate the modern world, and to think about those issues that are likely to concern you now and in the future. In this way we hope that you will not be merely a passive receiver of second-hand knowledge, but that you will produce your

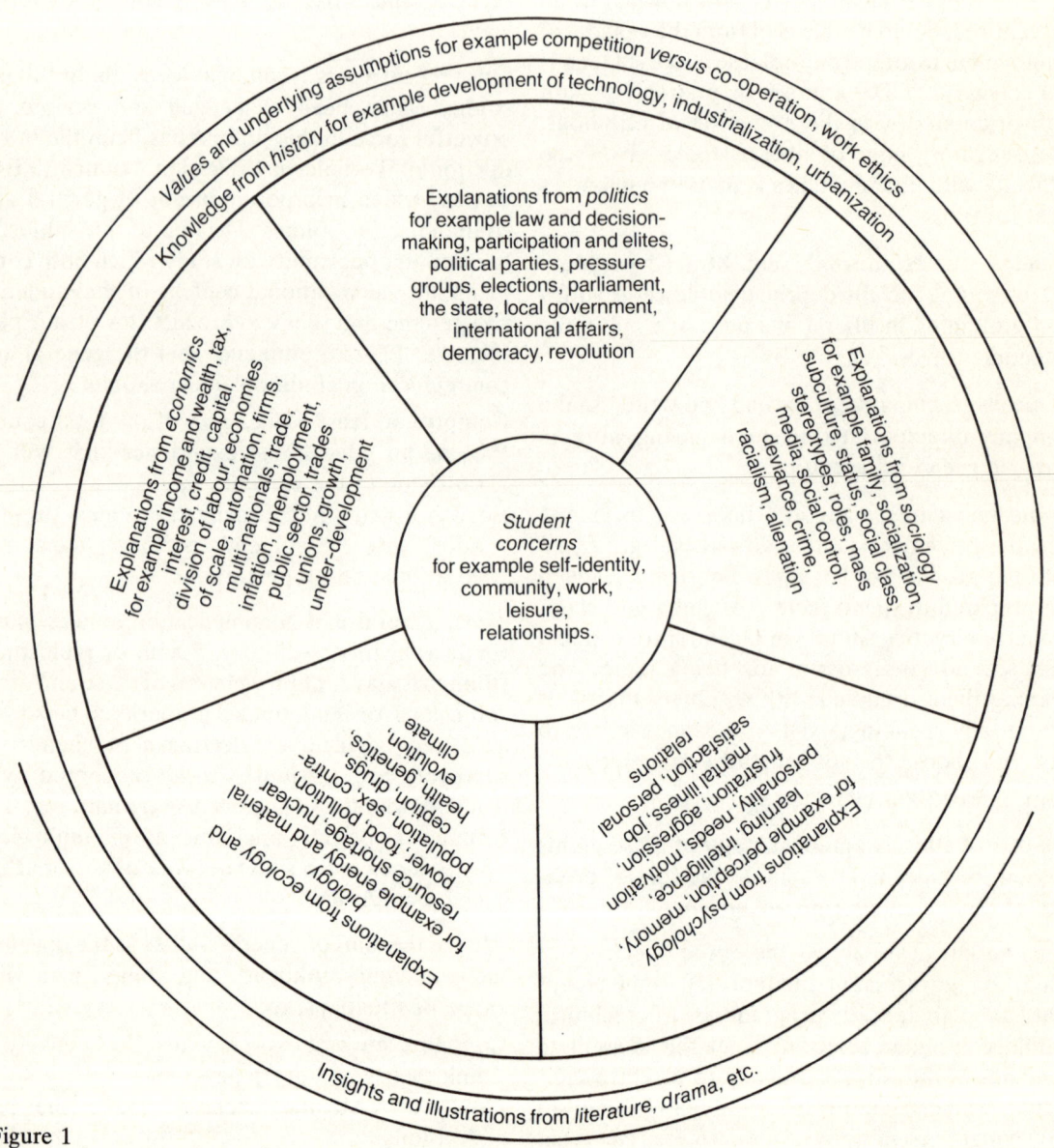

Figure 1

own insights and new perspectives. While the extent to which you can do this depends largely upon what you already know, everybody will be able to contribute something, however small. And whatever you get from general studies is likely to be in proportion to what you are prepared to put in.

Figure 1 shows what we think general studies is all about.

Paul Denham
Howard Bamforth
John Derbyshire

1 Mankind in time

The aim of this section is to help you to understand the time-scale of human evolution. You will be encouraged to consider the development of human skills and the major steps in man's progress from the level of intelligent apes towards the achievement of civilization.

Life on earth

All the planets and satellites in our solar system were formed more than 10,000 million years ago from a vast cloud of gas that used to surround the sun. For millions of years afterwards the planet earth was the scene of countless spectacular events: volcanic eruptions, earthquakes and lightning storms. But the most important events were happening slowly and undramatically in the shallow, muddy pools where the first forms of life would eventually appear.

Table 1 *The history of our planet: a comparative view*

Event	Approximate number of years ago	Comparative time: compressed into one year
Formation of first rocks	4,700,000,000	1 January
First primitive life in the oceans	3,000,000,000	13 May
Oxygen level in the atmosphere reaches 20 per cent; and earliest fish	500,000,000	23 November
Earliest land plants	430,000,000	28 November
Earliest insects	350,000,000	4 December
Earliest amphibians	300,000,000	8 December
Earliest land reptiles	250,000,000	12 December
The Age of the dinosaurs	200,000,000	16–24 December
Earliest birds and mammals	155,000,000	19 December
First primitive apes	40,000,000	28 December
First evidence of humans (*Homo habilis*)	3,000,000	6.25 p.m. 31 December
Modern man (*Homo sapiens sapiens*)	50,000	11.54 p.m. 31 December
End of last Ice Age in Britain	15,000	100 seconds to midnight
Invention of the wheel	5,500	37 seconds to midnight
Norman invasion of England	918	6.16 seconds to midnight
Colombus lands in the West Indies	492	3.30 seconds to midnight
James Watt's steam engine was built	202	1.36 seconds to midnight
Wright brothers' aeroplane was flown	81	0.54 seconds to midnight
First man on the moon	15	0.10 seconds to midnight
		midnight 31 December 1984

We will never know exactly how life first appeared, but one theory suggests that it started with chemical reaction in a hot, steamy atmosphere composed of hydrogen, methane, ammonia and water vapour. In 1953 a young American scientist called Miller set up a simple experiment to discover what would happen when lightning occurred in this kind of atmosphere. He used an electrical discharge to simulate lightning in a glass vessel containing water and the correct mixture of gases. After a few days he analysed the liquid in the flask and was surprised to find that the electrical discharge had caused the gases to react together to form *amino acids* (the building-blocks of protein that are important constituents of all living cells).

$$
\text{methane} \quad = \quad \begin{array}{c} H \\ | \\ H-C-H \\ | \\ H \end{array}
$$

$$
\text{ammonia} \quad = \quad H-N \big\langle \begin{array}{c} H \\ H \end{array}
$$

$$
\text{water} \quad = \quad H-O-H
$$

$$
\text{hydrogen} \quad = \quad H
$$

Alanine is one of the simplest of the twenty different amino acids that make up protein molecules.

$$
\begin{array}{c}
H \\
| \\
H-C-H \\
| \quad\quad H \\
H-C-N\big\langle \\
| \quad\quad H \\
\;\;\; C-O-H \\
\diagup \\
O
\end{array}
$$

In recent years a new theory has emerged which suggests that the primitive atmosphere consisted of carbon dioxide, water vapour, nitrogen and traces of other gases. The experiments were repeated using this mixture and, once again, amino acids were produced.

So these theories suggest that proteins and other complex long-chain molecules were synthesized from simple gases under the influence of lightning and/or ultra-violet radiation from the sun. They gradually accumulated in warm pools where this 'primeval soup' became more concentrated. Some of the complex chemicals congealed to form primitive living cells which were able to grow and multiply by absorbing simpler chemicals from the surrounding liquid.

The cells of all organisms on the planet contain a substance known as DNA (deoxyribonucleic acid) – evidence of a single origin for all life four billion years ago. DNA is the means by which genetic instructions are passed on from generation to generation. One molecule of DNA consists of two long strands, twisted together into a double helix. Each strand is made up of four different chemical units known as nucleotide bases, joined end-to-end in a long chain. The exact sequence forms a code which the cell can 'read' to provide instructions for the production of the correct proteins for the development of the cell.

Each nucleotide base is linked by a weak bond to a complementary base in the other strand. The complete DNA molecule comprises several thousand base-pairs. See Figure 2.

It is possible for the cell to make precise copies of its DNA by a process known as *replication*. During this process the weak links between the strands are broken one by one and the double helix begins to unravel from one end. The surrounding solution contains thousands of free bases which become linked to the unpaired bases in the strands according to simple bond-pairing rules – adenine can only be linked with thymine, and guanine with cytosine.

The newly aligned bases can now become permanently joined end-to-end to form new strands as the unzipping proceeds along the molecule. When the replication is complete, the cell contains two molecules of DNA (each identical to the original). The cell can now divide to produce two cells, each containing a full set of genetic information.

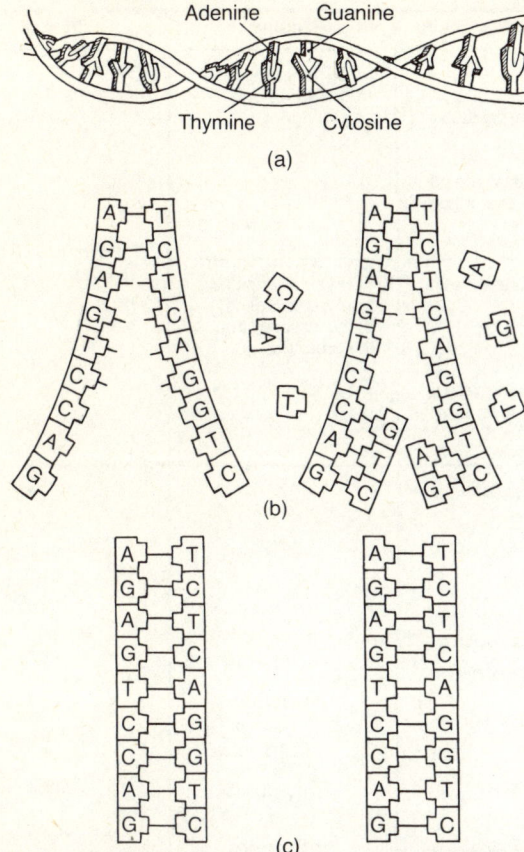

Figure 2 *The replication of DNA. The bases are shown fitting together like building blocks, but in fact their bond is chemical. The number of possible 'messages' even in a tiny segment of DNA is staggering: with the fifteen pairs of positions, there could be over a thousand million combinations*

Some cells were able to stay joined together after cell division, eventually forming a multi-cellular organism in which each cell took on its own distinct function.

Over a period of time some cells developed the ability to produce complex chemicals from simpler substances using the energy of sunlight (photosynthesis). A by-product of this process is oxygen.

These were the first stages in the process of evolution. About seventy million years ago, while dinosaurs were on the verge of extinction, another evolutionary branch had produced the first mammals. Some of these creatures were to develop into the most advanced organisms on the planet – *homo sapiens sapiens*.

The arrival of man

Man first appeared on earth about three million years ago, in the form of a species known as *homo habilis*. We are, therefore, a very recent arrival. Our impact on the planet during this relatively short time is really quite remarkable, especially when you consider the limitation of the earth's surface. When you add the frequent changes of climate and the hazards of a wide range of bacteria, viruses, fungi, insects and animals, it may seem surprising that mankind has survived at all.

On the other hand, the sheer scale, variety and complexity of these problems probably assisted man to attain dominance, for he proved to be the supreme adapter. Mankind was the life-form that could step into any environmental niche, whether Arctic snows, steaming swamp lands or arid deserts, and exploit its potential. Ultimately, man began to manipulate the environment to his own advantage.

The development of human skills (see Table 2)

Power grip and precision grip

Self-assessment questions

1 List the various ways in which you use both these grips in your everyday life and work.

2 Try to perform one of the tasks from your 'precision grip' list *without using your thumbs*.

Stereoscopic vision

Self-assessment question

3 Keep one eye closed and try to perform a precision manual task such as drawing a 29 millimetre equilateral triangle or lacing up your shoe. You will find that this is more difficult than usual because your ability to judge distance is impaired.

Years ago	Species Brain Size(cc average)	Habitat, Locomotion and Way of Life	Feeding	Period
25,000,000	*Dryopithecus* ? cc ape	Forests. Tree-top habitat away from predators. Brachiation: swinging from branch to branch. Walked on all fours when on the ground: quadrupedal locomotion.	Food gathering (fruits from trees).	Pre-human
12,000,000	*Ramapithecus* ape ? cc	Forest fringe, near open grassland. Lived in trees, but later species adapted to open grassland. Gradual change from quadrupedal to bipedal locomotion: walking upright on two legs.	Food gathering (fruits from trees. Seeds, bulbs, grasses from the ground).	
3,000,000	*Homo habilis* skilful man 750 cc	Open grassland near lakes or rivers. Bipedal locomotion.	Hunting and food gathering.	Old Stone Age (Palaeolithic Period)
1,000,000	*Homo erectus* upright man 1000 cc	Open grassland near lakes or rivers.		
500,000	*Homo sapiens* wise man 1300 cc	Nomadic tribes. Some cave dwelling.		
50,000	*Homo sapiens sapiens* 1400 cc modern man	Nomadic tribes. Some cave dwelling. Some permanent settlements, especially on lake-shores and sea-shores.	Advanced hunting, food gathering and fishing.	Middle Stone Age (Mesolithic Period)
10,000		Farming villages. Permanent settlements.	Subsistence farming, cultivation, stock-rearing.	New Stone Age (Neolithic Period)
5,500 present		Towns and cities, supported by agricultural surplus. Development of civilization. Growth of industry.	More productive farming. Agricultural surplus.	Bronze Age, Iron Age, Roman Empire, Dark Ages, Middle Ages, Renaissance, Industrial Period

Table 2

Technology	Notes
No evidence.	Characteristics of tree-dwelling apes: 1 A grasping hand with 'power grip' for holding on to tree branches. 2 Two front-set eyes with stereoscopic vision; allowed accurate judgement of distance when swinging from branch to branch. 3 Fast reactions and good co-ordination. Humans have inherited all these characteristics, but we have found other ways of using them!
No definite evidence of tool-using or tool-making. Might have *used* simple tools (for example sticks and stones) even if unable to modify natural materials to *make* tools.	Climatic changes turned large areas of forest into open grassland: Savanna. The new environment encouraged the survival of bipeds: 1 They could see above the long grass. 2 Their hands were free to carry their young. 3 They could carry food, and weapons of defence. 4 They could carry tools, for example digging sticks to help them find food. 5 They could use their hands to explore the resources of their surroundings.
Simple tool-making. Roughly-chipped stones. Roughly-shaped bones and wood.	The development of human characteristics: *Brain* 1 Receives and interprets information from all the senses. 2 Controls the actions of the body. 3 Stores knowledge and experiences. 4 Solves problems. 5 Designs tools, machines, processes, etc.
Use of fire: cooking; heating; light; protection from predators; hardening spear points. Wooden spear: wooden point sharpened with a stone knife and hardened by fire. Stone hand-axe: an all-purpose tool for cutting, scraping and digging. Made by removing flakes from a block of flint by hammering.	*Eyes* Stereoscopic vision: judgement of distance and depth. *Hands* Precision grip: 1 Man evolved with a long 'opposable' thumb which can meet the tip of the index finger in a delicate grip. 2 Man's advanced brain and nervous system can co-ordinate fine movements precisely. Power grip: 1 Relies on the strong grasp of long fingers. 2 Makes little use of the thumb. ape's hand man's hand power grip precision grip
Composite tools: flint-tipped spear; harpoon; bow and arrow; spear thrower; fishing tackle; bow-drill. Stone tools for working wood and bone.	*Communication* Man can communicate complex ideas through speech, drawing and writing: depends on advanced co-ordination between brain, mouth, eyes, ears and hands.
Ground and polished stone tools: hoe and sickle; spindle and loom for cloth making; tools for pottery and basket-making.	*Social groups* Living and working in groups allows large-scale achievements which individuals could not accomplish alone. *Transmission of culture* Man can pass on his skills, knowledge and way of life from one generation to the next.
Metal tools and weapons. Exploitation of a wider range of natural resources (materials and energy) on an increasingly large scale.	*Adaptability* Man's body and brain are not restricted to special situations such as swimming or flying; man can adapt to most environments, often with the aid of his technology.

Early technology

Self-assessment questions

4   Find drawings and photographs of Stone Age tools and weapons.

5   Visit museums to examine original specimens.

6   Find out from your local library how and when they were made.

7   Compare these skills and techniques with those of today's craftsmen.

The rise of the naked ape

Many creatures have superior physical characteristics to humans, for example the speed of the deer, strength of the ox, sight of the eagle, etc., but none of these creatures has such a well-balanced package of abilities. The behaviour of man is determined by genetic instructions, 'pre-wired' into our nervous systems before birth, to a far lesser extent than other organisms. Young humans are dependent upon their adult guardians, relative to our lifespan, far longer than any other species and this period of immense 'plasticity' has given us the greatest capacity for learning new behaviour and adapting to the environment.

Tool using was the most important stage in the accelerated pace of human development compared with other life-forms. It was both a cause and effect of our walking on two legs. In common with many other species, man had already developed a language composed of gestures (for example averting eyes and baring teeth). Some form of communication was an absolute necessity for co-operative hunting. However, with his hands free, man was able to extend this system of gestures and signals, and then to supplement and eventually replace this means of communication with spoken language.

The growing capacity of the human brain that enabled the creation of a verbal language also permitted greater scope for abstract thinking. Once learnt, a lesson stayed remembered and did not need to be mastered again when the same problem or situation was encountered. While birds, beavers, spiders, bees and ants may be said to 'work' when they build nests, dams, webs, and hives, their activities are for the most part instinctual. Man's work, on the other hand, is conscious and performed with a purpose. As Karl Marx said, 'The bee puts to shame many an architect in the construction of her cells, but what distinguishes the worst architect from the best of bees . . . is that the architect raises his structure in his imagination before he erects it in reality.' Man has been able to build on the labour, knowledge and experience of past generations.

The manufacture and use of simple tools made a new life-style possible. Gradually humans began to experiment with new materials: flint, clay and pigments. They began to think of matters other than the immediate essentials of survival. One early consequence of man's skill to anticipate the future was the widespread development of burial rituals. According to Carl Sagan, 'Man is probably the only organism on earth with a relatively clear view of the inevitability of his own end.'

Each of these stages was slow, but the process of solving one problem inevitably gave rise to new questions and the gradual acquisition of practical knowledge. Early man, living in small groups, made a meagre living by hunting and foraging: following the herds of wild animals; collecting berries, nuts and roots; and using fire to cook the fish he caught. The invention of the bow and arrow and the net greatly increased the productiveness of these activities.

The appearance of agriculture

In the fertile valleys of the Near East about 10,000 years ago a fundamental step took place: the domestication of animals and the planned growth of crops. Man no longer needed to rely on the foodstuffs that nature provided; from this point man could increase the productivity of nature through his own activity. The development of agriculture was associated with greater *specialization* of activities within society.

Segregation of sexes

The first 'division of labour' was between the sexes. In many groups women were in charge of the settlement, preparing food and clothing and making domestic utensils (for example pottery). Men's activities usually lay outside the home: hunting, fishing, and providing raw materials for simple tools. The 'pairing' of males and females for short or long periods developed out of earlier forms of group marriage. However, the development of agriculture changed the relationship between men and women. Although the primitive cultivation of crops and cereals was carried out around the settlement by women, the greatest progress was made in the taming and breeding of animals. It was the men who tended the herds of cattle and sheep, and their increased importance as producers of food assisted them asserting their dominance over their women at home. With the growth of private wealth in livestock came the spread of monogamous marriages as men were determined to pass on their possessions only to their own children.

The first farmers

Those groups that turned to pastoral farming were able to produce more and a greater variety of products, for example meat, milk, skins, wool, etc. This encouraged trading between tribes and the spreading of handicraft production. As knowledge and technology improved, agriculture became more productive and groups were able to produce more food than they needed for their own survival. This enabled some members of the group to give up farming and live on the surplus food their neighbours provided, as long as they could give them handicrafts or services in return. Over the years, the number of non-farming specialists grew to include wood and metal-workers, builders, weavers, soldiers and priests. The activities of the merchants who handled trade between producers were helped by the use of metal coins. Before the introduction of metal coins, cattle had been used as 'money'.

Self-assessment questions

8 Make a fuller list of specialist workers who might have been found in Ancient Mesopotamia, Egypt, Greece or Rome.
9 Describe what handicraft or service each worker would be able to provide to the farmers in return for their surplus food.

Tribal warfare

Disputes between tribes were often settled in battle. With increasing wealth, plunder became an additional reason for war, so tribes built wooden stockades around their farmsteads. Instead of killing their captives they employed them in the fields and workshops.

The growth of towns and cities

Men and women lived together in family groups which eventually became large tribes. Most of their property – huts, boats, land – was shared between them. There was a gradual process of amalgamation of tribes and their territories during which land was assigned to individual families. Pastoral farming was nomadic, but crop growing required permanent settlement. While farmers needed large areas of land around their homes, non-farming specialists were able to live in densely-populated settlements. The settlements began to develop as trading centres and walls were built around them to protect their wealth.

As a result of specialization, some families accumulated more wealth than others and so conflicts arose between the different tribes, the rich and the poor, farmers and town dwellers, and free men and slaves. A force was needed, therefore, to mediate when conflicts occurred and to moderate them. At first the urban settlements were governed by popular assemblies of citizens which elected their civic leaders and military commanders, but slowly these were replaced by hereditary succession and 'kings' appeared. An armed force was needed not only to restrain citizens but also to protect them from external enemies and, consequently, taxes were required to support it. When the same individual filled the roles of both king and priest, his authority was given divine reinforcement. The king's servants, who administered the *surplus production* of society, were the first group to have sufficient leisure time to develop the arts, crafts and scientific knowledge that we call *civilization*.

The first cities, the wheel and primitive writing made their appearance at about the same time, about 5500 years ago in Sumeria. A system of word-pictures (hieroglyphics) was created to keep records of commercial transactions, historical events and codes of law. Eventually pictograph writing was replaced by the more flexible alphabet system where letters represent sounds. At the same time units were developed to measure area, weight and time (for example plots of land, sacks of wheat, and the times for sowing and harvest). Writing was not only a powerful new means of communication; it also allowed people to store knowledge outside their bodies for the first time.

Self-assessment questions

10 Figure 3 has been simplified for reasons of clarity. What other connections or new factors would you add to make it more complete?

11 How is our society different from/similar to the economic unit shown in Figure 3?

12 Suggest possible reasons why some families became wealthier than others during the early development of civilization.

13 Make a list of the physical features of the environment that you would expect to find in an area where early civilizations appeared.

14 What was the part played by slave-labour in this system? Why did slavery only appear when the productivity of agriculture had exceeded the subsistence level (that is, when society could produce a food surplus)?

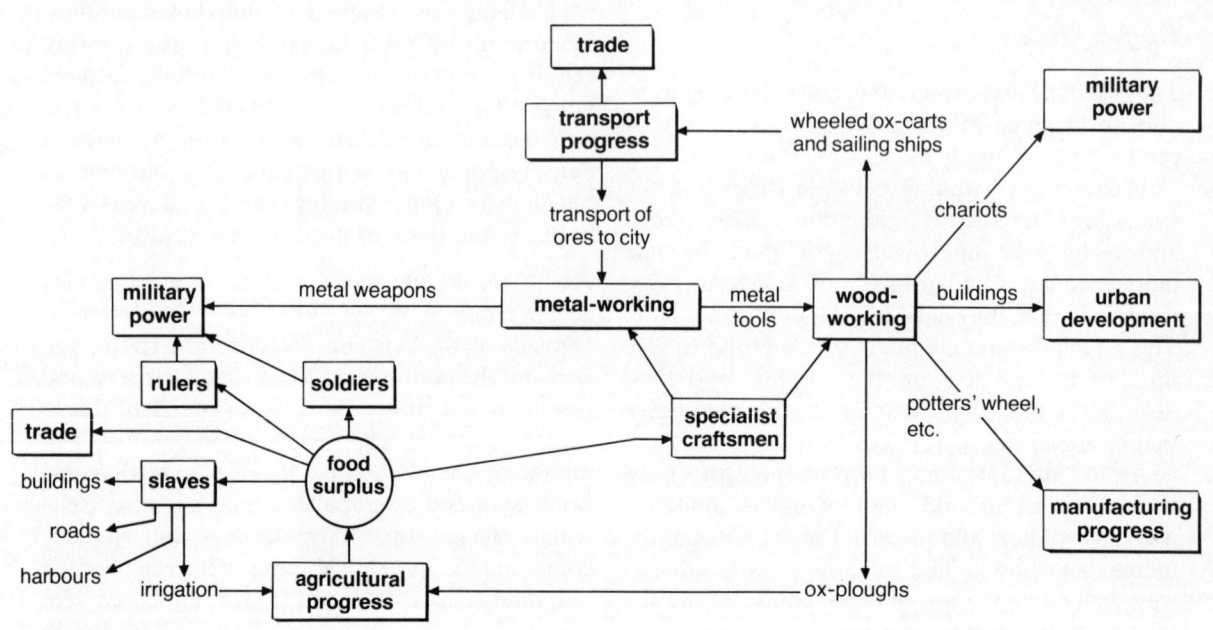

Figure 3   *The origins of civilization: a Bronze Age City in the Near East,* circa *3500 BC*

The development of civilization

Civilizations appeared 'spontaneously' in many parts of the globe, although the scale and pace of their development were influenced by such factors as climate and isolation. A number of distinct 'cradles of civilization' have been identified.

Each of the advanced areas shown in Figure 4 – with their metal-working, pottery, writing, sculpture, irrigation and brick or stone-built cities – acted as the springboards for development elsewhere. Western Europe can trace its heritage from Ancient Greece and Rome which in turn drew elements from the Middle East and Northern India.

In a number of instances, civilizations of great complexity were achieved which then collapsed from within – this could have happened in the case of the Maya Indians of Yucatan and the mysterious founders of Zimbabwe. Others went into decline and their development was terminated by conquest, for example Egyptian, Roman, Aztec and Inca civilizations. Sometimes features of the old civilization were incorporated into the society established by the conquerors but often almost everything was destroyed and lost forever.

In some areas, however, the process of development was halted at a very early stage by internal stagnation, for example the Amazon basin, Arctic wastes, Australasia, parts of Africa and North America. When colonists encountered the Plains Indians in the early nineteenth century they found them at a level of development similar to Europe during the early Neolithic period (New Stone Age). In remote parts of the world, the nomad and the hunter–gatherer can still be found though pressures from the modern world mean a constant dwindling of their numbers.

Self-assessment questions

15 Why did certain areas get 'stuck' at a primitive stage of development? Were these people 'less intelligent' or did they merely lack the stimulus that prompted others to progress?

16 What kinds of forces stimulate innovation and change?

17 Is a 'civilized' society always better than a 'primitive' society? In every respect?

18 Why do 'empires' stagnate and decline? What are the symptoms of this process?

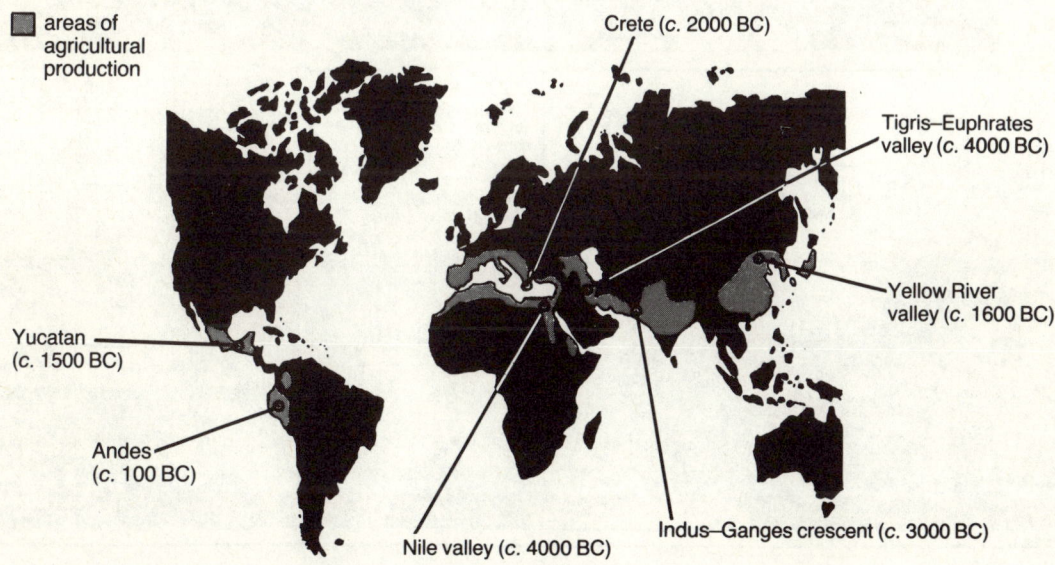

Figure 4 *Areas of advanced civilization*

2 Knowledge and ideas

The aim of this section is to explain the part played by theories and questioning in the development of human knowledge. You will be encouraged to consider some factors that hinder logical thinking and the relationship between ideas and change.

Figure 5

What is reality?

People who awake suddenly from a dream often experience a temporary period of disorientation while they work out what is 'real'. How do we *know* that our dream–fantasies are 'unreal' in comparison with the alarm of the bedside clock? What is the ability that enables us to distinguish between the reality of a TV news item and the artificial nature of drama? The fact that we do not constantly ask ourselves these kinds of questions is because, for the most part, reality is taken for granted. It's common sense, isn't it?

Imagine two people standing in the same place and gazing in the same direction. We may assume that they both receive the same visual stimuli. However, we cannot be sure that they perceive the same things – one may be colour blind, or under the influence of a psychedelic drug. Similarly, are we ever sure where perception ends and interpretation begins? The sight of a dog conveys a different meaning depending upon whether the observer is frightened of dogs, or if the dog is a faithful family pet. But that does not imply that we can see anything that we please. The ideas in our heads are created by using visual and other information from the material world in which we live.

Our impression of the world outside our bodies is organized around the idea of *here and now*, the time and space zone that is within reach or accessible to us. Our thinking is primarily concerned with central interests such as work and home, while our interest in far zones is less intense and urgent. You may like to think about cowboys and indians or what is happening in outer space, but this interest is a matter of private, 'leisure-time' choice rather than an immediate necessity of your everyday life.

You obviously share the world with other people who organize their perceptions around their own here and now. You also know that they have a perspective on this common world that is not identical with yours. Your 'here' is my 'there' and our 'nows' do not fully overlap. Nevertheless, there is a close similarity between the meanings that you and other people give to the shared world. *Common sense* is the knowledge that we share with others in the normal, self-evident routines of everyday life. While we take for granted the reality of our 'here and now', problems arise when we encounter areas of the world outside our experience.

Mental models

Each person has a mental picture of what the 'world out there' is like. This picture is shaped by two factors: our own personal experience and the access that we have to the experience of others. For centuries we acquired knowledge by *education*, but today there is another source that assumes an ever increasing importance. The *mass media* have created a nation of people who have opinions on just about every subject. We have mental pictures of places we have never visited, people we have never met, and events we have seen only as tiny images on a TV screen.

Our mental image or 'map' of the world is quite detailed in some areas, but only a rough sketch in others. Human psychology seems to demand that the general outline that we have acquired for ourselves through experience be filled in with details, and we use what we are taught by our parents, schools, friends, and mass media for that purpose. Often what we end up with are *stereotypes*.

Stereotypes

A stereotype is an over-simplified idea of something based on limited experience. For example, between the age of six and ten Graham lived in a street where there was a Polish family. This particular family was unable to keep a tidy house and garden, and people in the street used to talk about 'those scruffy Poles'. From this limited experience Graham generalized that all people from Poland were dirtier than British people. Graham never went to Poland, had never met any other Poles, and did little reading. When he married and had children he still made occasional remarks about 'scruffy Poles'. Graham's children also grew up believing that Poles were dirtier than British people.

It is a convenient mental device to apply the qualities of a small sample to an entire group because this helps us to deal with the vast amount of reality that we can never know in detail. The problem is that most stereotypes contain only a kernel of truth, and so are dangerous if taken to be the whole truth. Everyone holds some stereotypes because they give us a sense of security, a feeling that something complex is understood, and provide the illusion that we know our way around in strange territory. When our stereotypes are challenged we often consider that we are being personally attacked and vigorously defend these ideas.

The tendency is for the media to strengthen stereotypes rather than replace commonly-held images with a fuller picture. TV, for example, often shows 'cardboard characters' (people whose personalities are not developed in the plot). These characters – such as the dumb blonde secretary, the tough copper, the nagging wife – are easily recognized by viewers and can be used for laughs or instant plot development. The constant repetition of such characters tends to condition viewers to expect blonde secretaries to be dim, policemen to be tough, etc. People who belong to groups that are frequently stereotyped may find it difficult to overcome media-created expectations in others.

Self-assessment questions

1   Here are some groups that are part of the national store of stereotypes drawn upon by the TV and mass circulation newspapers. Choose a few of them, or any examples that you have thought of, and describe the main features of the stereotype.

Americans	mothers-in-law
Asians	motor-cyclists
civil servants	shop stewards
hippies	women's liberationists
homosexuals	vicars
Irishmen	overweight people

2   Are any of these groups unfairly stereotyped?

3   Choose a group that you belong to that is the target of occasional stereotyping and argue why you think it to be false.

4   What mental image do you think people in Western Europe or Russia, Japan or the USA have of the British, for example: polite, lazy, old fashioned, violent, etc?

Facts and values

What passes for knowledge in any group consists of two elements, and most situations must be understood in terms of both.

Values and language

There is no Berlin Wall between facts and values. In practice it is often difficult to identify which of our ideas are opinions and which are not. One

Table 3

Facts (cognitive statements)	*Values* (normative statements)
Simple descriptions	Opinions
Statements of what 'is' or 'was' or 'will be'	Evaluations of what is 'good' or 'bad'
	Statements of what 'ought' to be
	Moral judgements of what is 'right' or 'wrong'
Examples	*Examples*
This rose is red	I prefer roses to daffodils
Mercury expands when warmed and contracts when cooled	Young hooligans should be flogged
West Ham won the FA Cup in 1980	The Rolling Stones are the best rock band in the world

reason is that the language we use to express our ideas actually incorporates values. Words like 'vandal', 'scrounger', and 'massacre' are *not neutral*: they produce an emotional response arising from the images that we have previously learned to associate with them.

Self-assessment question

5 Look at the following ways of describing the same things

                    terrorist – freedom fighter
            overseas visitor – alien
                     execute – murder
            security service – secret police
                        drunk – merry
                        blunt – rude
                          mad – eccentric

Can you think of any more word-pairs that suggest favourable and unfavourable images? List as many as you can.

A further factor that prevents the separation of facts and values is that we do not attribute equal weight or significance to all the facts that we know. The facts rarely 'speak for themselves'. It is up to us to speak for them. The way that we present the facts will be influenced by our objectives.

Self-assessment question

6 There is a great 'pool' of facts about the Nazi concentration camps, and different accounts would be selected by:
   (a) A war criminal defending himself in court
   (b) A camp survivor giving evidence against him
   (c) A priest writing a sermon about hatred
   How do you think each person would decide:
   (i) What constitutes an important fact;
   (ii) How the facts should fit together into a pattern; and
   (iii) The way in which this knowledge is presented?

Remember: A fact is like a sack – it won't stand up until you put something in it!

Today, the term *propaganda* has unpleasant associations with totalitarian regimes that use their control of the mass media to distort the truth and manipulate the population. Not all forms of propaganda, however, are so sinister. The term really covers all the ways of presenting information so that it is likely to convince and persuade others.

Self-assessment questions

7 Find examples of good and bad propaganda.
8 What do 'good' and 'bad' mean in this context?
9 Are the following statements fact or value?
   (i) There are too many immigrants in this country.
   (ii) Marsupials carry their young in a pouch.
   (iii) The sun orbits the earth every twenty-four hours.
   (iv) Cigarettes can seriously damage your health.
   (v) Abortion is murder.
   (vi) Men are superior to women.

Suppose that we agree with the first statement and you don't. How could we decide who is right? First, of course, we would need to agree what is meant by the terms 'immigrant' and 'country'. Then we could establish the precise number of people in question – which requires that we agree to accept the same statistical evidence as valid. But this still does not bring us any nearer to a verdict because there is no measure of 'too many' that is independent of someone's personal opinion.

On the other hand, it is worthwhile to ask whether factual statements are true or false. There are two kinds of factual statement to consider. Some statements are merely definitions that refer to a general agreement in our community about what something means. Thus, marsupial *means* a mammal that carries its young in pouch. No one can deny this as long as we continue to classify species in this way. In everyday argument, we often construct sentences in such a way that they have a *built-in irrefutability*. For instance, the statement 'all patriots support this policy' is true if we define a patriot as someone who supports the policy.

A different kind of factual statement is one that makes an assertion about the world that can be investigated. Despite appearances, we now know that the sun does not orbit our planet. Until comparatively recently, however, most people believed that it did and the authorities went to great lengths to suppress any individuals who challenged this 'fact'. In 1616 the Church forbade anyone, on pain of death, to teach that the earth was not the centre of the universe. There are many more cases like the examples above where yesterday's heresies have become today's conventions.

Ways of thinking

How can we be sure that our mental models are the closest possible approximations to reality? One way is to observe the outside world as *objectively* as possible; that is, to minimize the personal (or 'subjective') factors arising from our own values and prejudices that get in the way and distort our observations.

Accurate observations are insufficient on their own: a process of *logical* thinking is required to make sense of them. We are more likely to think logically if we progress from one point to another by the established rules of rational argument. Table 4 shows two ways.

Table 4

Inductive reasoning	*Deductive reasoning*
Here we start with a large but limited number of observations from which we infer *generalizations* (that is universal statements or principles that summarize the observations).	Here we start with a *premise*: preferably a statement of truth that is so obvious and acceptable to everybody that it does not need proof. From one or more premises, we can deduce conclusions of a more limited nature.
Example From separate observations that air, hydrogen, carbon dioxide, ammonia, etc. expand when heated, we may conclude that '*all* gases expand when their temperature rises'.	*Example* We *know* that the efficiency of an abrasive depends upon its hardness and that carborundum is harder than talc. We may *conclude*, therefore, that carborundum is a better abrasive than talc.
But beware You should not generalize from a limited sample. Just because my Italian car is rusty, it doesn't follow that all Italian vehicles corrode easily.	*But beware* The premise may be wrong. 'All cats eat fish. Harry is my cat. Therefore Harry eats fish.' (But he won't!) A valid conclusion may still be deduced from a false premise.
Your observations may be accurate but your conclusion may be false. Just because you become drunk after consuming whisky and water, or gin and water, or rum and water, it does not follow that water is the intoxicating ingredient.	Your conclusion may be too sweeping (that is, it may go beyond the premise). For instance, we cannot say that carborundum is a better ingredient than talc in toilet powder.
Try this You observe that stones, coins and pieces of iron all sink in a pool of water, but that wood, oil and paper float. What general principal can you infer?	*Try this* Given time, you know that fairly pure water freezes at about 0°C. Your car radiator contains fairly pure water. What do you conclude will happen during a cold winter night?

Probability

According to inductive reasoning, if a large number of As are observed under a wide variety of conditions and without exception to possess property B, then we may safely conclude that all As have property B. Safely concluded but not guaranteed. Despite all past experience, it is conceivable that one day we may come across a stone that doesn't sink in the pool, or a pig that flies. Still, the greater the number of observations that form the basis of our conclusion, the greater are the chances that it is probably true.

Similarly, when a doctor says that 'nearly everyone given penicillin for a sore throat recovers quite quickly', he is not predicting with certainty what will happen in your particular case. Rather, he is talking in terms of probability (that is, some or 90 per cent of As have property B).

Cause and effect

We are frequently concerned to explain *why* something happens. We generally do this by reconstructing a chain of events in terms of cause and effect (for example, I am late *because* the bus broke down). If we discover that a particular event always occurs before a certain phenomenon with which it is associated, we may assume that the former event causes the latter (for example, whenever I eat liver, I feel sick).

One problem with causal explanations is that they imply that the effect was an inevitable consequence. I may say that a patch of ice 'caused' my car to skid, but this only happened because I was driving too fast for the road conditions. Moreover, the connection between two events may be purely coincidental or be caused by some third factor (for example, my alarm clock invariably rings before the newspaper is delivered, but it does not cause it to happen).

Quantitative and qualitative change

Which comes first, the chicken or the egg?

As long as we assume that things do not change,

this old puzzle is insoluble. Once we see it in the light of knowledge about the evolution of egg-laying creatures, it becomes answerable.

During its life-cycle, the butterfly goes through several stages of growth (egg, caterpillar, chrysalis, etc.). At particular junctures, simple growth gives way to fundamental change. In society it is not always so easy to recognize when a qualitative change has occurred. When does an ageing car become a pile of scrap? When does a friendship turn into hostility? When does democracy become a tyranny? When does a good idea become obsolete?

Theories

Just as you use stereotypes to help you understand the social world, scientists and technologists employ their own mental models to assist them explain, predict and control the natural world. These models are called *theories*.

We cannot see molecules or magnetic fields or electric currents: only the movements of iron filings and galvanometer needles. Thus, when we say that 'molecules of gas behave like tiny elastic billiard balls in random motion', we are using a theory to describe the activities of particles that we cannot observe.

Many people are sceptical about theories, associating them with idle speculation and flights of fancy. They say that it is important to get at the facts without being influenced by preconceived ideas. Yet sceptics would not have much confidence in a mechanic, called to tackle the problem of why their car won't start, who says, 'perhaps your car is angry or your neighbour has cast a spell on it'. Everyone expects a mechanic to make a reasonable assumption about what to look for and what to ignore: that is, to have a theory about what causes starting problems.

A mechanic's theory may derive from his own experience and intuition, technical manuals, attending college, etc. It will consist of a series of possible causes of non-starting, ranked in order of probability. If he believes that damp plugs are the most likely cause, he has a means of *testing* the theory by cleaning or replacing them. Should the car then start, he has *confirmed* his theory by applying it in practice. If, on the other hand, the car still won't start, he must *modify* his theory and try again (for example, by checking the fuel-gauge or charging the battery). At the end of the day he may even *reject* his theory completely and conclude that the vehicle really has been bewitched!

Scientific method

Or a 'model' of how scientists develop knowledge.

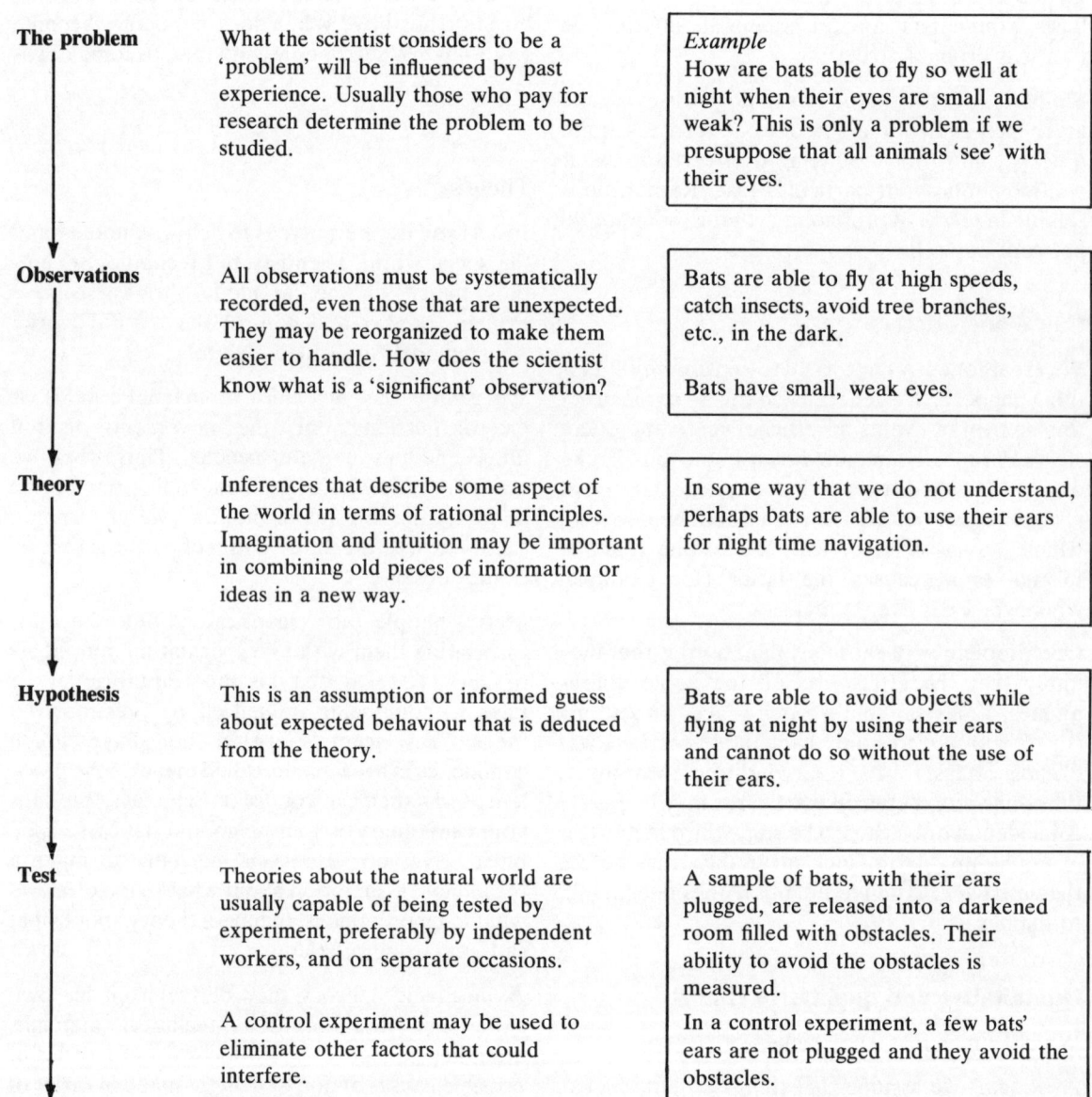

The problem

What the scientist considers to be a 'problem' will be influenced by past experience. Usually those who pay for research determine the problem to be studied.

Example
How are bats able to fly so well at night when their eyes are small and weak? This is only a problem if we presuppose that all animals 'see' with their eyes.

Observations

All observations must be systematically recorded, even those that are unexpected. They may be reorganized to make them easier to handle. How does the scientist know what is a 'significant' observation?

Bats are able to fly at high speeds, catch insects, avoid tree branches, etc., in the dark.

Bats have small, weak eyes.

Theory

Inferences that describe some aspect of the world in terms of rational principles. Imagination and intuition may be important in combining old pieces of information or ideas in a new way.

In some way that we do not understand, perhaps bats are able to use their ears for night time navigation.

Hypothesis

This is an assumption or informed guess about expected behaviour that is deduced from the theory.

Bats are able to avoid objects while flying at night by using their ears and cannot do so without the use of their ears.

Test

Theories about the natural world are usually capable of being tested by experiment, preferably by independent workers, and on separate occasions.

A control experiment may be used to eliminate other factors that could interfere.

A sample of bats, with their ears plugged, are released into a darkened room filled with obstacles. Their ability to avoid the obstacles is measured.

In a control experiment, a few bats' ears are not plugged and they avoid the obstacles.

Tentative acceptance

Scientists gather facts and perform experiments with the aim of falsifying their hypothesis. If this cannot be done, the theory is accepted as valid rather than true. Dalton's atomic theory, for example, could not be properly tested for over a century. His theory was provisionally accepted, however, pending further experimental evidence.

The hypothesis has not been disproved but may still be improved. It can be made more precise by modification to say that bats hear echoes of their own squeaks rebounding from objects.

This new hypothesis may be tested by silencing the bats before they are released into the room. The bats collide with the obstacles again and the hypothesis is supported.

Theory confirmed

While one instance or example may prove that a theory is false, it is very difficult to prove that one is definitely true. There is always the possibility that future experiments or events will disprove the theory. Scientists, therefore, generally think in terms of probability of correctness.

A tried and tested theory that is well supported by the weight of experimental evidence may become accepted as a *scientific law* or 'theorem', for example Boyle's law.

It is still possible that new factors will be discovered to show that this theory is wrong. Perhaps bats detect echoes, not with their ears, but with sensitive areas near to their ears, the functioning of which was impaired by the plugs. Or perhaps different bats detect obstacles in different ways, so the sample was not representative.

Where do new ideas come from?

During the seventeenth century, scientists believed that all combustible materials contained a substance called phlogiston which was ejected from burning bodies (in the form of heat, flame and light) and then absorbed into the air. This theory fitted and explained the known facts:

(i) Bodies burned because they were rich in phlogiston.

(ii) Metals had many properties in common with each other (compared, for instance, with their oxides) because all metals were composed of phlogiston and a different 'earth'.

However, it wasn't long before scientists made discoveries which puzzled them. Although organic materials such as wood lost weight when burned, some metals actually appeared to gain weight when heated. The theory was therefore *modified* to take this into account. Phlogiston, it was claimed, had a 'negative weight' while fire and other particles sometimes entered a body as phlogiston left.

The invention of the air pump led to the discovery that air was an active ingredient in chemical reactions, and a number of different gases were separated in laboratory experiments. By the mid-eighteenth century, the phlogiston theory was in a state of crisis: it could not explain all the known facts.

In 1774 Joseph Priestley heated red oxide of mercury and collected the gas emitted. He called it *dephlogisticated air*. Although a brilliant scientist,

Priestley was unable to see that the gas was oxygen because he was committed to the phlogiston theory.

Meanwhile, Antoine Lavoisier was conducting similar experiments with gases. Unlike Priestley, he began with the assumption that there was something wrong with the phlogiston theory and that burning bodies absorbed part of the atmosphere. By 1777 he had developed the oxygen theory of combustion that initiated a revolution in scientific theory which led to the development of modern chemistry. Why did the oxygen theory overthrow the phlogiston theory and replace it completely within a decade?

Although the phlogiston theory had been unsatisfactory and had stifled the development of chemistry for over a century, it could only be rejected when an alternative theory became available. The oxygen theory was a *better* theory and was accepted because it was the most successful in solving problems. Lavoisier's theory enabled scientists to see old problems in new ways:

(i)   To make more precise and reliable observations when looking at old objects with old instruments.
(ii) To predict the relationship between a gas and its weight.
(iii) To provide a correct explanation of respiration.
(iv) To require a new classification of chemical substances to fit in with the theory.

At the same time, the oxygen theory generated further research to answer problems that it could not solve (that is, why metals are so alike). All our current theories, such as those associated with Copernicus, Newton and Einstein, are the result of scientific revolutions that overturned earlier ideas. Indeed, Einstein's theory of relativity can only be accepted if you recognize that Newton's laws of motion are wrong. Newtonian dynamics are still used by engineers but predictions derived from them are only valid in a small number of restricted conditions (that is, when the relative velocity of bodies is small compared with the speed of light).

Ideas and change

If you lived in thirteenth-century Britain, you would have seen a society comprised of different groups, each with its own function – priests prayed, barons ruled, merchants traded, knights fought and peasants tilled the soil. Each group was supposed to receive rewards appropriate to its station in life. If you were born a peasant, you would almost certainly die a peasant and no other kind of life seemed conceivable. There was a world to come where those who had patiently endured the tribulations of this 'vale of tears' would enjoy eternal bliss and the wicked would suffer in torment. The 'rights' and 'functions' of the different groups were necessary, and therefore, in a sense, just. Today, these ideas seem absurd to us, but they were plausible at the time because society was relatively stable and they reflected the actual relations between people.

Today it is taken for granted that we live in a world of constant change. Anyone over the age of sixty can remember a time when the Indian peninsula was a British colony; when there were no contraceptive pills or atomic bombs or National Health Service; when Gracie Fields was everybody's sweetheart; when Huddersfield was in Division I; and when the EEC (European Economic Community) had not been thought of.

Self-assessment questions

10 What are the most important changes that have occurred in *your* life-time?

11 What changes are going on at the moment?

12 (i) Which changes that have taken place are for the better and which are for the worse?
    (ii) What can you do to encourage or resist these changes?

Learning to learn

Much of the knowledge that you have accumulated in your head is already obsolete and a great deal of the rest is in the process of becoming old-fashioned. Those of us who learned how to use a slide-rule found that we needed to acquire a new skill to operate an electronic calculator. It is obvious today – if it wasn't before – that the knowledge and skills that we are taught in schools and colleges must be updated continuously during the rest of our lives. It is therefore necessary to learn how to learn.

In their book *Teaching as a Subversive Activity* Neil Postman and Charles Weingartner argue that we learn by asking questions, particularly by asking new questions about old problems. In school, they say, students are not taught how to ask questions: rather they are restricted to memorizing somebody else's answers to somebody else's questions. Students are accustomed to teachers deciding in advance what information they should know and even the order in which it should be taught. Most of this 'knowledge', they claim, has little in common with the problems faced by young people today. As a result, many students end up unable to decide for themselves what they want or need to know.

As a way out of this situation, Postman and Weingartner propose that courses should be based on students' answers to the question 'what is worth knowing?'. They come up with a series of 'open-ended' questions to which there is no single 'correct' answer, but rather a range of possible answers. For example:

  (i)   What do you worry about most of all?
 (ii)   What, if anything, seems worth dying for?
(iii)   How can you tell 'good guys' from 'bad guys'?

Part of the process of learning is to be able to rephrase or break down these open-ended questions into a series of answerable 'worth knowing' questions. To illustrate their point, they present a problem similar to the one below.

Study the following questions and then answer the self-assessment questions.

  (i)   What is the name of your school/college?
 (ii)   Are the children of middle-class parents more intelligent than working-class children?
(iii)   Who invented the automobile?
 (iv)   Who is the most powerful person in Britain?
  (v)   Will the sun rise tomorrow?
 (vi)   How are you?
(vii)   Will you succeed in your career?
(viii) Is 'love' a verb or a noun?
 (ix)   Is it right for a person to smoke cigarettes?
  (x)   Are the people on Mars more advanced than the people on earth?
 (xi)   Why do people kill each other?
(xii)   Are you the same person that you were yesterday?

Self-assessment questions

13 Which of the questions above can you answer with absolute certainty?

14 How can you be certain of your answer?

15 What information would enable you to answer the other questions with absolute certainty?

16 Which questions restrict you to giving factual information? Which questions require no facts at all?

17 Which questions need to be rephrased before you try to answer them?

18 How can they be rephrased to make them answerable?

19 Which questions require the testimony of experts?

20 Which questions assume that the answerer is an expert?

21 Which questions may have false assumptions?

22 Which questions require a prediction as the answer?

23 What kinds of information may improve the quality of your predictions?

You may find that the answer to a great many questions is merely another question. But at each stage of rephrasing and refining, the nature of the original problem becomes clearer and one step closer to solution. However, a fair proportion of questions that appear immediately answerable at first glance, turn out to be more complex.

In the modern world hardly anyone possesses the entire range of specialized skills that are required to deal with the variety of situations that arise in the course of everyday life. We do not need to worry unduly that we lack a particular piece of knowledge as long as we can obtain it when required. On these occasions we turn to experts for assistance: doctors, mechanics, meteorogists, etc. These people have authority because of what they know (although occasionally experts get things wrong). In particular, we must be on our guard against accepting the word of an authority simply because of *who* the person is. Most of us have a deeply rooted habit of believing a person because he *occupies* a responsible position.

In any organization those at the top have access to more information and therefore have a fuller picture of what is going on than anyone else. We assume that those lower down the organization will have incomplete information and therefore their view of the situation will be partial and distorted. Thus, whenever there is a controversy about what the facts of a particular situation actually are, we usually trust the party that is most powerful and respectable. People tend to accept the word of doctors rather then patients, foremen rather than apprentices, and college lecturers rather than students.

Self-assessment question

24 You are the producer of a TV/radio panel programme in which experts comment upon contemporary problems and issues. Which four of the following would you select to make up a balanced and authoritative panel? Which four do you think would have least of relevance or interest to say?

bishop	peer
business tycoon	pop star
coal miner	professional sportsperson
college student	senior policeman
doctor	trade union leader
housewife	unemployed person
journalist	university professor
MP	

Continuing education

Learning for employment

You will probably need to change jobs several times during your working life and, even if you don't, your job will change. Here are a few ways that you can keep abreast of new developments.

Colleges

Colleges provide the following types of courses.

(i) *Short courses* about new technology (for example numerically controlled machine tools). Firms usually pay for their employees to attend if they think that the knowledge gained will benefit the company.

(ii) *Evening classes* in GCE O- and A-levels, and other courses for those who want to gain further qualifications. Students normally pay their own fees.

(iii) *Full-time courses* are an option for those who want to gain new qualifications in order to change their jobs. This could be expensive, unless you are eligible for a local authority grant (which will probably still be less than your normal pay).

Correspondence courses

These courses are offered by private organizations for a fee in a wide variety of general and technical subjects. Useful for those who prefer to work alone, but there is no one to talk to when you get into difficulties.

The Open University

The Open University provides an attractive way of studying for a degree in your spare time without having to give up your job. No special entry qualifications are needed. The course arrives in the post and you send off your written work to a tutor for assessment. The BBC broadcasts special TV and radio programmes for each course unit, and there are residential summer schools where students can receive personal tuition.

Government-sponsored retraining schemes

Sponsored schemes were introduced to encourage

people to learn new skills, especially in areas of high unemployment. The Training Opportunities Scheme (TOPS) sponsors a wide range of programmes, but the emphasis has been on short intensive courses in manual skills such as plumbing and bricklaying.

Trade unions

Shop stewards are now legally entitled to take time off work with pay to attend training courses approved by their union or the TUC (Trades Union Congress). There are now about 160 centres offering day-release courses on such topics as health and safety, and collective bargaining. There are also postal courses, and study groups organized by the Workers' Educational Association.

Learning as a leisure activity

It is likely that we shall have more spare time in the future, either through new technology leading to a reduction in working hours or because more of us will be unemployed. Learning as a leisure activity already exists in many forms.

Television and radio

Adult education broadcasts cover a wide range of interests from gardening to foreign languages. You don't have to enrol on a course or pay a special fee, but on the other hand you don't get a certificate. There are books published in association with many of these programmes.

Adult education classes

Most local authorities run evening classes in leisure activities ranging from judo to pottery to car maintenance. You have to pay a fee but there is no examination at the end. Your local town hall will tell you which courses are offered (and if the course you want isn't listed, write to ask whether it will be considered for the following year).

Libraries

A hundred years ago only wealthy people had access to large numbers of books, but today you can walk freely into your local library and enjoy a vast collection of books worth hundreds of thousands of pounds. Libraries keep reference books, journals, fiction and non-fiction and local history books. If you need to borrow any special books the librarian will probably be able to obtain them from another library.

Computer-assisted learning

Relatively inexpensive micro-computers are already available, and you will probably own one yourself within the next ten or twenty years. You will be able to acquire 'software', for example by linking into a vast national data bank, to turn your computer terminal into an advanced teaching machine.

Self-assessment question

25 What new learning opportunities can you foresee arising in the future?

3 Personality

The aim of this section is to explain the functions of the brain and to investigate the factors that make up your personality. You will be encouraged to consider human motivation and personal relationships, and the meaning of mental illness.

Looks can be deceptive

Look at Figure 6. What do you see? A young woman or an old woman? The drawing is only a combination of lines, yet the shape is not understood by simply adding together the separate items. Indeed, they were *organized* into a distinct pattern.

We are usually able to see an object 'as it really is' even when it is presented under unusual or distorting conditions. Distance, for example, is judged from various visual clues. People look 'life-size' although seen at great distances. We can predict which shapes you will see under given circumstances as can be seen in Table 5.

Figure 6

The senses

Every normal human body possesses a set of receivers (eyes, ears, tongue, finger tips, etc.) that are sensitive to changes in energy: lightwaves, soundwaves, pressure and temperature.

It is estimated that your brain receives 100 million separate coded messages every second. This wealth of information is processed to filter out whatever is irrelevant. Therefore, we are more likely to notice or recognize items that interest us. In one experiment, hungry people identified more 'nonsense' pictures as being related to food than well-fed people.

Self-assessment questions

1 Which are the main senses?
2 Which is most sensitive to change and which most limited in range and distance?
3 How do human senses compare with those of other animals?

Self-assessment question

4 What distracting messages might interfere with your concentration in class or while driving if this filtering process did not occur?

Small enclosed areas are more likely to be viewed as distinct units than large open areas	
Objects that are close together are more likely to be understood as related	How many shapes are there here? III III III III III
You expect the element that naturally finishes an incomplete pattern	Which letter comes next? T E C H N O L O G _
Where there is more than one element to choose from, you select the one that is simplest to see	Do you see as or ?
Straight lines appear to bend	
The white bands appear whiter than they actually are and grey spots appear at intersections	
Which circle is largest, A or B?	
These impossible shapes are only credible as two-dimensional figures	

Table 5

The brain's muscle-operating circuits

If the human body were proportioned in the same way as the brain's muscle-operating circuits, it would look something like the one shown in Figure 7. The largest motor areas in the brain are associated with the hand, followed by the mouth and tongue. Only a small area of the brain controls the legs and torso.

The more I look at human beings, the more impressed I become with the vast bands of intelligence they can use. We often say of a job 'it's as easy as crossing a road', yet as a technologist I am ever impressed with people's ability to do just that. They go to the edge of the pavement and work out the velocity of the cars coming in both directions by calling up a massive memory bank which will establish whether it is a mini or a bus because there is significance in the actual size. Then they work out the rate of change of the image and from this assess the velocity. They do this for vehicles in both directions in order to assess the closing velocity between them. At the same time they are working out the width of the road and their own acceleration and peak velocity. When they decide they can go, they will just fit in between the vehicles.

The above computation is one of the simpler ones we do, but you should watch one of our skilled workers at Lucas Aerospace going through the diagnostic procedures of finding out what has gone wrong with an aircraft generator. There you see real intelligence at work. A human being using total information processing capability can bring to bear synaptic connections of 10^{14}, but the most complicated robotic device with pattern recognition capability has only about 10^3 intelligence units.

Mike Cooley, *Architect or Bee* (Hand and Brain Publications 1980)

Learning

Learning is *any experience that changes our beliefs or behaviour*. A number of theories have been proposed to explain how we learn.

Classical conditioning

Ivan Pavlov noticed that hungry dogs salivate at the sight of food, in anticipation of eating. He

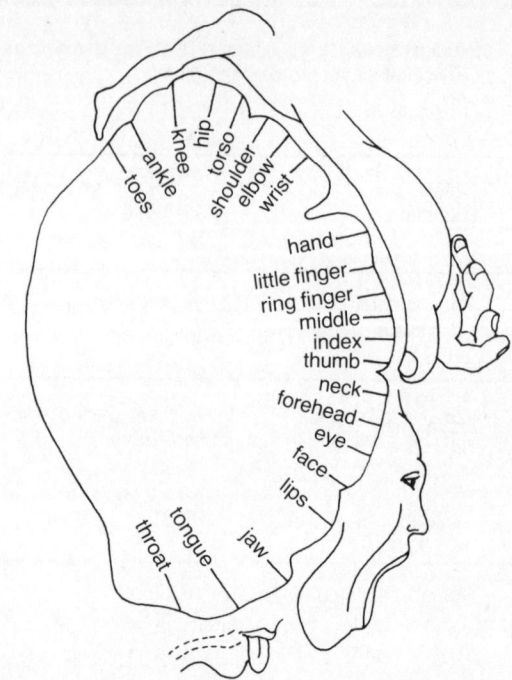

Figure 7   *Wilder Penfield's model of the brain's muscle-operating circuits*

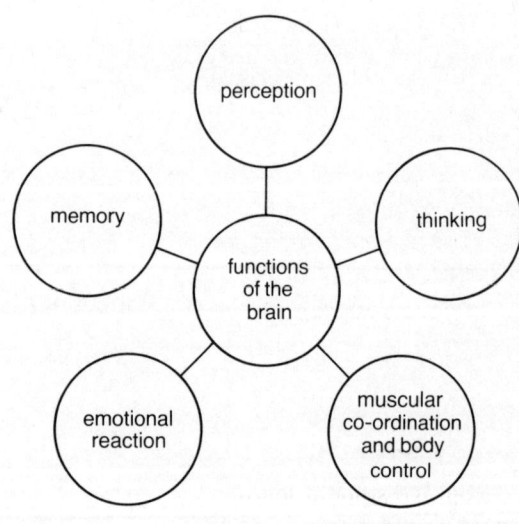

Figure 8

taught the dogs to associate the sound of a bell with the appearance of food. After a time he found that the dogs would respond (by salivating) to the signal (bell), even when food did not appear. The dogs were later taught (or 'conditioned') to associate the bell with a light, and were seen to salivate to the light alone.

signal → response

You take longer to 'un-learn' a response than to learn one. Pavlov showed that when the bell was frequently sounded to the dogs – but the food never presented – the response gradually diminished and eventually stopped. Even then, after a long period of time, the neutral stimulus (bell signal) could occasionally cause the conditioned response.

Have you learned to respond in particular ways to signals (clock alarms, door bell)?

Operant conditioning

B. F. Skinner experimented with pigeons in specially designed boxes. Motivated by hunger or curiosity, the bird moved around the box in a random manner and eventually – by accident – depressed a lever. This lever operated a mechanism that delivered a reward (food pellet) to the pigeon. After a while the bird learned to work the lever in order to obtain food. Skinner concluded that rewards reinforce desired behaviour and encourage the subject to learn more quickly.

response → reward

Satisfying experiences tend to be repeated whenever possible, and painful ones avoided. Responses that become associated in your brain with rewards (even when the reward itself is absent) are often regarded as pleasant in themselves.

Self-assessment questions

5　What kind of rewards are used in colleges to encourage student learning?

6　Will punishments encourage slow learners?

If we combine these two theories we have a single process of learning.

signal → response → reward

Latent learning

Animals can also learn without conditioning and rewards. Psychologists have tried to measure learning ability by training rats to obtain food by successfully navigating their way through a maze. It was discovered that rats who were allowed to explore the maze out of curiosity would later learn to 'run the maze' more quickly than other rats without prior experience.

In another experiment, it was noticed that the brains of rats kept in a lively and varied environment were more developed than those of rats bred in dull, repetitive environment. This suggests that physiological changes accompany intellectual experience and that a stimulating environment during childhood makes future learning easier.

Self-assessment questions

7　What is the best way for you to learn?

8　Can too much motivation actually hinder learning?

Feedback

We learn more effectively if we have an indication of our past performance. This information is called feedback. For example, a darts player whose first throw falls too low will take appropriate action to aim his second dart for a higher number.

Try this experiment
Ask a student to *estimate* the length of a minute.
Plot the answer on a graph but do not say how accurate the estimate was.
Repeat this exercise another nine times.
Now carry out the experiment again, but this time give the student details of accuracy of performance after each estimate.
Does the student learn the skill of estimating units of time more effectively with or without feedback?

Self-assessment questions

9 What feedback do you receive about your performance at college and work?

10 What additional information would be helpful?

Concentration

It is easier to learn to drive, swim or speak a foreign language if we receive short but frequent periods of instruction and practice. The reason is quite simply that we are unable to concentrate our attention on a single subject for long periods. After a while our minds inevitably begin to wander. Yet after a short break we may be able to return to the matter with renewed interest. A variety of learning activities, for example listening, talking, reading, etc., can help to increase our ability to concentrate. However, the most important factor that influences the span and intensity of concentration is our degree of *motivation* to learn.

Self-assessment question

11 Suppose that you were to plot a graph to show the amount of attention that you pay to particular subjects and activities during the course of a day in college.

  (i) What would it look like?

  (ii) What is your longest period of concentration?

  (iii) What do you lose interest in most quickly?

  (iv) What factors affect the intensity of your concentration?

  (v) What changes might increase your powers of concentration?

Memory

Dr Wilder Penfield has shown that the brain functions as a high quality video recorder. Not only are past experiences recorded, but also the feelings with which they are linked. These memories are permanently available for replay and so provide information on which to base today's decisions.

Unfortunately we are only able to remember (that is, recall voluntarily) a small proportion of our previous experience. Although we often say that we have 'forgotten' the rest, it has not really been lost. Indeed, we can only gain access to this information with the help of some external stimulus. A smell or a sound, for example, may spontaneously trigger off unexpected memories. Often the effect is a little startling, because not only do we recall these experiences but we actually *relive* them. Our feelings (of embarrassment, anger, disgust, compassion, etc.) appear as vivid as when they originally happened, even after many years. Indeed, some memories seem so real that we have the impression of being in two worlds simultaneously.

We tend to

Remember	Forget
Recent events.	Past events (although very old people often recall their youth more clearly than events of yesterday).
Experiences associated with intense emotion (for example a serious accident, your first date).	Material we do not use frequently (although this does not seem to apply to motor skills such as cycling and swimming).
	Material that we have not learned properly because something interfered with the process.

Try this experiment

Ask a student to stand between two others.

The students to the left and right should read aloud slowly from different texts.

The student in the middle should attempt to ignore one recital and write down the other as it is received.

What can the student recall of the disregarded recital?

12   How many different things are you capable of doing at once?

13   Do you ever realize that you have not been paying enough attention to something you are doing?

Have you ever looked up a number in a telephone directory and then forgotten it before you have completed dialling? Even if you have, you are still unlikely to forget important numbers or those you dial frequently. The reason is that memory operates on two levels: *short-term* and *long-term*. The difference between them is similar to that between a refrigerator and a deep-freeze. We may store for a while new information in the short-term memory but it will eventually be forgotten unless it is transferred to the long-term memory. This process may involve certain physiological changes in the brain.

If you have a poor short-term memory, there is not much that you can do about it. Here is a test to see how good your memory is.

Read a list of numbers, say seven to begin with, to a listener.

Ask the listener to repeat them back immediately. What is the maximum number of digits that you and other students can recall?

We have more memories in our store than we realize, but often we cannot recall them without the appropriate cue.

Mnemonic is a device which helps trigger recall. Thus, the sentence 'Every Good Boy Deserves Favour' reminds us of the notes of the treble clef, E G B D F, in music.

Associate a clear visual image with material that you are trying to learn, since you are more likely to recall the image and, therefore, the related ideas in the future (for example *apple – laws of motion*).

It is difficult to remember a large number of unrelated details, so transform raw data into a pattern before storage. This requires that you fully understand the material and that you reorganize it into categories and groups.

Write brief notes in the form of *keywords* or phrases that remind you of a wider range of ideas.

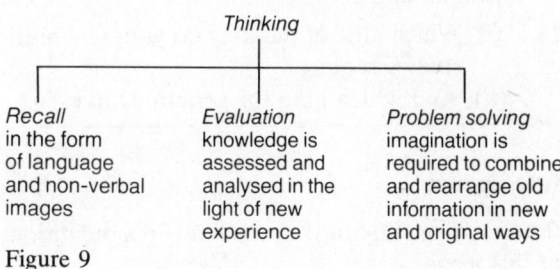

Figure 9

Although the different parts of the brain must co-operate and interact in the process of thinking, there is evidence that specific areas deal with particular intellectual functions. The left hemisphere of the brain has been associated with *rational* thinking, and the right hemisphere with *intuition*.

Table 6

Left hemisphere functions	*Right hemisphere functions*
main language centre	pattern recognition
speech	non-verbal ideas
writing	musical ability
calculations	thinking of things as a whole

This distinction is reflected in two types of thinking:

convergent thinking	divergent thinking
uses previously learned information to arrive at	
one correct answer	a large number of possible answers

Example of a question to test your ability at this kind of thinking:

What is the quickest way to travel from London to Manchester?	How many ways are there to travel from London to Manchester?

Self-assessment questions

14   Which type of thinking are you best at?

15   Does an artist need to think in a different way from an engineer?

16   (i)   Which kind of thinking do your technical studies require?
　　　(ii)   And which kind for general studies?

Intelligence

Before you go any further write down a definition of this term.

You have probably come up with something like this: 'the ability to solve problems', 'mental quickness' or 'brain power'. Your answer probably has something to do with intellectual effort and ability.

The aspect of intelligence that psychologists appear to be most concerned with is its measurement. Their research stems from the work of Binet and Simon who studied children at the beginning of this century. Dr Binet assumed that all children, whether bright or dull, were basically the same and that it was their *rate* of intellectual development which was different, not the process itself.

Binet devised a series of tests to measure 'mental age', the ability-level he considered typical of a particular age group. Intelligence tests gave rise to the expression intelligence quotient (IQ):

$$\frac{\text{mental age}}{\text{calendar age}} \times 100 = \text{IQ}$$

The average IQ for the population as a whole is 100. If a ten year old child is found to have a mental age of nine, his IQ is $\frac{9}{10} \times 100 = 90$. What is his IQ if his mental age is eleven?

The Binet tests are only suitable for individual school children. Professor Eysenck and others have attempted to refine IQ measurement and to devise tests appropriate for adults. Scores are 'standardized' so that comparisons may be made across the whole population.

IQ testers have long realized that intelligence involves a number of separate mental abilities:

memory, judgement, originality, concentration, etc. They have, therefore, attempted to assess a range of factors. Here are four typical questions.

(i)   *Numerical ability*
　　　Insert the missing number
　　　50   44   38   ___   26

(ii)   *Verbal ability*
　　　Insert the three letter word that completes the first word and starts the second (clue: insect)
　　　CH(___)IQUE

(iii)   *Spatial perception*
　　　Complete this pattern by filling the vacant square.

(iv)   *General reasoning*
　　　Underline the odd one out.
　　　cow   giraffe   rabbit   herring   sheep

Some criticisms of IQ tests

Psychologists and teachers are both sharply divided over the accuracy and usefulness of IQ tests as a measure of intelligence and an indicator of future performance. The critics argue that IQ test scores:

(i)   *Often do not reflect actual ability*
　　　Some students may be 'coached' in IQ-type questions to improve their performance, while others who are ill, anxious or lack motivation will do worse than their true abilities merit. Those who advocate IQ tests claim that these problems can be minimized by better testing procedures.

(ii)   *Do not measure intelligence*
　　　IQ tests are prepared by well-educated, middle class people. They naturally assume

that the skills and knowledge valued and respected by their group constitute intelligence. An Eskimo hunter is intelligent enough to survive in an environment where most university professors would perish, but he would probably score very poorly in an IQ test. The proponents of IQ tests say that their tests are 'culture-free' and show fairly the important intellectual skills.

A further criticism is that IQ questions are biased in favour of those who think convergently. (If you had underlined *giraffe* as the odd one out because it is not normally eaten in Britain, were you wrong?)

(iii) *Are self-fulfilling prophecies*
Test scores are used as a basis for separating children into groups, such as A and D streams in school. A child who is treated as 'bright' or 'thick' may alter his image of himself and consequently his behaviour. One researcher found that, between the ages of 8 and 11 years, the measured intelligence of children in the top streams increased while the intelligence of those in the bottom streams actually declined.

(iv) *Condemn individuals to menial jobs from an early age*
IQ tests are used to predict future performance. It is assumed that those who do well in IQ tests will also benefit from further education and succeed in certain jobs. One

authority, for example, proposed that people with IQs of 130 are suited to professional and managerial jobs, while those who score less than 90 are only capable of learning repetitive skills involving a limited range of decisions. Moreover, IQ testers assume that intelligence is fixed and constant; that scores will not vary significantly over time. Except in rare circumstances IQ tests do not allow for 'late developers'.

Smart rats?

Some years ago at Harvard University some experimenters were falsely told that a group of rats had been specially bred for intelligence. In test after test these rats were found to perform far better than other rats. Surprisingly, the same group of rats consistently turned in poor performances after the testers had been told that these rodents were particularly stupid.

What had happened was this. Because the experimenters knew in advance that the rats were bright or unintelligent, they selected only those aspects of the rats' behaviour that were consistent with that conclusion and disregarded all the rest.

Self-assessment question

17 Design your own test to measure the intelligence of students in your group (including your lecturer).

Answers
(i) 32
(ii) ANT
(iii) ⌐□
(iv) herring (the only fish)

Personality

Personality is the complex pattern of behaviour, habits, feelings, attitudes, and emotions that characterize a person. Scientists disagree over the question of whether personality (and in particular your level of intelligence) is determined mainly by:

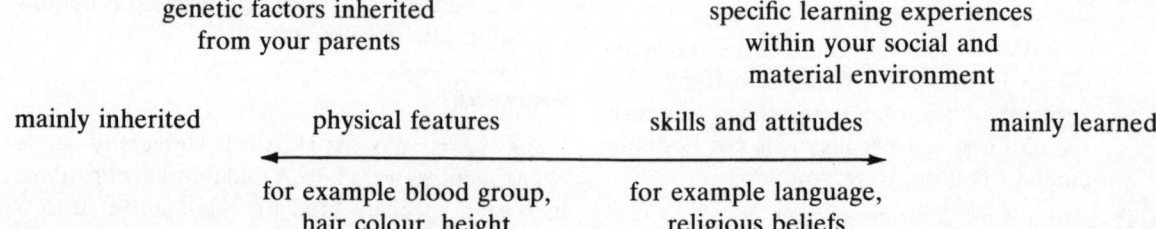

| *Nature* | or | *Nurture* |
| genetic factors inherited from your parents | | specific learning experiences within your social and material environment |

mainly inherited   physical features   skills and attitudes   mainly learned

for example blood group, hair colour, height   for example language, religious beliefs

Some psychologists (notably Jensen and Eysenck) argue that individual differences in intelligence arise overwhelmingly from heredity. Their evidence is based largely on controversial studies of identical and non-identical twins. They conclude that *groups* who score consistently well in IQ tests (for example middle class and white people) are more intelligent than groups who do not (for example working class and black people).

Their opponents argue that the explanation lies in deprived educational and other facilities. For example, a child who grows up in a home containing books and magazines, and who receives constant parental encouragement, is likely to learn to read faster than a child who lacks this kind of intellectual stimulation. In school, the ability to deal easily with written material will make possible the rapid development of other mental skills.

We may say that a person is honest, friendly, talkative, emotional and clever. This kind of description identifies the important traits or characteristics of an individual's personality. We assume that a person's pattern of behaviour, attitudes, etc. will remain constant over a period of time, and in different situations. The shy, timid student usually becomes a quiet and bashful young worker. This does not mean that your personality is forever fixed and unchanging: we often comment that a person is acting 'out of character'.

Personality traits are usually expressed as pairs of opposed qualities which represent extremes of behaviour, for example impulsive – cautious, cheerful – depressed, self-confident – insecure, suspicious – trusting.

Self-assessment question

18 How much do you 'take after' your parents? Why do you think this is?
19 Select a person whom you know quite well (a friend, relative, workmate, etc.) and write down a brief description of their personality.

Self-assessment question

20 Make up your own tests to 'measure' these and other important traits. Ask friends if they think the results are accurate.

Are you a lion or a mouse?

A personality test – but please don't take it too seriously

1 After a quarrel with your girl- or boy-friend, are you the first to apologize
   (a) always
   (b) usually
   (c) occasionally
   (d) never

2 Do the people that you work with think that you are
   (a) mild and obedient
   (b) quiet and conforming
   (c) assertive and independent
   (d) aggressive and stubborn

3 In a restaurant, your food is badly cooked. Do you
   (a) say nothing but decide not to come back
   (b) ask the waiter to put matters right
   (c) refuse to pay for the meal
   (d) insist on making a complaint to the cook

4 In politics, do you think of yourself as
   (a) neutral
   (b) moderate
   (c) independent
   (d) an extremist

5 Someone who started at work after you is promoted before you. Do you
   (a) accept that he must be better qualified than you are
   (b) feel miserable but try not to show it
   (c) try to find out from your boss why
   (d) tell the other person that he must be a bootlicker

6 If you found a youngster stealing apples from the tree in your garden, would you
   (a) tell him to clear off but let him keep a few
   (b) make him give back your apples
   (c) phone the police
   (d) hit him

7 When taking part in competitive games
   (a) do you play just for the fun of it
   (b) do you try to win but don't mind losing
   (c) do you hate losing
   (d) must you win at all costs

8 After waiting a long time, the bus comes and a little old lady jumps the queue. Do you
   (a) help her on to the bus
   (b) feel angry but say nothing
   (c) mumble under your breath about queue jumpers
   (d) try to push past her

9 You are out for a drive in the country. Do you
   (a) drive slowly so that other drivers can overtake you easily
   (b) not mind how many drivers overtake you
   (c) try to overtake the driver who has just passed you
   (d) drive so that other motorists cannot overtake you

10 You want to go to a disco but your girl- or boy-friend wants to stay in and watch TV. Do you
   (a) watch TV
   (b) toss a coin to decide what you're going to do
   (c) go to the disco alone
   (d) go to the disco together

Scoring: all questions
(a) 1   (b) 2   (c) 3   (d) 4

Your score
Under 20   You are fairly submissive and allow others to take decisions for you and boss you about. Try standing up for yourself occasionally.

20–30   You are about average, neither too assertive nor too meek and mild.

Over 30   You like to be dominant. You're independent but you could put people off.

If you scored over 35 it can't be much fun having you around!

Human motivation

We are usually interested in the reasons *why* people behave as they do, for example their *motives* for committing a crime.

How many reasons are there for a person buying a newspaper? We might want to discover last night's soccer results, or obtain some change for a parking meter, or make a date with the shop assistant. Many different motives may result in the same behaviour.

Self-assessment question

21 Suggest five possible motives for a person:
  (i)   Drinking a glass of beer.
  (ii) Attending a course at a technical college.
  (iii) Growing a beard.
  (iv) Buying a particular model of motor car.

Similarly, very different kinds of action may result from the same motive. Suppose that you have fallen out with your parents or a friend. Suggest five possible ways to regain their affection.

We cannot explain specific, individual actions without reference to the particular conditions in each case. The study of motivation in general, however, can help us to understand the underlying reasons for human behaviour.

Needs

Maslow has suggested a *hierarchy of human needs*. A *need* is an inward urge that prompts behaviour that is either physically or emotionally satisfying. Human needs are presented as a hierarchy in order to show that the lower or basic needs are essential for human survival. If we fail to satisfy our basic physical needs, we will become ill and in extreme cases even die. Once we have achieved these primary requirements, we become aware of another urge that drives us on to ensure our personal safety. When this is satisfied, the need to feel that we are an accepted member of society comes to the fore.

As we move up the scale we achieve a greater amount of personal fulfilment. If our secondary needs (largely psychological requirements) are not satisfied, we suffer from some degree of stress. The amount of stress will decline as we approach the condition of self-realization. Acute stress, however, may cause physical illness or abnormal behaviour.

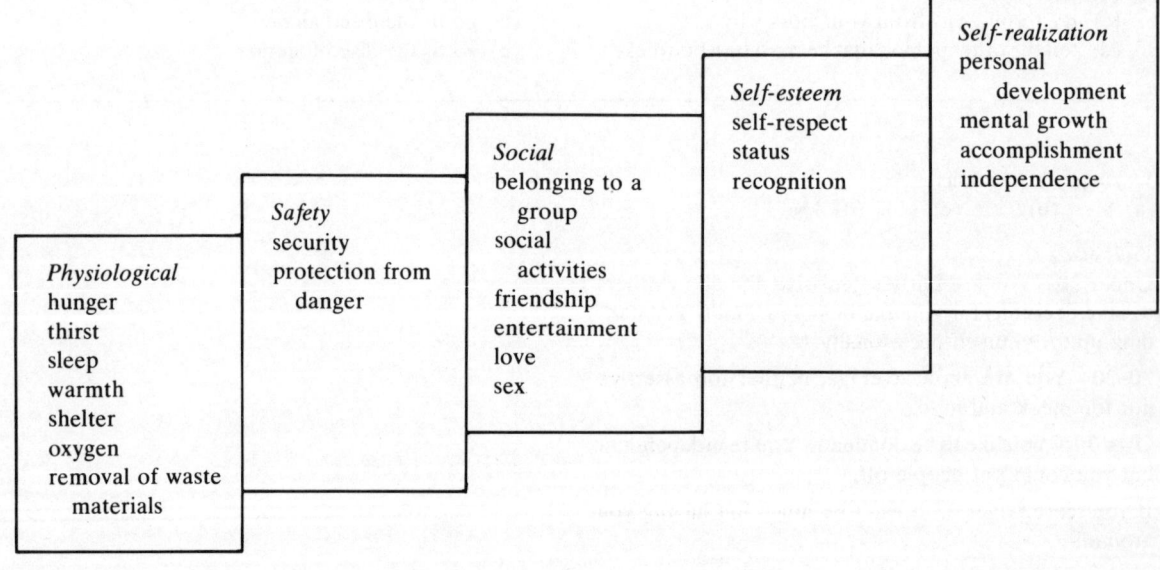

Physiological
hunger
thirst
sleep
warmth
shelter
oxygen
removal of waste
   materials

Safety
security
protection from
   danger

Social
belonging to a
   group
social
   activities
friendship
entertainment
love
sex

Self-esteem
self-respect
status
recognition

Self-realization
personal
   development
mental growth
accomplishment
independence

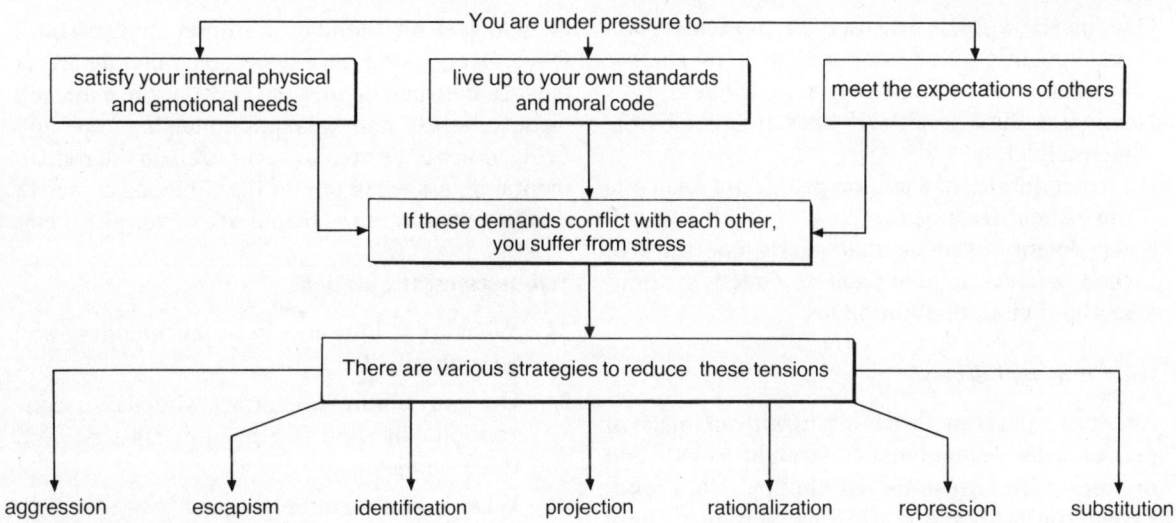

Figure 10

Defence mechanisms

Aggression you become angry, shout, or come to blows. Aggression may be directed against the cause of frustration, some innocent and harmless object, or the world in general. We usually find ways to contain and limit the scope of our aggression in order to minimize the damage that it may cause (for example, by substituting verbal insults and threatening gestures for real violence).

Escapism you take refuge in fantasy in order to avoid facing disagreeable facts (for example, daydreams about murdering your boss or next year's holidays).

Identification you attempt to overcome your own personal weakness by association with some source of strength (for example, Nazi stormtroopers, gangs of football supporters).

Projection you blame others for your problems and project your own bad feelings on to someone else. (For example, a person who is sexually frustrated may accuse others of immorality.)

Rationalization you make excuses to justify your behaviour (for example, 'what I did was all right because those people ain't normal', 'it was an accident', 'I couldn't help myself', etc.).

Repression you push sad memories to the 'back' of your mind or deny the existence of a problem.

Substitution you find alternative satisfactions to compensate for frustrated aspirations (for example, you enjoy your leisure after a boring day at work).

Mental illness

Consider the distinction between physical illness (for example, sore throat, cancer) and physical handicap (for example, blindness). A similar difference exists as far as mental health is concerned. Mental handicaps are forms of brain damage, arising at birth, resulting from accidents or serious physical illness. Handicaps can rarely be 'cured', but individuals can live full and worthwhile lives within certain limits. Mental illness, on the other hand, can be a temporary state from which we recover after medical treatment or a period of natural restoration.

We are all vulnerable to mental illness, although it is not infectious.

One in six women and one in nine men will undergo in-patient treatment in a psychiatric hospital at some stage during their lives.

Nearly one-third of all NHS beds are filled by the mentally ill.

A further quarter of a million people are receiving out-patient treatment.

Some doctors estimate that nearly one-third of their patients are complaining directly or indirectly of emotional problems.

What is mental illness?

Literature and comedy has left us with an image of padded cells, raving lunatics, straight jackets and people with illusions of being Napoleon. Psychiatric medicine is still relatively new: until the end of the nineteenth century the mentally ill were generally treated with great brutality and inhumanity (see Hogarth's *Bedlam Asylum*). During the Middle Ages symptoms of mental illness were interpreted as being possessed by the devil and were 'treated' by exorcism, torture and execution.

Our moods and feelings are constantly fluctuating in response to changing events and situations. How do you feel on Monday mornings or Christmas Day? Over a long period we generally achieve a balance between depression and elation, calm and anxiety, stress and relaxation, feeling 'up' and being 'down'. We are, however, well on the road to mental illness when one of these moods comes to dominate our lives and begins to exclude all others.

Self-assessment questions

22   What is the difference between 'madness' and 'eccentricity'?

23   Do you admire eccentrics who flaunt convention, or find them embarrassing and threatening?

24   What is abnormal behaviour?

25   Have you ever committed a mad action?

26   How often can you break the rules of acceptable behaviour before society labels you?

Just as there are many forms of physical illness, so too are there many forms of mental illness, as can be seen in Table 7.

Table 7

Neuroses (chronic mental illness – minor illnesses which can last a long time)	Psychoses (acute mental illness – major illnesses which can last a short time)
Neurotic depression and anxiety state Extreme forms of depression and anxiety (for example nervous breakdowns). May be sufficiently serious to totally incapacitate or drive a person to suicide.	*Manic depression* Violent swings between extreme depression and elation.
Phobia An irrational fear (for example, fear of spiders or open spaces).	*Paranoia* Unreasonable feelings of persecution by either some particular source or the world in general.
Obsession An unreasonable preoccupation (for example with your health – hypochondria).	*Schizophrenia* A fantasy existence in addition to your real existence. Associated with delusions and hallucinations.
	Senile dementia Accelerated ageing. Associated with vagueness and disorientation.

What causes mental illness?

If you are suffering from a cold, you know that you have been infected by a virus. There are, however, no simple explanations for mental illness. We sometimes say that a particular situation is enough to drive a person mad, but it is more likely that abnormal behaviour arises from several inter-linked causes. The following have been suggested as underlying factors that contribute towards mental illness in general:

(i) Heredity
(ii) Individual predisposition
(iii) Physical illness
(iv) Stress

A group of radical psychologists (notably R. D. Laing) have argued that it is a mistake to diagnose certain kinds of abnormal behaviour as mental illness at all. Indeed, the so-called mentally ill are merely acting in a perfectly reasonable way when faced with crazy situations in which normal behaviour is inappropriate. We generally consider that a mentally ill person is not, partly or entirely, responsible for his actions. When conflicts and problems exist within a group (for example, a family), it may be convenient to label a person as mad in order to provide a scapegoat. That person's statements and actions can then be seen, not as a challenge to the group, but merely as symptoms of illness. An uncomfortable or threatening situation is thereby 'resolved' without the need to tackle the original problem.

Self-assessment question

27 (i) What are the consequences of labelling a person as mentally ill?
    (ii) What are the consequences for the person concerned?
    (iii) What are the consequences for those who apply the label?

How is mental illness cured?

Is there more mental illness today than in previous periods? On the basis of figures showing the numbers diagnosed as mentally ill and receiving treat-ment, it would appear that there is. One reason for this increase is that more patients are prepared to seek medical help and doctors are more likely to diagnose a psychiatric disorder and refer a patient for treatment. Previously, many hid their illness from fear of the consequences. Today, we are more likely to encounter a sympathetic attitude from doctors, friends and relatives, and we have more confidence that the treatment will be effec-tive.

Most psychiatric patients who require a spell in hospital stay only a short time: nearly half are discharged in less than a month. The majority receive out-patient treatment. The actual diag-nosis of the illness will determine the form of treatment (therapy) that is suitable. Treatment includes:

(i) Drugs
(ii) Group discussion – sharing problems with staff and fellow patients in order to under-stand the origins of the illness.
(iii) Psychotherapy – talks with specialized med-ical staff.
(iv) Occupational therapy – practical activities to restore confidence.
(v) Behaviour therapy – specialized treatment to overcome irrational fears.
(vi) Electroconvulsant therapy (ECT) – the patient is anaesthetized and an electric cur-rent passed through the brain in order to cause a spasm. Many patients have benefited from this treatment, although it has been associated with disorientation, memory-loss, and listlessness.

Some psychiatrists argue that physical treatments (that is, drugs and ECT) are used primarily to control patients and treat symptoms, but do not really uncover the underlying causes of mental illness.

Self-assessment question

28 (i) What image have the media and comedy presented of psychiatric treatment?
    (ii) Do you think this image is accurate?

4 Social relations

The aim of this section is to help you to understand the part played by social groups in shaping your ideas, your life-style, and your relationships. You will be encouraged to consider those social groups to which you belong and your attitudes towards other people.

Who are you?

Write ten answers to this question.
'I am . . .'

You have probably defined yourself in terms of your name, age, sex, occupation, physical appearance, leisure interests, preferences and friendships.

Here you are indicating the *social groups* that you belong to:

(i)   Your family
(ii)   Your peer group (peer means equal)
(iii) Your social class

These groups, and the larger society as a whole, have a great influence in shaping our personality, opinions, expectations and the image that we have of ourselves. From them we get our accent, our preferences in clothes and politics, and even our attitude to sex. The process by which we become a member of society by learning the appropriate behaviour and attitudes of the groups to which we belong is known as *socialization*.

A complex society like Britain is composed of numerous sub-groups that, through their inter-relationships, make up our culture or way of life. Indicate whether you feel that you are any of the following:

biker	middle class
Catholic	Mod
English	teenager
football supporter	Ted
male	working class

Clearly we all belong to several different (though overlapping) sub-groups. At the same time, we also believe that we are personally unique. While no two of the four billion people on this planet are truly identical, there are many ways in which we identify with other people.

Self-assessment question

1   Rank these factors in order of their importance in helping you to identify with others:

accent	language
age	leisure interests
blood group	nationality
diet	political attitudes
education	religion
gender (male/female)	skin colour
height	social class
intelligence	style of dress
job	wealth

You have probably realized that several of these factors are frequently inter-related, for example:

nationality – language – skin colour
education – job – social class – wealth

Self-assessment questions

2   Are there any other sets of features that are usually linked together?

3   How do you explain these connections?

4   You are about to meet a total stranger, but know only *three* of these factors about him/her in advance.
   (i) Which factors would be most useful in helping you to assess what this person will be like?
   (ii) Should we assume that all people with the same characteristic are much the same?

Your children continue the game

60 RETIREMENT	58 VOTES	56 APPOINTED	54 OCCUPATIONAL ILLNESS	52 CONGRATULATIONS!
golden handshake +20	Conservative	to the Board	obesity – three weeks at a health farm	100–1 outsider at Ascot +20
index-linked company pension +10	Liberal	Justice of the Peace	ulcers – six months on milk and eggs	Premium Bond win +50
at 65 with state pension	Labour	shop steward	dermatitis – industrial injury benefit	win the pools +100

22 CAREER	24 GIRL-FRIEND	26 CAR	28 RECREATION	30 INCOMES POLICY
merchant banker +50	several	sports +10	polo, hunting and shooting	dividends up +5
computer programmer +20	living together	firm's +5	jogging, squash and sailing	salary frozen but annual increment +2
mechanic +10	pregnant so you get married	second-hand	pool, darts and fishing	wages frozen

20 MAJOR ACHIEVEMENT	19 ARRESTED	18 FURTHER EDUCATION	17 PASS DRIVING TEST	16 EXAMINATION TIME
'blue' for rowing	for smashing up a bar on rugby tour −10	Oxbridge university +15	father buys a car +10	fail exams, must resit −5
on *University Challenge*	at a student sit-in −10	redbrick university +10	borrow daddy's car	pass exams and go to sixth form +5
pub's darts team star	at a football match −10	day-release at college +5	steal a car	leave for apprenticeship +5

Year

1 YOUR FATHER IS A	2 YOU LIVE IN	3 YOU ARE LOOKED AFTER BY	4 CHILDHOOD ILLNESS	5 PRIMARY SCHOOL
stockbroker +50	Virginia Water +50	*au pair* +5	German measles −2	prep school – small class +10
school teacher +20	Milton Keynes +10	nursery school +10	whooping cough −5	average-size class
bricklayer +10	Middlesbrough	baby-minder	pneumonia −10	large class and free milk −10

START LIFE HERE

Try This Game of LIFE CHANCES

FOR THREE OR MORE PLAYERS

- Throw dice to decide who your father is.
- Use a counter to indicate each player's position.
- Using a dice, work your way around the board.
- Add up the total scores of the squares you land on.
- How do you know who has won?
- How can you modify this game to make it more realistic?

50 HOUSE	48 OPEN DAY AT SCHOOL	46 BOUND OVER FOR	44 MARRIAGE PROBLEMS	42 MEMBER OF	40 ALL CHANGE?
detached +15	take sherry with the headmaster +5	assaulting hunt saboteur −5	keep a mistress	golf and country club	rumbled by fraud squad
semi-detached +10	talk to maths teacher +10	disturbance at motorway inquiry −5	go to a Marriage Guidance Council	bridge and tennis club	sell product to Arabs – make money
council house +5	don't attend −10	punch-up on picket line −5	wife gets legal separation	United supporters' football club	study at night school

32 AT WORK YOU WEAR	34 FOR LUNCH YOU EAT	36 CHILDREN	38 MENTAL STRESS
pin-stripe suit	expense account lunch +5	Sarah, Julian, James, Lucinda, Clare, Sebastian	visit a psychiatrist
casual clothes	health food and real ale	Thomas and Kerry	take Librium −10
overalls and boots	fish and chips −5	Wayne, Steven and Sandra	take aspirins −5

15 STUDIES	14 AT SCHOOL	13 READS	12 HOLIDAY
classics −10	officer training corps	father's *Daily Telegraph* +5	Barbados +5
science and a language +20	school prefect	comics and adventure stories +5	exchange with pen-friend in France +5
metal-work and technical drawing +10	on detention for playing truant −5	very little	holiday camp at Blackpool

6 ACCIDENT – FALL OFF	7 CHRISTMAS PRESENT	8 WHERE IS MUM?	9 MEMBER OF	10 SOCIAL MOBILITY?	11 SECONDARY SCHOOL
pony at gymkhana	trust fund +10	mother is on holiday abroad	house at school	father loses money on stock exchange	boards at public school +10
swing in garden	electronics kit +5	mummy does not work +10	cubs		comprehensive GCE stream +5
bicycle in road	football strip +2	mum works	street gang	if you can name the local school with best exam results	comprehensive CSE stream

Social class

Unless you were 'born' into the 'right family' you will have found it very difficult to win our life chances game. Is this just as it is in real life?

There is not any single, accepted model of the class system that exists in society today. Here are two very different views.

Separate groups with opposing interests

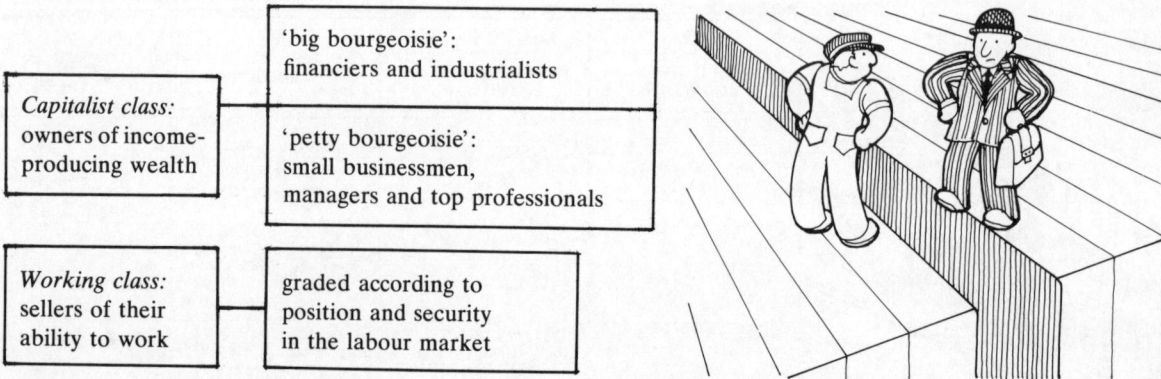

Capitalist class: owners of income-producing wealth

- 'big bourgeoisie': financiers and industrialists
- 'petty bourgeoisie': small businessmen, managers and top professionals

Working class: sellers of their ability to work

- graded according to position and security in the labour market

Separate grades on the social ladder

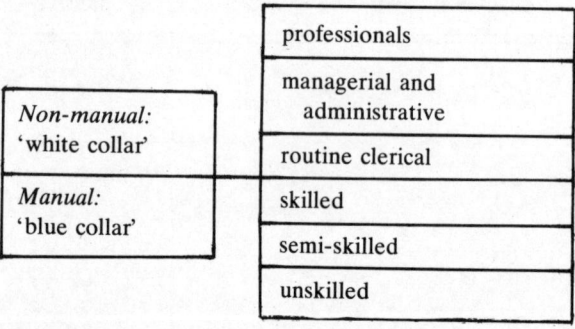

Non-manual: 'white collar'

- professionals
- managerial and administrative
- routine clerical

Manual: 'blue collar'

- skilled
- semi-skilled
- unskilled

The Registrar General (the official responsible for the collection of Census information) has produced a classification of social class based on the second model. He has found it necessary to modify his classification over time to reflect shifts in the occupational structure. The growth of the white collar sector largely reflects an increase in clerical employment for women. Many routine non-manual jobs now offer worse pay and security than skilled manual occupations.

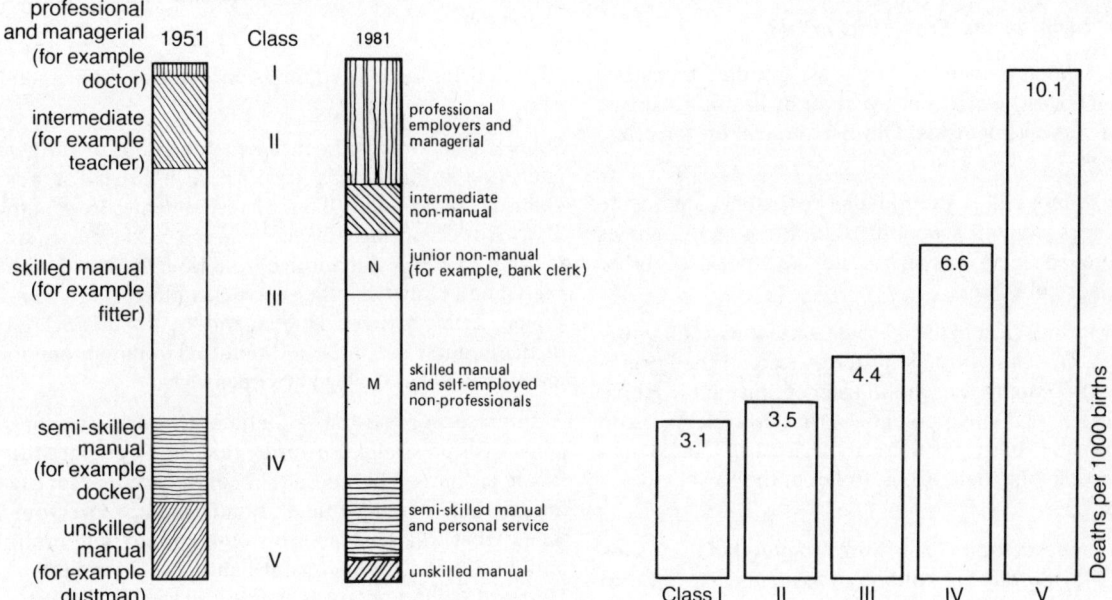

Figure 11   *Based on the occupation of the chief economic supporter of each household and excluding those not classified (students, retired people, armed forces, 'economically inactive' people)*

Figure 12   *Post neonatal deaths: England and Wales, 1975*

The class distinctions of disease

The table below gives the increased or decreased risk – in percentage terms – of a man from each of five social classes dying from certain causes. The particular work he does is not the main contributory factor as similar differences of risk exist for wives of men in these categories. Diet and lifestyle are major influences.

Table 8

Cause of death	Unskilled	Semi-skilled	Skilled	Managerial	Professional
All causes	+43	+ 3	average	−19	−24
Tuberculosis	+85	+ 8	−4	−46	−60
Stomach cancer	+63	+14	+1	−37	−51
Lung cancer	+48	+ 4	−7	−28	−37
Coronary disease	+12	− 4	−6	− 5	− 2
Bronchitis	+94	+16	−3	−50	−72
Duodenal ulcer	+73	+ 7	−4	−25	−52

Source: World Health Organization, Office of Population Censuses and Surveys

Who's who in the Eton class of '48

Most schools – even the best – are gratified by half-a-dozen Oxbridge places in a year; or by having a score or so of very distinguished Old Boys to call on for prize-givings.

Eton is above all that. From one year alone, among the 209 boys who left school in 1948, there are 33 names mentioned in *Who's Who*, not to speak of other accolades of success.

They include, just in the present Conservative administration, Douglas Hurd (Minister of State at the Foreign Office); Timothy Raison (Minister of State at the Home Office); – that's two potential Prime Ministers – Lord Mansfield (Minister of State at the Scottish Office); and Spencer le Marchant, Comptroller of the Royal Household.

The Ambassador to Spain, Sir Antony Acland, left Eton in 1948. So did Sir Anthony Lloyd, the High Court judge. Two royal equerries were their contemporaries: Randle Cooke (Duke of Edinburgh) and Lord Napier and Ettrick (Princess Margaret). It was Lord Snowdon's leaving year, too.

Among the rich men, perhaps the most famous are Sir James Goldsmith, Basil de Ferranti and Charles Hambro (of the bank of that name). The Marquess of Hertford, high up in the stately homes league with Ragley Hall, was there. So was Gay Kindersley, the famous amateur jockey and trainer; Julian Slade, the composer; the Hon. Robert Erskine, of TV art-programme fame. So, even, was the Dean of Wells, the Very Rev. Patrick Reynolds.

Nineteen are titled.

The Old Etonians, class of '48, are now aged just about 50: at the peak of their careers. We sent out a questionnaire to all of them and the 63 who replied often did so in gratifying detail. We asked about their education, their careers, positions, land-holdings; about their families.

Alliances forged on the playing fields (or indeed the river) of Eton last for a long time – especially amongst those who would not regard themselves as among nature's intellectuals. It was the same year in which Lord Snowdon ('Tiny' Armstrong-Jones, as he was known) coxed the Eton boat.

After school, all that generation were faced with National Service. The regiments they went into were mostly predictable: Coldstream, Scots, Life, Grenadier and Royal Horse Guards, 5th Royal Horse Artillery; 5th Royal Inniskilling Dragoons; the Buffs. Of our sample, 13 opted for regular commissions varying from three years on up.

Soldiering may have been taken for granted: further education certainly was not. Where it existed it was Oxbridge or nothing. Of our 63 respondents, 36 went to Oxford or Cambridge: five of them to Christ Church, six to King's College Cambridge, traditionally linked with the school. Only two other university places were mentioned: Trinty College, Dublin, and the London School of Economics. Six of the 63 went to Sandhurst; one to the Royal Naval College at Greenwich.

Eton protectiveness lasts a lifetime. Of our correspondents, six said straightforwardly that they went into the family business. This doesn't, of course, account for the innumerable family-friend ramifications. Everyone 'knew' that Charles Hambro would go into, and probably take over, the merchant bank. The Marquess of Hertford's inheritance was assured; so was Basil de Ferranti's entrance into his family firm.

Extrapolating from our sample, probably one in six of the Class of '48 are stockbrokers (though that doesn't necessarily mean they practise broking); and as many as one in ten Lloyds underwriters, either working for others, or just in their own names. Most are company directors, even if of only limited companies dealing with their own money, for tax purposes. Charles Hambro probably tops the list, with no less than 26 major directorships.

Outside the City and the world of money in general, what does seem odd is the under-representation – from the 'best school in the world' – of the professions. Two senior churchmen; three senior serving officers; six lawyers. We found one senior don, Mr Timothy Ryder, reader in Classics at Hull University. Not one of our correspondents was a school-teacher or a medical doctor: artists, in the widest sense, don't seem to have existed.

Many are landed gentry. We expected (correctly, as it turned out) reticence on this question. The Earl of Mansfield's estates in Perthshire are estimated at 33,880 acres. Of those prepared to describe their holdings, Mr James Morrison said he farmed 3,700 acres in Wiltshire, plus 2,000 acres woodland and 'land let'.

It is a truism that 90 per cent of Etonians are imbued with a particular kind of self-assurance, an off-handed but sometimes arrogant charm, which gives them a head start in life over other public schoolboys.

Guardian November 1979

As several studies have shown, patterns of class advantage and disadvantage have little changed in over fifty years. A survey by the Oxford Social Mobility Group indicated that the chances of 'lower class' people entering the 'higher class' have not changed since the 1920s.

Similarly, the Diamond Report on the distribution of wealth showed that the working class post-war improvement in living standards was not based on a bigger slice redistribution of the national wealth, but on an overall growth of the economic cake. As such, those living standards are vulnerable to any slow down in economic growth.

As judged by 'middle class' standards working class people are deficient in a whole range of factors, everything from intelligence and the ability to conceptualize, to health, social mobility, education and jobs. For instance it has been shown that children of Class V parents (unskilled manual), are more likely than others to:

be born abnormally early or late
be abnormally light or short
be bedwetters or nail biters
come from broken homes
have less well-educated parents
be unimmunized or vaccinated
be less frequent attenders of classes
have parents who are reluctant to consult teachers
have homes which are overcrowded or lack such basic
   amenities as hot water or a bath
go to the dentist less frequently
be aggressive and destructive
reject adult standards
speak unintelligibly
have poor general knowledge
be poor readers or poor at arithmetic
be classed as not specially creative
do less well at school
die
David Donnison, *A Pattern of Disadvantage* (National Foundation for Educational Research 1972)

It is some of these facts that the life chances game tries to simulate. People in the higher social groups will, in general, have better life chances and be able to pass these on to their children because they have:

(i) Greater awareness of their rights and the ability to get the 'system' to work for their benefit and that of their children.

(ii) Similar attitudes to other people in influential positions and there is a tendency for them to be given preferential treatment, if only unconsciously.

(iii) A higher income and better conditions of employment.

(iv) Greater job security and better access to mortgage and credit facilities.

(v) Better housing and personal transport.

(vi) Longer education leading to higher qualifications.

(vii) Better health and greater life expectancy.

Self-assessment questions

5 There are differing attitudes to social class. It is sometimes said that we are all becoming middle class, with the upper and working classes moving towards the centre.
   What evidence supports or contradicts this conclusion?

6 It is sometimes said that young people are 'classless' with similar tastes in clothes and music.
   (i) Is this true?
   (ii) What class do you belong to?
   (iii) What class do other people think you belong to?

7 There are differing attitudes to society, with the middle class tending to emphasize hard work and ability, and working class people stressing luck and 'who you know'.
   (i) What factors assist you to get on in life?
   (ii) Do you see society in terms of the 'social ladder' or 'us and them'?

Saying it with clothes

Class is a matter of economic position and the inequalities of wealth, power, opportunities and security that result from it. This situation is obscured by the preoccupation of many people with the *symbols* of social ranking: what sociologists call 'status'. We all judge one another by an unconscious and unspoken language of status. This code communicates by signs: in this exercise it works in terms of clothes.

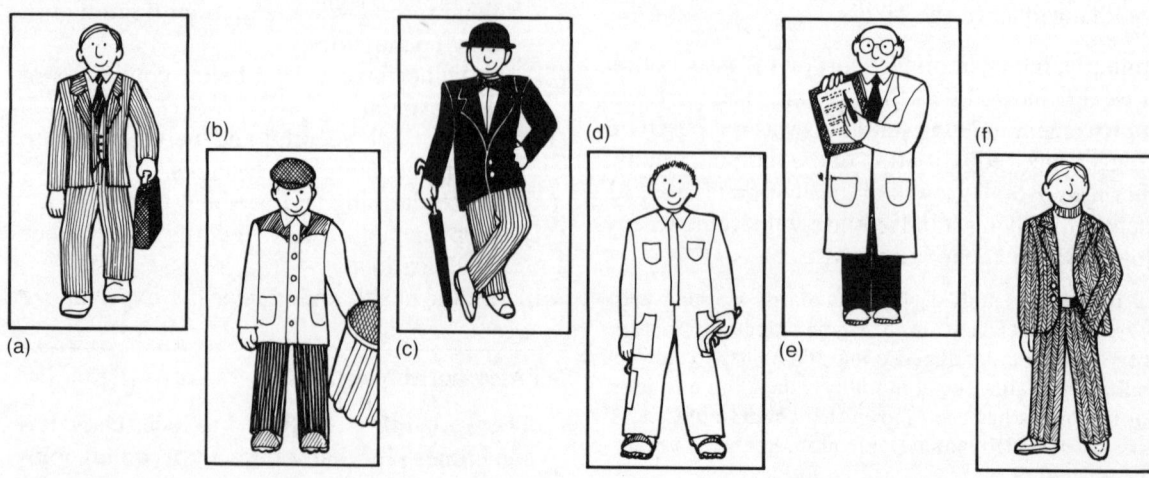

Figure 13

8 Rank the outfits shown in Figure 13 in order of status. Then compare your results with the rest of your group.

Clothes not only indicate our social status but also the peer group to which we belong within the wider culture. It is during our teens and early twenties that these peer groups become an increasingly important influence and sociologists have suggested the existence of a 'youth culture'. The peer groups formed at school, for example, help us develop our individual and social identities. Paul Willis has analysed the importance of one such group as a means for 'the lads' to resist their teachers and gain superiority over conformist students.

The first signs of a lad 'coming out' is a fairly rapid change in his clothes and hairstyle. The particular form of this alternative dress is determined by outside influences, especially fashions current in the wider symbolic system of youth culture. Whatever the particular form of dress, it is most certainly not school uniform, rarely includes a tie (the second best for many heads if uniform cannot be enforced), and exploits colours calculated to give the maximum distinction from institutional drabness and conformity. There is a clear stereotypical notion of what constitutes institutional clothes – Spike, for instance, trying to describe the shape of a collar: 'You know, like a teacher's!'

Paul Willis, *Learning to Labour* (Saxon House 1978)

There is a close connection between the needs of young people to assert their own distinctive identity, and the trends in clothes, music and dancing that are exploited commercially by the fashion and entertainment industries.

9 Consider the list of youth-cultural styles in Table 9 with their approximate year of emergence, some of the features of their visual style and the values associated with them.
Fill in the missing information and complete the table. Add any other styles which have recently appeared.

Table 9

Year	Group	Clothes		Hair		Music and dance	Attitudes and image
		Male	Female	Male	Female		
1956	Teds	Draped jacket Drain-pipe trousers Beetle-crusher shoes Velvet collar Bootlace tie	Tight sweater Full skirt Bobby sox	DA Quiff Brylcreamed hair	Pony- tail	Rock 'n' roll Bill Haley Elvis Presley Jiving	Being masculine and aggressive
1958	Beatniks						
1962	Beatle people						
1965	Mods						
1965	Rockers						
1967	Hippies						
1968	Skinheads						
1976	Punk rockers						

Peer groups in action

Peer groups are more than a means of reinforcing *individual* identity through clothes, hair and music etc. They are a means to express our *collective* identity through group action in which individuals act out distinctive roles.

In a recent report on soccer violence it was suggested that many of the fans involved are younger people with particular problems: they are either unemployed, socially deprived, bored, or frustrated by what they see as a 'sick society'. Unable to achieve status from their activities at school, work and home, these young people find an expression for their frustrations only in a working class youth culture of violence. Their groups applaud those activities that they can be good at: fighting, heavy drinking, group loyalty and gaining control of a territory. A soccer match is seen as a 'natural arena' which 'offers an acknowledged meeting place, a carnival atmosphere in exciting contrast to the drabness of the workaday week and scope for belonging to a loosely constructed group'.

This explanation does not claim that there is a single, easily tackled cause of soccer violence. Indeed, it sees the problem as part of a general revolt of vulnerable young people against an unsympathetic adult society.

10 (i)   What other groups, beside those of young people, seek a distinct identity for themselves in any of the following?

> special clothes
> fighting skills
> heavy drinking
> territorial control
> group loyalty

(ii)   Are they all presented unfavourably by the mass media?

(iii) Is the above explanation of soccer violence too 'soft' on the 'hooligan'?

Male and female

The socializing function of the family and peer groups is particularly important in forming our attitudes to the opposite sex. Do you agree or disagree with the following five statements?

(i)   Women are better cooks than men.
(ii)   Men are more mechanically minded than women.
(iii) It is natural for women to look after children.
(iv)   A man should buy the drinks for his lady in a bar.
(v)   A husband who isn't the breadwinner must lose his self-respect.

While we are still small children we learn the appropriate behaviour and attitudes for boys and girls. Young boys are told that it is 'sissy' to play with their sister's doll and that 'big boys don't cry'. Dad takes little Johnny to the park for a game of football while young Susie is encouraged to help mum with the washing-up. By the time we go to school the patterns of our sex-roles are already determined.

These attitudes reflect the situation in an industrial society in which earning a living occurs on an individual basis outside the home. Even when husbands and wives both work, the woman usually has the lower income and she is the one who leaves her job to look after children.

Is this situation inevitable? In the seventeenth century hand-loom weaving was carried out as shared, family activity inside the home. Why can't work be carried out on a shared and equal basis today? Or perhaps couples could alternate spells of employment and child care. Why should housework be a woman's job?

These prevailing attitudes are reinforced in our peer groups. Paul Willis has characterized a typically working class male attitude:

There is a traditional conflict in their view of women: they are both sexual objects and domestic comforters. In essence this means that whilst women must be sexually attractive, they cannot be sexually experienced . . . she is a sex object, a commodity, she is actually diminished by sex . . . she has been romantically and materially partly consumed. The 'girl-friend' is a very different category from an 'easy lay'. She represents the human value that is squandered by promiscuity. She is the loyal domestic partner. She cannot be held to be sexually experienced – or at least not with others. Circulated stories about the sexual adventures of the 'missus' are a first rate challenge to masculinity and pride. . . .

Working class girls often resolve the contradiction between being sexually desirable but not sexually experienced by retreating into a world of romanticism (readily encouraged by teenage magazines). Girlish behaviour such as the 'crush' and message-sending within the protective circle of the informal female group only strengthens boys' sense of superiority.

Men's lib?

Social pressure to conform to our traditional sex-roles does not only restrict the lives of women: it may also cause anxiety for men. In Sweden an official report, based on interviews with men from a wide range of backgrounds, revealed some of their deepest worries.

Loneliness
Most of the men had no close friends (apart from their wives and girl-friends) with whom they could discuss their anxieties and frustrations. As a result they were convinced that other men – unlike them-

selves – were never fearful, never miserable, never frustrated, always hunting after sexual adventure, and were tough and virile like James Bond. While men form a far wider range of 'secondary friend-ships' – with workmates and others who share their interests – they have much greater difficulty than women in developing intimate friendships. It is from lack of a confidant that men develop peculiar ideas about each other, and also about women.

Loss of virility
Many men reported that they were inhibited by the constant emphasis in magazines, films, etc. on sex-ual performance. They felt under strong pressure to make love frequently. For most of the men interviewed, to be 'free' meant to be promiscuous. Yet only one man in five was regularly unfaithful, chasing girls all the time. These men insisted that it was nothing to do with emotion; it was a question of proving 'you were a man'.

Unsatisfactory family life
Many of the men thought that their preoccupation with work prevented them from enjoying to the full their role as householders and fathers. They frequently believed that their wives encouraged this state of affairs, to keep their supremacy in the home. The report said that too many mothers try to guard their possessive mother-role and avoid sharing it with the father. Men even suffer from their wives' reluctance to let them do housework. One man told his interviewer: 'It's no good my doing it, she only does it all over again'.

In Sweden, as in Britain, most of the decision-makers in public affairs are men. They are so busy taking decisions that they never have time to cook, do housework or take care of their children: so they never learn what life is like for most people. The report questions whether the widely-accepted differences between men and women are real, and if not, whether they should be perpetuated. 'What the world needs today is not toughness,' it says. 'The world needs capacity for involvement, a will to co-operate, human understanding and tender-ness. This can only be achieved by giving a fair and equal share of the responsibilities of life to both sexes.'

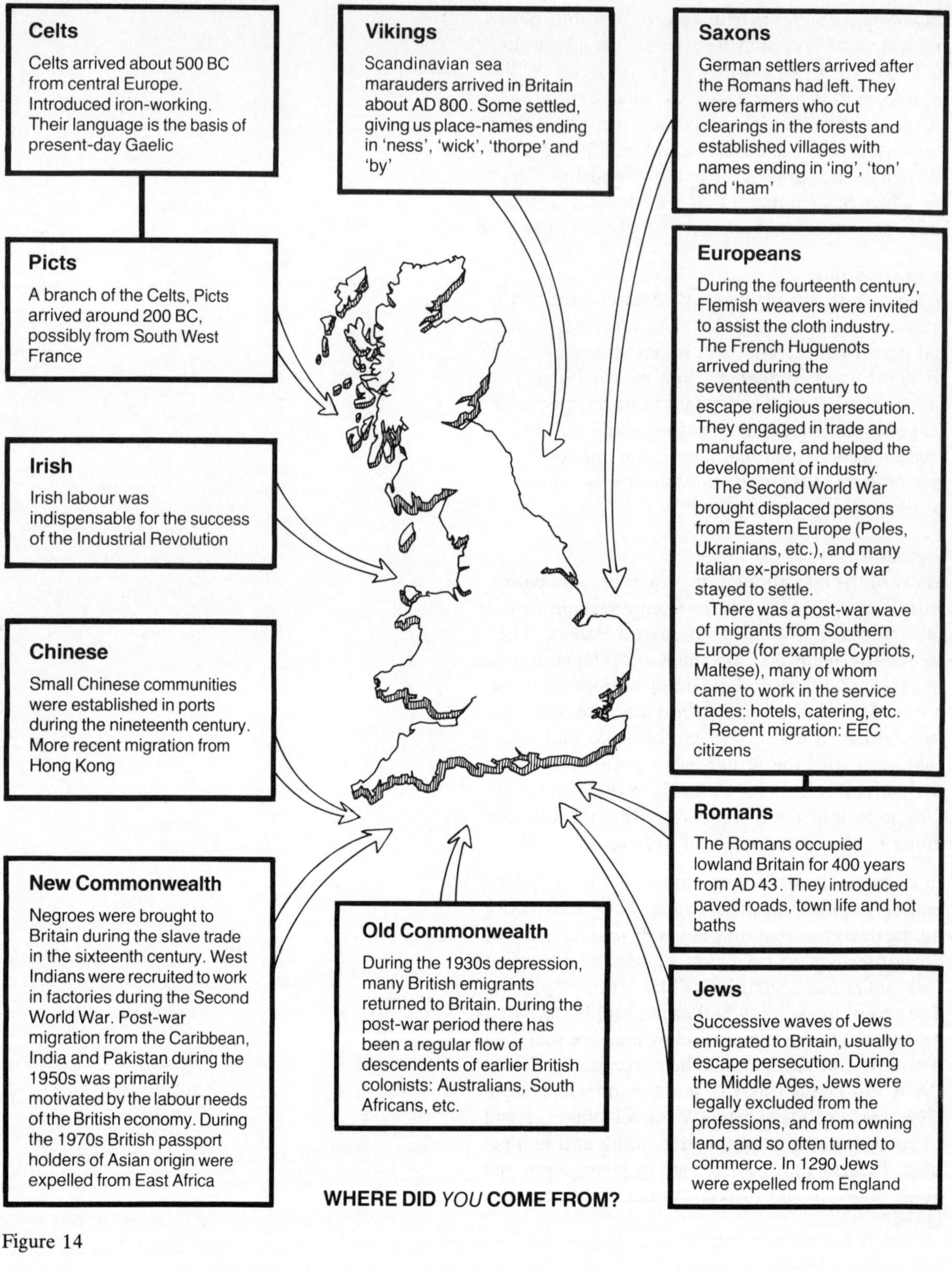

Celts

Celts arrived about 500 BC from central Europe. Introduced iron-working. Their language is the basis of present-day Gaelic

Vikings

Scandinavian sea marauders arrived in Britain about AD 800. Some settled, giving us place-names ending in 'ness', 'wick', 'thorpe' and 'by'

Saxons

German settlers arrived after the Romans had left. They were farmers who cut clearings in the forests and established villages with names ending in 'ing', 'ton' and 'ham'

Picts

A branch of the Celts, Picts arrived around 200 BC, possibly from South West France

Europeans

During the fourteenth century, Flemish weavers were invited to assist the cloth industry. The French Huguenots arrived during the seventeenth century to escape religious persecution. They engaged in trade and manufacture, and helped the development of industry.

The Second World War brought displaced persons from Eastern Europe (Poles, Ukrainians, etc.), and many Italian ex-prisoners of war stayed to settle.

There was a post-war wave of migrants from Southern Europe (for example Cypriots, Maltese), many of whom came to work in the service trades: hotels, catering, etc.

Recent migration: EEC citizens

Irish

Irish labour was indispensable for the success of the Industrial Revolution

Chinese

Small Chinese communities were established in ports during the nineteenth century. More recent migration from Hong Kong

Romans

The Romans occupied lowland Britain for 400 years from AD 43. They introduced paved roads, town life and hot baths

New Commonwealth

Negroes were brought to Britain during the slave trade in the sixteenth century. West Indians were recruited to work in factories during the Second World War. Post-war migration from the Caribbean, India and Pakistan during the 1950s was primarily motivated by the labour needs of the British economy. During the 1970s British passport holders of Asian origin were expelled from East Africa

Old Commonwealth

During the 1930s depression, many British emigrants returned to Britain. During the post-war period there has been a regular flow of descendants of earlier British colonists: Australians, South Africans, etc.

Jews

Successive waves of Jews emigrated to Britain, usually to escape persecution. During the Middle Ages, Jews were legally excluded from the professions, and from owning land, and so often turned to commerce. In 1290 Jews were expelled from England

WHERE DID *YOU* COME FROM?

Figure 14

Racialism

Immigration is often seen by the 'host' population as a threat from 'outsiders'. The process is more likely to be associated with tension and conflict when:

(i) The immigrants have distinctive and different appearance, customs and beliefs.

(ii) There is already competition for such things as jobs and housing.

Additionally, Britain has the legacy of a colonial mentality that sees black people as 'savages' whom it was the 'white man's burden' to civilize. Often these ideas were merely presented as a justification for slavery and colonial exploitation, but now they have become part of the popular stereotype of 'Pakis' and 'coons'.

Should we expect immigrant groups to:

(i) abandon their own culture (religion, diet, dress, marriage customs, festivals, etc.) and adopt the culture of the host society; or

(ii) Retain their own culture as a distinctive part of the wider society?

The latter course was the one which was followed by virtually all British settlers who migrated to foreign lands.

Self-assessment questions

11 Find out about British people who emigrated from this country during the nineteenth and twentieth centuries.

12 What impact did *they* have upon the host populations?

13 If there was a world-wide policy of sending home all immigrants and their descendants, how many would be arriving back in Britain from America, Canada, Australia, South Africa, etc.?

Immigration: what do you think?

Self-assessment question

14 Indicate whether you think that the following statements are true or false.

(i) There is uncontrolled immigration into this country.

(ii) Immigration is making Britain an overcrowded island.

(iii) White people are leaving this country and are being replaced by black immigrants.

(iv) There are over five million black people in this country.

(v) There are large numbers of illegal immigrants entering the country.

(vi) All immigrants are the same.

(vii) Immigrants get priority in housing.

(viii) Blacks come here to sponge off the welfare state.

(ix) Immigrants come here and take white people's jobs.

(x) The Race Relations Act gives black people rights that whites don't have.

Immigration: the evidence

(i) Under the 1971 Immigration Act very few categories of people can come and settle in Britain. They are:

(a) Commonwealth citizens whose parents or grandparents were born here.

(b) Spouses, fiances and specified dependents of those already here.

(c) Certain people with British passports who have no other citizenship.

All EEC nationals have a right to work in any EEC country.

(ii) The chart in Figure 15 shows immigration and emigration trends in Britain from 1965 to 1981.

(iii) Well under half of the people who come to Britain are black (from areas such as India, Caribbean and other 'New Commonwealth' countries). Most immigrants

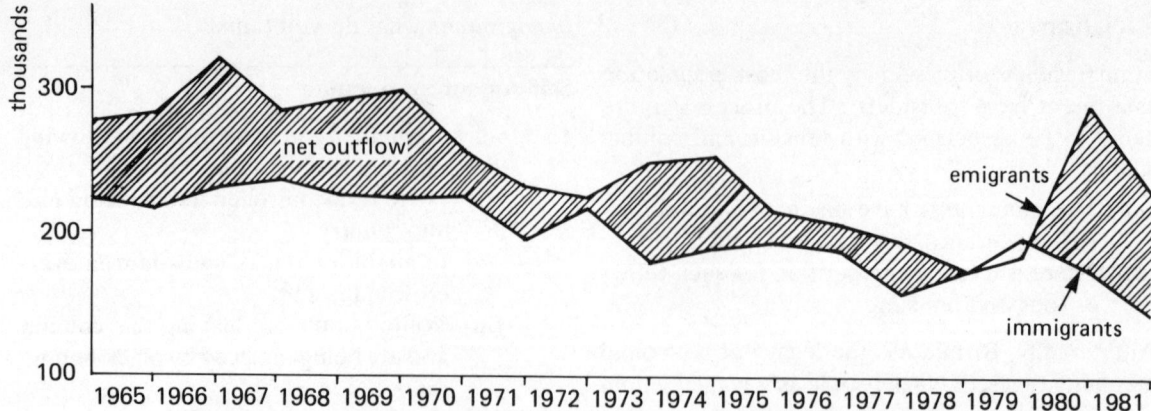

Figure 15

are from the United States of America, Canada and countries of the EEC.

(iv)   The latest estimate of the size of the non-white population is 2.7 millions (5 per cent of the total population). About half of these people are not foreigners at all as they were born in Britain. Why do people think that a large group of coloured people is a 'problem'?

(v)   It is impossible for anyone to know how many illegal immigrants there are, but only a couple of hundred are arrested each year. In 1974 the government announced an amnesty for illegal immigrants and after one year less than 2,000 people had applied.

(vi)   Black people, like everybody else, are different from each other. Although there is a tendency to see no difference between people with the same colour skin, there is probably little in common between a Pakistani doctor and a hospital porter from Trinidad except their concern for patients. Another example is that West Indians and Asians have very different attitudes to marriage. People from the Indian subcontinent may be Hindus, Sikhs or Moslems.

(vii)   In 1977 34 per cent of white families lived in council housing but only 24 per cent of coloured families.

(viii)   Although discrimination results in higher rates of unemployment among black teenagers in some areas, a higher proportion of immigrant males are working compared to white men. The reason for this is quite simple: blacks as a group are younger than whites so there are more of them working and, therefore, paying tax and national insurance.

Since there are proportionately fewer old people in the black community, they take much less from the state than the white population (for example, in old age pensions). Indeed, one study has shown that black people are likely to receive only 85 per cent as much as their fellow citizens from state funds for health, welfare, education, social services and housing.

(ix)   During the 1950s and 1960s, when there was a shortage of labour, many industrialized countries turned to the underdeveloped world to help them out. West Germany, France and Switzerland have a greater proportion of migrants in the total workforce than Britain. As a French industrialist states: 'What worries me is the rising aspirations of the French worker. . . . They are increasingly looking for white collar jobs and the only way we can match this outflow is by using immigrants. Nearly 25 per cent of Renault's workforce is now immigrant'. In 1976 nine out of ten workers on the production line at Ford's Cologne plant were migrants from countries such as Turkey, Greece, Yugoslavia, Italy, Portugal and Morocco.

It is now very difficult for a New Commonwealth citizen to get a work permit in Britain since they are not issued if the job can be filled by a local person.

(x) The Race Relations Act gives protection to all of us against discrimination on grounds of colour, race and ethnic origin. It is now an offence to stir up racial hatred. There is still concern, however, among some immigrant communities about:

  (a) The level of intimidation and violence they suffer from gangs of white youths.
  (b) The government's methods of enforcing immigration laws.
  (c) The 'unfair' use of police powers against West Indian youths.

We have argued that all the statements on page 59 are false. A prejudiced person will not have been convinced by our evidence. But then, such a person tars every member of a group with the same brush and reacts to people because of *who they are* (... Pakis, United supporters, Mods, Catholics ...) rather than because of *what they do*.

5 A life of your own

The aim of this section is to outline some of the problems faced by young people today. You will be encouraged to consider the questions of employment, accommodation, sources of information, emotional and sexual relationships and contraception.

Adolescence and change

When a boy grows up in a primitive society, say among the Australian aborigines, and he reaches a particular stage of physical development, the men of the tribe will take him away from the village and out into the bush for a few days. There the boy is initiated into the secrets of the tribe. When he returns to the village he will be treated as a man, with adult rights and responsibilities. The transformation from 'child' to 'adult' has occurred virtually overnight.

Growing up in Britain isn't so straightforward. The period from the end of puberty around the age of sixteen (the rapid growth spurt) to the time when many young people get married in their early twenties, is a period of change and contradictions. Sometimes adults regard adolescents as equals and at other times they treat them as kids. Therefore, on occasions young people feel mature and independent and on others they find themselves behaving childishly and irresponsibly. What do appeals to 'act your age' really mean? The law reflects this confusion:

At *12* you can be sent to a community home.

At *13* you can buy a pet.

At *14* you can own an air rifle and pawn an article.

At *15* you may be sentenced to a Borstal Institution.

At *16* you may legally buy fireworks and cigarettes, join the armed forces and get married with your parents' permission.

At *17* you may be sentenced to prison and hold a licence to drive a car.

At *18* you may legally see adult-rated films, buy drinks in a pub, place a bet, give blood, vote and sign a binding contract.

At *21* you can stand for Parliament.

Adolescence is a period when young people go through a series of complex physical, sexual and intellectual changes. During this time youngsters normally:

(i)   Become independent from their parents.

(ii) Develop new kinds of social and working arrangements.

(iii) Develop a sense of their own identity.

(iv) Clarify their views about the world.

(v)   Take decisions that affect their future.

Parents

One study of 16,000 teenagers found that 86 per cent of them got on well with their mothers and 80 per cent of them with their fathers. Where friction did occur the main problems were hairstyles and dress, followed by coming-in times. These problems reflect two sources of conflict:

(i)   Parents are reluctant to accept that their son or daughter is no longer a child and that old rules and regulations are no longer appropriate.

(ii) Young people realize that their parents' standards and patterns of behaviour are not the only possible ones, and that they actually prefer to adopt some of the alternatives. Influences from outside the family – friends and 'idols' – become more important.

Some parents try to enforce petty restrictions merely in order to prop up their slipping authority; others are genuinely concerned that their children should not adopt an adult life-style before they are responsible enough to handle it.

Self-assessment questions

1 How much control should parents retain over adolescents?
2 What do you dislike most about parents?
3 The main complaint of most young people is lack of privacy (for example, over one-third share a bedroom). Why do you think this is a problem?

Employment

Probably the most important decision that adolescents face concerns the question 'What are you going to do when you leave school?' At the age of 16, when teenagers have finished their compulsory education they have several main choices of what to do, as can be seen in Figure 16.

Self-assessment question

4 What are the advantages and problems associated with the possibilities listed in Figure 16?

Sooner or later, you must consider the question of employment. Some of your freedom of choice has been reduced by the time you leave school, for example by the subjects that you studied. Equally important is the availability of employment in your area. One of the consequences of increasing competition for jobs is to raise the standard of qualifications that are normally required for entry.

How do you select a suitable job, bearing in mind that your decision may affect the kind of work that you do for the next 45 years? Do you scramble for the first vacancy? Or calmly match your skills, abilities and interests with the qualities and requirements of different jobs? Here are some factors to take into account:

(i) What combination of mental and physical effort does the job require?
(ii) What unusual conditions are involved (travel, shifts, dangers, etc.)?
(iii) What are the short and long term prospects of the job?
(iv) How is your job likely to change as you become older and more experienced?
(v) Will you learn a skill that can easily be transferred to a new employer, area or trade?

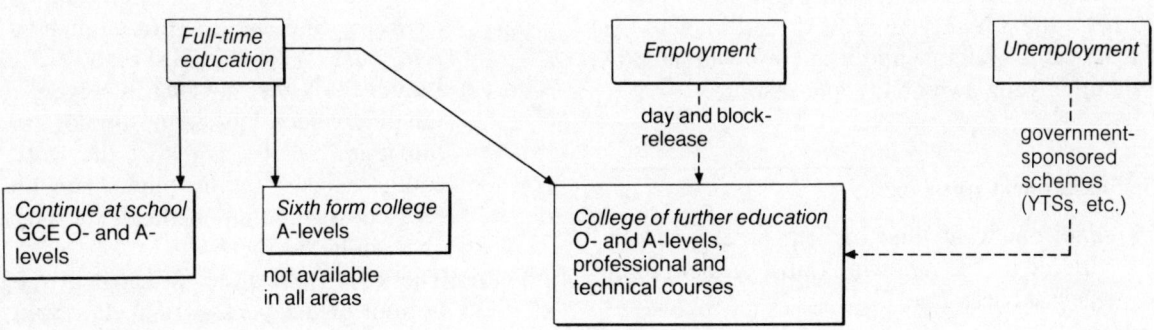

Figure 16

Self-assessment questions

5   (i)   What careers advice did you receive from teachers, careers services, firms, relations, etc.

(ii)   How reliable and useful was it?

6   How did you find out about the opportunities available (from friends, media, etc.)?

7   How could young people be given a clearer idea of what different kinds of work are really like?

8   (i)   Rank the following features according to how important they were in your choice of a job:

chances of promotion	near to home
friendly workmates	pleasant working conditions
friendly management	responsibility
good holidays	safe working conditions
good pay	social club
interesting work	status of job
job security	training
	travel

(ii)   How many are met by your job?

(iii)   What kind of work would satisfy all your requirements?

(iv)   Are you in the right job?

Useful sources of advice and information

Being independent means solving the problems of everyday life for yourself. But whatever problem you have, there is usually someone whose job it is to help and advise you. You should know what assistance is available and when you will need to rely upon your own ability and resources.

Self-assessment questions

9   Find out what kind of help or expertise is offered by the following (most of them offer their services free).

(i)   *Individuals*: doctors, solicitors (some work in Law Centres), social workers, student councillors, local councillors, MPs.

(ii)   *State-funded agencies*: Citizen's Advice Bureaux, libraries, Department of Health and Social Security, Job Centres, Family Planning clinics, local authority departments, police.

(iii)   *Voluntary organizations*: trade unions, Women's Aid, National Society for the Prevention of Cruelty to Children.

10   Where would you go to obtain advice in order to solve these problems?

(i)   A bloke drove into my bike yesterday. He admitted liability at the time but this morning came round to say that his insurance had expired and he can't afford to pay for the repair. He now says that the accident was my fault anyway.

(ii)   The people next door have a dog that barks all night. When I went round to complain, my neighbour threatened to let it loose on me. What can I do?

(iii)   My boss at the garage where I work says that unless I get my hair cut and smarten my appearance he'll give me the sack. Have I got the right to dress how I like?

(iv)   My girl-friend had a big row with her parents and they threw her out of the house. She stayed at my place last night but my parents reckon she ought to go home. She doesn't want to go crawling back and, anyway, I don't think they'd have her. She doesn't earn enough to rent a flat. What should she do?

(v)   I don't think that my local is serving a full pint of beer. I asked the landlord to top it up, but he said that the froth counts as part of the pint. Then he refused to serve me again. Is he right and can he do that?

(vi)   There's an old dried-up canal at the bottom of our back garden. It's been used as a rubbish dump and now it's rat infested and smells horribly in the

summer. The local kids play there –
they need a decent adventure play-
ground.

(vii) I've been round to see my granny. She's
on her own now that my parents have
moved to Leeds. The neighbours said
that they hadn't seen her all week. I
broke the door lock and found her in
bed. I think she's dead.

(viii) My brother is away at university. During his summer vacation I found him
smoking dope. I think that he may be
into hard drugs too. My parents would
go berserk if I told them.

(ix) My landlord wants to double my rent. I
said that I won't pay more until he fixes
the water heater. He says that if I don't
pay he'll throw me out. I'm worried
that I'll come home and find all my gear
on the street.

(x) My sister is married with three young
kids. Her husband doesn't earn much
and they can't make ends meet. Is there
any way they can get some financial
help?

A home of your own

If you are living at home, your own room is often
the place where you try to express your personality: wallposters, colour schemes, degree of untidi-
ness, etc. But you may still feel restricted: 'Don't
play your records too loud'. You probably pay
something towards your board. How much would
it cost you to provide all these services for yourself
(for example, laundry, food, heating, rent, rates,
refrigerator, TV)?

Leaving home marks a major step towards independence. Students often leave home quite early
when they go away to university, but most young
workers live with their parents until they get married. Even then, newly married couples frequently
live at home with one set of parents for a time until
they can afford to get their own home.

There are one million more *homes* than *house-*

11 What are the advantages and disadvantages
of:
(i) Living with in-laws.
(ii) Rented accommodation.
(iii) Buying your own home.

Housing

In Britain there are more than 20 million dwellings. Of every ten homes, approximately:

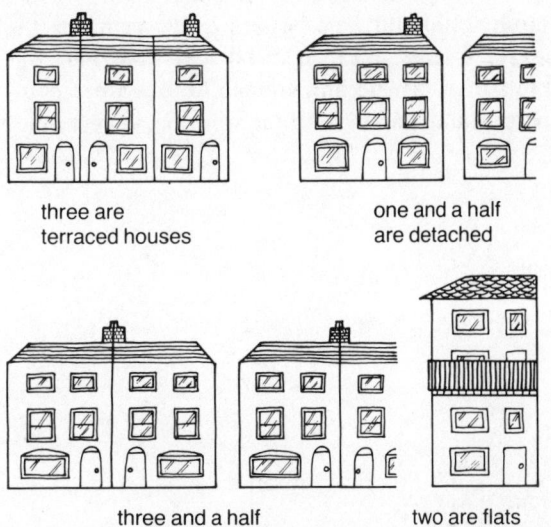

three are
terraced houses

one and a half
are detached

three and a half
are semi-detached

two are flats
and maisonettes

holds, so why do people talk about a 'housing
problem'? There are several reasons why:

(i) Over 70,000 people are actually *homeless*:
they have nowhere permanent to live.
(ii) Over one million houses have been
declared *unfit* for human habitation.
(iii) Another million, while not actually slums,
lack one or more of the *basic amenities*:
what most of us take for granted as everyday
essential fittings (for example, a bathroom,
a hot water system, an inside lavatory).
(iv) The total number of housing units includes
190,000 'second homes' and even more
empty properties (630,000 in England
according to a 1982 survey – 100,000 of
them council owned).

(v) Many properties are *under-occupied*, for example by elderly people whose relatives have died or moved away.

(vi) The homes are not always where people need them.

(vii) There needs to be a reserve of vacant houses to allow people to move about.

New households are constantly being formed while older houses continue to fall into disrepair. It has been estimated that an extra 300,000 houses must be built each year to meet these basic needs. To actually replace the existing slums would require 500,000 new houses every year for the next 15 years. Yet, in 1980 less than half this number of private and council houses were completed, and the 1981 total was the lowest since 1951. With housing earmarked to contribute over two-thirds of the total net reduction in public expenditure by 1984, it is unlikely that the situation will improve much in the near future.

Table 10   *Housing standards in 1981*

Type of tenure	Overcrowding (more than one person per room)	Lacking basic facilities. Without exclusive use of:	
		bath or shower	inside WC
Owner-occupied	2%	2%	2%
Rented from local authority/new town	8%	1%	1%
Rented privately	4%	15%	15%
All tenures	4%	3%	4%

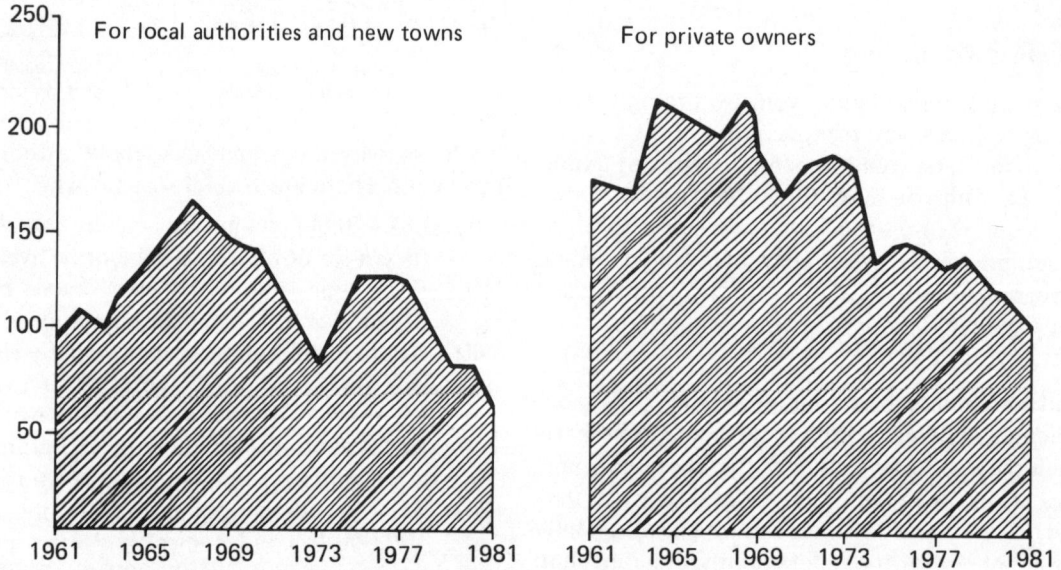

Figure 17   *Houses and flats completed 1961–81 in England and Wales*
Source: Housing and Construction Statistics (HMSO)

Sector A, in Figure 18, contains a large proportion of the oldest and poorest housing: three-quarters were built before 1919 (compared to one-third of all houses); many lack a basic amenity.

For many years, landlords have been selling their best property for owner-occupation.

Although private tenants are generally the poorest group of householders, they are the worst off for financial assistance from the government.

In Scotland 54 per cent of all houses are in Sector B, but less than a quarter in South West England. In London two-thirds of council properties are flats, but only 30 per cent in Manchester. The standard of these dwellings is reasonably good: two-thirds have been built since 1945.

In Sector C we have the owner-occupiers. The Conservative Party believes that councils should be legally obliged to sell their homes to sitting tenants who are now entitled to discounts of 33–50 per cent off the market value and 100 per cent council mortgages on demand. The Labour Party argues that selling houses reduces the stock of homes available and that only those of poorer quality will be left for the million people on council waiting lists.

Buying a house

Most people cannot afford to buy a house outright, so they borrow money from a building society and pay back the loan, plus interest, over 20 or 30 years. This is called a mortgage. House prices depend upon:

(i) The costs of construction (including the purchase of building land).
(ii) The number of homes for sale.
(iii) The amount of cash available to buy them.

Building societies are cautious about whom they lend money to and what type of properties they will consider. This can pose difficulties for people:

(i) On low incomes (you can usually borrow about 2½ times your annual income).
(ii) Buying older properties or flats.

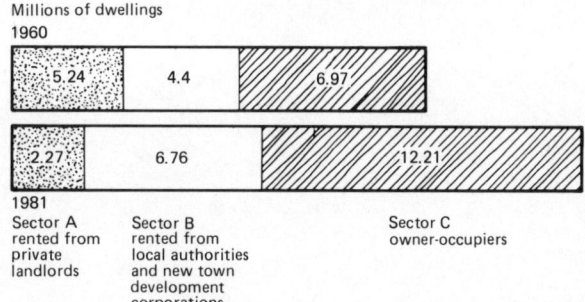

Millions of dwellings
1960
Sector A rented from private landlords
Sector B rented from local authorities and new town development corporations
Sector C owner-occupiers

Figure 18

(iii) Who cannot find a large deposit (usually 10 per cent of the total purchase price) from their savings.

Although owner-occupiers as a group are more prosperous than other householders, they enjoy a state subsidy in the form of tax relief on mortgage interest payments; improvement grants from the local council; and free capital gains when owners sell their houses. On the other hand, there are a lot of additional expenses involved in house purchase: valuation and conveyancing fees, deposit, insurance premiums, etc.

Housing survey

Carry out a survey of housing in your area. You will probably be able to obtain useful statistics and maps from your local library and town hall. Here are a few questions to consider:

When were different parts of the town built?
Was housing planned or did it 'just happen'?
Have housing needs changed over time (for example large Victorian houses built for rich families with servants may have been divided into flats for multiple occupation)?
What do you think are 'basic amenities' (for example, does it include central heating)?
What proportion of houses have gardens and garages?
Are they in a good state of repair and decoration?
Are they near to shops, schools, bus routes and play areas?

Are streets wide, well-lit, tree-lined, etc?

How many people are homeless or on the council waiting list?

What sort of people are they?

What provision exists for homeless people?

Has your council carried out a programme of slum clearance?

Where were people re-housed? *What* do they think about the change?

How many new homes (public and private) were completed in your area last year?

How many houses will be needed in the future? And *what* type?

Where should the resources come from?

The Housing Department

Imagine you are an official in the local authority housing department. A three-bedroomed council house has become available on a new estate and there are three applicants at the top of the waiting list. It is your job to select the applicant who qualifies.

Self-assessment question

12 Now that you have these facts look at the three different application forms (Figures 19, 20 and 21) and assess each one using the points system. Which applicant should have priority?

Bursley Metropolitan Borough
Rules regarding eligibility for council housing

The applicant must have been resident within the Borough for at least two years; *or*

If resident outside the Borough, must have been employed within the Borough for at least three years; *or*

If over 60 years of age, must have close relatives in the Borough who have been resident for two years and will give supportive assistance.

All applicants must be over 18 years of age and must have been on the waiting list for at least six months before an offer of tenancy can be made.

Joint applications will be accepted from engaged couples. After six months have elapsed, applicants will be pointed as if living with the least over-crowded parent but no tenancy will be granted until the applicants are actually married.

Points system

In the present situation where there is high demand for council housing, the points system will allow the council to allocate the available dwellings fairly and justly on the basis of need. The number of points allocated reflects the degree of eligibility.

Classifications

0 points – owner-occupiers/modern property/no overcrowding
private tenants/modern property/no overcrowding

4 points – owner-occupiers/old property
service tenants (that is caretakers, publicans, resident domestics, etc.)

6 points – private tenants/old houses/no overcrowding

8 points – non-householders/outside the Borough/working in Bursley

12 points – private tenants/modern houses/overcrowding
owner-occupiers/old houses/overcrowding

14 points – lodger applicants (that is c/o in-laws, in rooms, lodgings, etc.)/no overcrowding

16 points – lodger applicants/overcrowding
private tenants/old houses/overcrowding

Overcrowding   The Housing Committee considers the following a reasonable standard of overcrowding. Exclusive use of one bedroom for:

a man and wife;
a widow or widower;
a single person or two single males or two single females of the same family;
one child or two children under the age of 7 of the same family.

Combined rooms   (for example bedsitters) are not counted as bedrooms. Rooms less than 50 square feet, attics and bedrooms used as a passageway by other occupants are disregarded.

Old houses   means houses and flats which do not have their own bath, inside WC and water heating system.

Modern houses   means houses which do have these amenities.

Extra points

In order to allow the greatest flexibility in dealing with special circumstances:

Up to 10 points – severe medical cases recommended by the Council's medical officer.

Up to 16 points – special circumstances and social factors at the discretion of the Housing Committee.

APPLICATION FOR ACCOMMODATION

BURSLEY
METROPOLITAN BOROUGH
Housing Department Town Hall

1 Full name of applicant *YUSEF ALI PANGGABEAN*

2 Address *57 FILBERT STREET*

3 Are you

✓	married
	single
	widowed
	divorced

4 Are you at present

	a lodger
✓	a tenant
	an owner–occupier

5 Is your accommodation

	a house
✓	a flat
	a bed-sitter
	a hostel

6 Name and address of employer *OLD TRAFFORD MILL, CARROW ROAD*

7 Weekly income *£75*

8 Length of residence in the borough *18 YRS*

9 Give details of present accommodation (tick appropriate column)

	Exclusive use	Shared use	None
Kitchen	✓		
Living room	✓		
Bedroom 1	✓		
Bedroom 2			✓
Bathroom	✓		
Any other room			✓
Internal water closet	✓		
Hot water supply	✓		

10 List persons to be rehoused as a result of application

Surname	Forename	Sex	Date of birth	Relationship to applicant
Applicant	—	M	19/2/35	—
PANGGABEAN	JEMILLA	F	2/9/46	WIFE
PANGGABEAN	ANWAR	F	5/7/09	MOTHER
PANGGABEAN	KHALDA	F	17/10/63	DAUGHTER
PANGGABEAN	NAJMA	F	3/3/65	DAUGHTER

11 Give details of any medical consideration or special circumstances to be taken into account when assessment of your application is made

MY ELDEST DAUGHTER IS PARTIALLY PARALYSED AS A RESULT OF A CAR ACCIDENT WHEN SHE WAS A CHILD. BOTH SHE AND MY ELDERLY MOTHER HAVE GREAT DIFFICULTY CLIMBING THE STAIRS TO OUR FLAT.

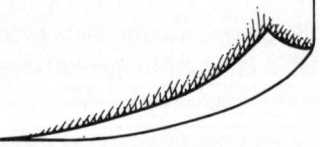

Figure 19

APPLICATION FOR ACCOMMODATION

BURSLEY
METROPOLITAN BOROUGH
Housing Department Town Hall

1 Full name of applicant _SHIRLEY TAYLOR_

2 Address _42 MAINE ROAD_

3 Are you

X	married
	single
	widowed
	divorced

4 Are you at present

	a lodger
X	a tenant
	an owner–occupier

5 Is your accommodation

	a house
X	a flat
	a bed-sitter
	a hostel

6 Name and address of employer _House wife_

7 Weekly income _Supplementary Benefit_

8 Length of residence in the borough _3_

9 Give details of present accommodation (tick appropriate column)

	Exclusive use	Shared use	None
Kitchen		X	
Living room	X		
Bedroom 1	X		
Bedroom 2			X
Bathroom		X	
Any other room			X
Internal water closet			X
Hot water supply		X	

10 List persons to be rehoused as a result of application

Surname	Forename	Sex	Date of birth	Relationship to applicant
Applicant	–	F	10/3/46	–
TAYLOR	Brenda	F	22/6/69	Daughter
TAYLOR	Steven	M	14/8/73	Son

11 Give details of any medical consideration or special circumstances to be taken into account when assessment of your application is made

I have received a notice of eviction from my landlord at the end of this month. My husband is in prison & is due to be released in eighteen months time & I would like a nice home for him when he comes out.

Also my son has been mixing with a bad crowd and has been in trouble with the police. I would like him to move to a better neighbourhood.

Figure 20

APPLICATION FOR ACCOMMODATION

BURSLEY
METROPOLITAN BOROUGH
Housing Department Town Hall

1 Full name of applicant ___Kevin Kelly___

2 Address ___21 Bramhall Lane___

3 Are you

X	married
	single
	widowed
	divorced

4 Are you at present

X	a lodger
	a tenant
	an owner–occupier

5 Is your accommodation

X	a house
	a flat
	a bed-sitter
	a hostel

6 Name and address of employer ___Anfield Engineering Elland Road___

7 Weekly income ___£100___

8 Length of residence in the borough ___20___

9 Give details of present accommodation (tick appropriate column)

	Exclusive use	Shared use	None
Kitchen		X	
Living room		X	
Bedroom 1	X	X	
Bedroom 2			
Bathroom		X	
Any other room		X	
Internal water closet		X	
Hot water supply		X	

10 List persons to be rehoused as a result of application

Surname	Forename	Sex	Date of birth	Relationship to applicant
Applicant	Kevin	Male	1961	—
Kelly	Sandra	Female	1962	My wife

11 Give details of any medical consideration or special circumstances to be taken into account when assessment of your application is made

I get on very badly with my wifes mother who we live with. The stress of living on top of each other has produced very bad feeling all round. This resulted in my wife attempting suicide last Christmas.

Figure 21

Sex and contraception

According to one survey, most young people expect to get married between the age of 20 and 25, and over half think that it is best to have two children. And this is what generally happens. Indeed, marriage is so widespread that there is even a tendency to regard people who remain single after their thirties as abnormal! But are there any alternatives to marriage as a way of organizing family life?

Today, one in three new marriages are expected to end in divorce and the number of one-parent families has risen dramatically (about one in eight children now live with a single parent). The popularity of cohabitation has increased, though 'living together' is usually a prelude to marriage. Thousands of young couples still get married during their teens, often because the girl is pregnant, and some end up with partners they might not have chosen had the circumstances been different.

It's normal to be different

Some people are attracted to the opposite sex, some to both sexes and others to their own sex. The latter are called homosexuals (gays or queers). It is estimated that about 10 per cent of the population has homosexual tendencies and many young people go through a temporary 'homosexual phase'. Male homosexuality is legal in England and Wales between consenting males over 21, in private. Homosexuals are still persecuted by ignorant people, however, and particularly by young men who want to demonstrate their own masculinity.

Adolescence is inevitably a time of sexual discovery and temporary relationships. In or outside marriage, sex is a matter of personal choice but it is worth remembering that:

(i) People should be honest with one another about what they are looking for in a sexual relationship (love, security, sexual satisfaction, status, children, etc.). A girl is an equal human being with her own feelings, not just a 'good lay'.

(ii) A lot of young people, especially boys, feel under pressure because others in their class or group boast about an active sex life.

(iii) Over half of all young people do not use any form of contraception, at least for their first sexual experience.

Self-assessment question

13 Giving commonsense advice, write your own replies to the following letters which are similar to those published in newspapers and women's magazines.

Problem Page

Dear Problem Page

When I go out with boys, they're only interested in one thing. Some girls seem to be able to go out with a boy and get to know him well without him expecting anything more than a goodnight kiss. The boys I go out with never stop at kissing. Things often go a lot further than I intend simply because I can't stop their advances without getting them annoyed. How can I have a friendship with a man where we can spend an evening together without me having to fight him off?

Josephine

Dear Problem Page

All my mates either have steady girl-friends or go out with lots of women. I don't meet many girls at work or where I live, and I'm too shy to go up to a stranger in a pub or disco as I just wouldn't know what to say. While I wouldn't win a beauty contest, I'm not unattractive, and I have a good sense of humour. But even so, I don't seem to be interesting enough for any girl to fancy me. In a few years all my friends will be married and I'll be left on the shelf.

John

Contraception

Table 11 lists the types of contraceptives available and gives pros and cons for each one.

Table 11 *Types of contraceptives available*

How is it used?	How does it work?	How safe is it?
Pill Women take a pill daily (for twenty-one days each month or continuously throughout the menstrual cycle, depending on the type of pill). The pill must be prescribed by a doctor.	Chemicals (synthetic hormones) in the pill stop the female egg (ovum) from being formed and fertilized.	In theory, 100 per cent reliable. (The pill doesn't work if it is left on the dressing-room table!) Unsuitable for some women, for example, those with high blood pressure. Others may gain weight.
Condom (French letter, sheath, Durex, etc.) Very thin rubber sheath unrolled over the penis before intercourse. The most common method of contraception and is available from chemists' shops, men's hairdressers', vending machines, through the post, etc.	Sperm is trapped at the end of the protective.	Electronically-tested brands are very reliable if used properly (for example before any sexual contact occurs).
Diaphragm (Dutch cap) Dome-shaped rubber device, kept in shape by a springy rim. It is inserted into the vagina over the entrance to the womb before intercourse, and it should be left there for about eight hours afterwards. Must initially be supplied by a doctor or Family Planning clinic to ensure correct fit.	The cap acts as a barrier to prevent the sperms getting into the womb.	Very reliable, but a spermicidal cream or jelly must always be applied to the diaphragm before use.
Spermicidal chemicals (jellies, creams, aerosol foams, suppositories, etc.) They should be allowed to melt and/or spread in the vagina before intercourse. They can be bought from chemists' shops, or free from Family Planning clinics.	The chemicals act as a barrier by killing sperms.	Unreliable on their own: effectiveness depends upon how well the chemical spreads. Best used as a back-up for condoms and diaphragms. Some women find that the chemicals cause itchiness.
Intra-uterine device (IUD, coil, loop) A small device, usually plastic, that is put into the womb and left there indefinitely. Usually	It is thought that this device prevents the fertilized egg from attaching itself to the wall of the womb.	Very reliable, but there is a slight possibility that the IUD might drop out without women realizing it.

only prescribed to women who have already had a baby. They should be changed every six months.

Safe period (rhythm method)
Abstain from intercourse for ten days or more each month, when women are most likely to conceive. The 'safe' period may be identified with the help of a calendar or thermometer and temperature chart (there is a slight rise in a woman's body temperature a couple of days after ovulation). The billings (mucus) method relies on the detection of changes in cervical mucus which occur near the time of ovulation. Some women notice a clear, jelly-like discharge from the vagina or experience a sensation of 'wetness' around the time that the egg is released.

For example, menstrual cycle of twenty-eight days.

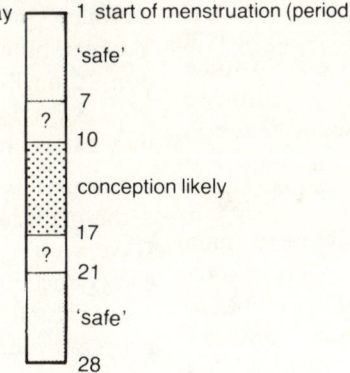

day — 1 start of menstruation (period)
'safe'
7
? 10
conception likely
17
? 21
'safe'
28

Conception is most likely just after ovulation when the egg moves from the ovary into the womb.

Reliability of this method varies according to the regularity of the woman's menstrual cycle. Up to 40 per cent of women using this method may become pregnant over the course of a year. A doctor can advise you about this method. It may be the only method of family planning for some couples whose religious beliefs prevent them from using other methods such as the pill or barrier methods.

Withdrawal
A man withdraws his penis from the vagina before ejaculation.

Withdrawal prevents semen getting into the vagina.

Not only highly unreliable but also very unsatisfying. Men may release sperms before ejaculation without realizing it.

Vasectomy (male sterilization)
Minor operation on the ducts leading to the testicles.

This operation stops sperm being released with the semen.

Completely reliable but these operations are usually irreversible so doctors will normally only perform them on adults who have completed their families.

Female sterilization
The fallopian tubes between the ovaries and uterus are cut or closed.

This operation stops ova from being fertilized.

Abortion

This is not a form of contraception but rather the termination of an unwanted pregnancy. Legal abortions are permitted if doctors believe that birth would:

(i)   Involve serious risk to the life of the mother.
(ii) Injure her physical or mental health.
(iii) Involve risk that the child will be born with a serious mental or physical handicap.

The most common method of abortion for women who are less than three months pregnant is the vacuum aspiration method. This entails sucking the foetus out of the womb with a special vacuum tube, the patient having had a local or general anaesthetic. It is a simple operation and women usually go home the same day.

If a girl wants an abortion she should consult a doctor as soon as she discovers she is pregnant, since it takes time to go through the formalities. Doctors have great discretion to decide whether a girl should have an abortion. One doctor might consider the fact that a girl is only 16 and has no means to support herself and the baby as sufficient grounds, and another doctor might not. In some areas so many doctors refuse that it is quite difficult to obtain an abortion (there are many fewer in Birmingham than in Newcastle, for instance). For those willing to pay, there are private clinics.

Abortion is a contentious issue. Some women argue that a child has a right to grow up in good conditions and that all women should be able to choose whether they want to become mothers. Anti-abortionists are disturbed by the fact that even a small foetus has recognizable human features (even though it is incapable of surviving for more than a few hours outside the womb).

Sexually transmitted diseases

There has been a steady increase in the number of cases of diseases spread from person to person by sexual contact (intercourse, oral-genital or anal-genital). These diseases include:

Syphilis ('pox')
Gonorrhoea ('clap')
Urethritis (NSU)
Pubic lice ('crabs')
Scabies ('the itch')
Genital herpes
Genital warts

Different infections cause different symptoms. You can obtain leaflets from The Health Education Council (78 New Oxford Street, London WC1A 1AH) that explain what they are and how they can be treated. But remember, if you:

Suffer unusual itching, soreness, or discharge from the penis, anus, or vagina;

Have a sore, lump, or rash on the genital area;

Experience increased frequency of passing water or discomfort when passing water;

Have put yourself at risk by having sexual relations with someone whom you suspect may be infected;

Then:

(i)   Stop all sexual activity.

(ii) Get medical advice without delay. Either see your GP or look in the telephone directory under the heading 'Venereal Diseases' for a clinic. Serious complications can be avoided by early diagnosis and treatment.

6 Money matters

The aim of this section is to deal with some aspects of personal finance. You will be encouraged to consider various systems of payment to employees, deductions from your wages, savings and borrowing, consumer rights and advertising.

How are you paid?

The wages (or salary) you receive may be determined by a combination of two or more of the following methods.

Time work

A payment for each hour that you are available for work, usually with a higher rate for overtime or unsocial hours. Pay may be deducted for arriving late at work or non-attendance.

Piecework

A payment by results system that is based on the number of units of work performed. These may be measured in terms of:

(i)   The number of items produced.
(ii) Time allowed for particular jobs as established by work measurement techniques.

Incremental scale

A fixed increase, or increment, is paid each year until employees reach a maximum salary at the top of the scale.

Commission

Here the worker receives a percentage of the money obtained from sales or other transactions.

Fee payment

For self-employed people who offer specialist services.

Fringe benefits

These may be in the form of cash – such as a clothing allowance – or take the form of cheap goods from the firm, luncheon vouchers or subsidized meals, company car, longer holidays, cheap loans, non-contributory pension schemes and expense accounts.

Self-assessment question

1   Find examples of occupations that are paid in each of the ways listed above.

Pay slips

Wages are usually paid at weekly intervals, often in arrears. You can receive them in several ways: cash in a sealed wage packet, cheque or paid directly into your bank account. Manual workers must be paid in cash unless employees agree to some other method. A salary usually comes in twelve, equal, monthly payments. Your employer is legally obliged to give you a pay slip each time you are paid, and it is advisable to check it – mistakes can happen. Pay slips come in different

			Pay Slip Advice				
Universal Engineering Division 42							
Department	Employee	Week/month number	Tax code	Clock hours	Overtime hours	Mr B. Sheene	
05	4301	16	137L	46.00	3.00	NI number WA01861A	
Basic pay	Piecework pay	Overtime pay	Bonus pay	Other pay		Total gross pay	
60.00	15.35	4.50	0.00	0.00		79.85	
National Insurance	Superannuation	Tax this week/ month	Voluntary deductions	Other deductions		Total deductions	
3.97	4.79	14.61	0.00	0.00		23.37	
Gross pay to date		Tax to date	Superannuation to date	Holiday res.		Net pay	
1280.82		234.73	76.85	0.00		56.48	

Figure 22   *Pay slip advice*

shapes and sizes (an example is shown in Figure 22), but most contain the following:

A works reference number
A number by which your employer recognizes you on his pay-roll records.

Tax week number
These go from 1 to 52 (or 53) and begin on 6 April each year.

Your tax code
This is an indication to your employer of what tax allowances you are entitled to. It is made up of:

(i)   A number – the amount of your allowances without the last unit (thus 178 means £1785); and
(ii) A letter – L means single person or married woman; H means married man.

Your employer has a set of tax tables which he uses to work out how much income tax to deduct.

Your basic pay
Your basic pay plus any additional 'credits' such as overtime, a bonus, holiday pay or special allowances (for example unsocial hours) are added together to give the *total gross pay*.

National Insurance
A proportion of your earnings (9 per cent for tax

year 1983–4) is paid as a compulsory weekly contribution into this fund. Your employer also has to make a similar contribution for you and his other employees. This money goes to the Department of Health and Social Security and entitles you to such cash payments as sickness, unemployment, and maternity benefit.

Superannuation
Although you may not be entitled to it for another forty years or more, your retirement pension is a form of deferred pay and you earn it during your working life. In addition to the state pension, an increasing number of firms run their own company schemes.

Voluntary deductions
Deductions such as trade union contributions and regular savings under the SAYE (Save As You Earn) scheme.

Other deductions
The only other deductions permitted are for fuel, food, tools or accommodation supplied by the employer, or maintenance payments to a divorced wife.

Net pay
Net pay is what you actually receive after your total deductions have been taken from your gross pay.

Income tax

This is likely to be your largest deduction. It is a tax on all income, whether from earnings, pensions or investments. Some professional and self-employed people settle their tax bills in a lump sum at the end of each tax year, but most of us pay our debt to the Inland Revenue through our wage packet: hence, Pay As You Earn (PAYE). PAYE is a way of collecting tax whereby employers are responsible for deducting it from employees and handing it over to the taxman. The Chancellor of the Exchequer decides the rates of tax and often announces changes as part of his Budget.

Everyone is entitled to certain *allowances*: part of your income that is tax-free. These include:

(i) Personal allowance
    for a woman or   – £1785 in
    single man   1983–4 tax year
    for a married man – £2795 in
                  1983–4 tax year

(ii) Other allowances
    These include contributions to most employer's pension schemes (but not state scheme), mortgage interest payments, fees to professional organizations.

You may also claim for *outgoings*: money that you spend 'wholly, exclusively and necessarily in the performance of the duties of your employment'. For example, the cost of replacing, cleaning and repairing protective clothing (boots, overalls, etc.) necessary for your job and which you are required to provide. In trades where it is usual for workers to provide their own tools and clothing, trade unions often agree a fixed deduction with the Inland Revenue. Check with your union representative if such a scheme applies to you. You can claim the full amount, even if you don't spend it. Keep any receipts in case you need to support your claim.

Let us suppose that you earn £5000 per annum (just over £96 per week), and that you are a single person with only your personal allowance. You don't have to pay tax on the first £1785 of your income. You therefore have 5000 − 1785 = £3215 of *taxable pay* on which you will pay tax at the basic rate (at present 30 per cent). 3215 × 30% = £964.50. Your tax allowance is spread over the whole year so you will pay £18.55 each week. Tax bands and rates change occasionally so you should check with your local tax office for the current figures. (*Note*: £18.55 is an *average*, not necessarily the exact amount you pay in tax each week.)

Tax forms

Tax Return (P1)

The Inland Revenue knows about your full-time earnings from your employer, but it is your responsibility to inform them about any allowance or expenses for which you are eligible (although building societies and assurance companies may do this in some cases). You do this by filling in a tax return. Some people are automatically sent one every year (in March or April) but if your tax position is fairly straightforward you may receive one every few years. If you are entitled to an allowance which you haven't claimed (for example you recently got married), you should inform the tax office. This form is a little complicated because it refers to two separate years: information about your incomings and outgoings relate to the last tax year and you are claiming allowances for the coming year.

Notice of Coding (P2)

This notice informs you of your tax code and how it is worked out.

P60

Your employer should give you one of these forms each year, usually in April. It gives details of your total pay, tax deducted, etc. for the tax year which has just ended. Use it to fill in your tax forms.

P45

If you leave a job your employer will give you a P45 form which shows the total National Insurance contribution made, the amount of money earned and the total amount of tax deducted.

Saving for the future

Why save at all?

Some people believe that it is better to spend the money we earn immediately and enjoy the goods and services we can buy. Inflation is constantly eroding the purchasing power of our money: if prices are rising at 15 per cent per annum the ten-pound note we salt away in the tea-caddy on New Year's Day will only be worth £8.50 by the following Christmas.

Nevertheless, we all need to save. When we are young we have to save for clothes, records, or larger items such as motor-cycles and holidays. As we get older and take on more responsibility, saving is necessary in order to set up a home, and to be ready for the unexpected expenses that occur with a family and car ownership. Looking even further ahead, saving is important so that we may survive during periods of unemployment, or live more comfortably in retirement.

How and where we can save

There are hundreds of institutions eager to help us save our money and, before deciding how and where to invest, it is advisable to consider:

(i)   The rate of interest paid (expressed as a percentage of the sum invested).
(ii) Whether you pay tax on your interest.
(iii) Whether you can pay in as little or as much as you like, or if you must save a fixed amount at regular intervals.
(iv) Whether you plan to save for a short or long term.
(v)   How quickly you can get your money back in an emergency.

Some of these factors change from time to time. *Money Which?*, published by the Consumers' Association, contains a useful and up to date guide for investors and borrowers.

Different forms of saving

High Street Bank $\begin{cases} \text{current account} \\ \text{deposit and savings accounts} \end{cases}$

Trustee Savings Banks
National Savings Bank
Building Societies
British Savings Bonds
National Savings Certificates
Save As You Earn (SAYE) schemes
Unit Trusts
Life Insurance
Premium Savings Bonds

Go to your local High Street and pick up the free leaflets which are available at Post Offices, banks, building societies, etc.

Self-assessment question

2   You are saving up for a new motor-cycle, price £800. You already have £300 and reckon that you can save a further £10 each week. Which form(s) of saving would you choose? Remember that you may want to retrieve your money quickly in the event that you come across a second-hand bargain in the meantime.

Borrowing money

Suppose you can't wait to save up until you have enough money to buy the motor-cycle. You would have to borrow money from someone. The following extracts from a motor-cycle magazine explain the different ways of obtaining credit.

Begging for credit

The cheapest way to buy a bike is to use your own cash, or to borrow cash from parents or friends. If this sort of money isn't available, the next best bet is to arrange your own loan at the lowest rates you can get – and then pay cash at the dealer of your choice. If that attempt fails, you're stuck with the finance offered by dealers – but not all dealers charge the same commission, which is why it is not always cheaper to buy a bike advertised at a discount price.

The interest rates quoted by the various people trying to lend you money are confusing. Banks always quote the true rate of interest you pay on your loan for every year or part of a year you are in debt. You only pay interest on the amount you owe, so the interest gets lower as you pay off the debt. Finance companies, on the other hand, generally quote a flat rate percentage on the whole loan right up to the day when you cough up the last penny. As a rough guide, true rate = 2 × flat rate + 1%.

People offering revolving credit go even further by quoting the interest they charge per month. Typical figures like 1.9% work out at a true rate of around 20% p.a. Like bank loans, the interest charged gets smaller as you pay off your debt.

Bank personal loans

Banks lend money in several ways, but not all of them are suitable – or even available – for buying a bike. With a personal loan, you arrange with your bank manager to borrow a lump sum at a rate of interest which is fixed at the time the agreement is made. This is definitely the cheapest source of money and should be number one on your list.

Bank personal loans are less easy to get than finance company credit. They are unlikely to consider you unless you already have a bank account – which means a known financial record. The manager will normally ask for about 25% deposit and is unlikely to consider repayment over more than three years. The upper loan limit varies between £1000 and £2000 from bank to bank. The loan will have to be in your parents' name if you are under 18 years old, but the bank will arrange for the repayments to be made from your account if you wish.

Other advantages are that you can pay off the loan at any time and so save paying any more interest (some finance company loans have a penalty charge if you pay back early). Your contract with the bank is only to borrow money so the bike is yours from the start and can't be repossessed, although the bank can still take you to court to recover the money you owe them if you don't pay. It is more likely, if you get in trouble with your payments, that your manager will try to work out some arrangement that will get you over a temporary setback.

Revolving credit

There are two main types of revolving credit, but in both cases you start by agreeing a loan limit with the lender based on the maximum amount you can afford to repay each month. At any time you can borrow any amount of money, either in one lump sum or in separate smaller amounts, as long as the total amount outstanding never exceeds your loan limit.

As you pay off the debt you can borrow more and there is no limit to the length of time you can be in debt up to the loan limit. You are free to spend the money on whatever you choose, and there is no need for a deposit.

The most common form of revolving credit is the credit card (Visa and Access). The other schemes available are the Midland Bank Personal Credit Plan and the Forward Trust Easy Riding Plan. Revolving credit comes second only to bank personal loans as a cheap way to borrow money – but there is a catch. The figures are calculated on the assumption that you use these schemes to borrow one lump sum (to buy a bike, say) and then pay off the debt as quickly as you would any other sort of loan, without topping up the loan with any more purchases. If you are weak-willed and pay off the debt more slowly, or if you can't resist the temptation to continually top up the loan by buying more goodies, the cost of this kind of borrowing can be astronomical. You have been warned.

Finance companies

Most of the High Street banks own one of the finance companies that specialize in lending more expensive money for buying cars and bikes. People tend to refer to their bike finance deals as hire purchase, but only about 5% of today's finance is hire purchase. The rest are personal loans, conditional sales and credit sales.

With hire purchase you hire the bike by making fixed monthly payments for a fixed period of time. You buy the bike by making a nominal payment (usually the last instalment) at the end of the agreement. You do not own the bike until the last payment has been made, so it is not yours to sell. If you want to sell the bike you may have to pay what you still owe in one lump sum.

A credit sale is where you buy a bike by paying in five or more instalments. You own the bike straight away so it can't be repossessed, but the agreement will probably state that you must cough up all the instalments immediately if you sell the bike.

Finance company personal loans are unsecured loans in the same way as bank personal loans. The advantage is that you don't have to have a bank account. Because they charge more, finance companies are prepared to take bigger risks – so they may lend you money after the bank has turned you down.

The personal loans that you arrange through your bike dealer must be used to buy a bike. But you can also go direct to some finance companies and get a personal loan for just about anything – house improvements, furniture, landscaped garden gnomes, you name it. As long as you are a credit-worthy person (i.e. they think you will pay up) the finance company won't ask too many questions about what you are going to spend the money on. Because there is no dealer's commission to be paid, this sort of loan is cheaper than a loan from the same company to buy a bike. The vast amounts of commission paid to dealers (rumoured to be up to 20% of the interest charged) are what make finance companies so secretive about their rates. By giving up all or part of their commission, dealers can reduce some prices by well over £100. As bike prices go up and less people can afford to buy, more dealers are looking to credit as a service to help sell bikes rather than as another source of profit.

Finance companies have a legal responsibility for the quality of the goods bought with their money. So, if you are borrowing money for a specific bike rather than just borrowing money, you will find it hard to get finance to buy a second-hand bike privately. Even second-hand bikes in dealers' showrooms will be turned down by some companies, and others will probably ask for a bigger deposit and will charge a higher rate of interest.

Paying for extras
It is essential to borrow as little as possible. You are already paying through the nose for your bike, but you'll need money coming out of every orifice in your body if you add insurance, accessories and clothing to the loan – especially insurance, which runs out after one year even though you spend three years paying for it on credit.

Insurance
Most, but certainly not all, finance deals include life insurance. Everyone is well advised to get some form of instalment insurance. It's good to know that you won't get into legal hassles up to your neck just because you missed a couple of payments through illness or an accident.

Golden rules
1   When shopping around for a bike that you are going to buy on credit don't pay much attention to interest rates quoted or the advertised price of the bike. Always ask for the TOTAL CREDIT PRICE (including deposit). If in doubt, work it out.
2   Always try every possible source of credit. They can only say no.
3   Work out all the costs in advance, not forgetting insurance. Remember running costs – don't try to make repayments so high that you've got nothing left for petrol, repair bills and clothing.
4   Make the biggest deposit you can.

Neil Millen, *Motorcycling* (June 1979)

Table 12

Repayment guide: £500 borrowed: Credit price (percentage interest paid)

| | Repayment period | | |
	1 year	2 years	3 years
Bank personal loan	546 (9%)	591 (18%)	636 (27%)
Credit card	557 (11%)	627 (25%)	695 (39%)
Finance company personal loan (not specific			
motor-cycle loan)	575 (15%)	650 (30%)	725 (45%)
UDT* motor-cycle finance			
new bike	598 (20%)	693 (39%)	788 (58%)
used bike (over 3 years)	628 (26%)	753 (51%)	878 (76%)

*United Dominions Trust

Consumer's rights

The Office of Fair Trading produces a range of useful leaflets and pamphlets which are free from Consumer Advice Centres. See in particular *Fair Deal: a shopper's guide*.

Figure 23   *This advice is taken from the excellent leaflet* How to put things right *produced by the Office of Fair Trading*

Do you know your rights?

(i) Your new camera won't focus properly. The shop assistant points to a sign saying 'No goods exchanged', but offers to take it back for repair. Must you accept?

(ii) You ask to see the manager. She says, 'This camera is under guarantee. You will have to take this up with the manufacturer. The address is on the box. Good day.' What can you do?

(iii) You tried on a pair of shoes in a shoe shop. One shoe felt tight but you expected it to stretch with wear. After a week it is still cutting into your foot. Can you get these shoes replaced with a larger size?

(iv) You discover that the record you've just bought is scratched. You return to the shop and ask for a replacement. The assistant says that the store has sold out of that title, but she offers you a cash refund. Can you insist on a replacement?

(v) The garage mechanic has given you an estimate of £65 for a repair to your vehicle. When you call to collect it, he says that the job took longer than he expected and the bill is £75. Must you pay the extra?

(vi) You agree to buy a vehicle on credit. The terms are: cash price £800, deposit £200, instalments of £45 per month for two years. What is the total credit price?

(vii) You are passing a motor-cycle showroom when you notice your dream bike in the window. After a test drive the dealer says he can arrange credit and you agree to buy it for £1000. Next morning you realize that you can't really afford it. Can you cancel the order?

(viii) What do the following symbols mean?

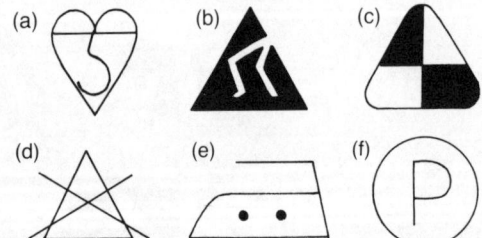

Advertising

It has been estimated that by the time you are 60 years old, you will have seen or heard approximately 50 million advertising messages. You will have found some helpful, others misleading but you will have ignored most of them. In Britain about 1 per cent of total national spending goes on advertising. Which kinds of product are most heavily advertised? Do they have anything in common? Before you go any further, make two lists:

(i) The ways in which advertising is helpful; and

(ii) The ways in which it is unhelpful or even harmful.

The first point to decide is helpful to whom? Manufacturers, retailers, advertising agencies, the media or consumers? The champions of advertising argue that it introduces customers to new products that they want, and lets them know where to find the best value. However, most adverts do neither of these things: they are purely concerned with keeping established brands and 'brand-images' in the consumers' minds.

The critics of advertising claim that it can create a demand where previously people didn't want or need an item, or it can mislead them into thinking that a particular brand is better than it really is. A voluntary 'code of practice' says that all advertising should be decent, honest and truthful. Unless advertisers make positively false claims, however, there is little control over what they can and cannot say.

To make advertising serve rather than mislead you, there are two important skills to learn. The first is the ability to determine exactly what facts are presented in the advert. The second is to be able to recognize how the advert is trying to make the product appealing. These sound like two simple skills, but advertisers spend many thousands of pounds to make the job difficult.

Almost every advert makes a claim: it says something about its product. For example, 'Nirvana Powder kills ants within ten seconds' claims very clearly that Nirvana Powder kills ants within ten seconds. That sounds simple, yet claims are rarely as clear as that made for Nirvana Powder.

Self-assessment question

3 Look at the three advertisements in Figure 24 which are similar to adverts constantly appearing on TV, on commercial radio or in the press. Write down:
   (i) What information you know about the product; and
   (ii) The way in which the advert makes the product appealing.

   Rate each claim according to whether it provides helpful or misleading information.

Nine out of ten dentists
agree that *EVERBRIGHT*,
with its special ingredient XT–40,
helps fight tooth decay.

(celebrity holds deodorant and says)
'If *ZAP* can keep me smelling sweet,
it can do the same for you.'

Figure 24

Analysing adverts

Everbright   All this means is that the manufacturer (or the advertising agency) could find nine dentists who agreed that the product *helps* fight tooth decay. However, so does water, toothpicks and all other toothpastes: the advert doesn't claim to *prevent* decay. XT–40 is merely the name that the makers have given to one of the ingredients: it may also be in all the other brands or it could even be totally ineffective.

Coco Chock   A beautiful young couple are shown in an attractive natural setting. The image suggests glamour, love, health, happiness and freedom. The basis of the advert is an emotional appeal: you associate the product with pleasant settings and warm feelings.

Zap   The endorsement or testimonial type of advert. Celebrities are paid large sums of money to hold, eat, wear, drink and smoke certain products. Rarely do they say that they use them all the time. The celebrities are carefully chosen according to the kind of feelings that they communicate to the public and the image that advertisers want associated with their product. Men may think that they can be like a rugged and successful sports-star if they use the same deodorant.

Nearly every advert (except the purely factual, like a list of prices) attempts to appeal to you by involving your feelings, wishes and dreams. Products are presented as luxurious, modern, sexy, healthy, patriotic, etc. Many studies have shown that a person's choice of a product is often based on feelings rather than a specific claim.

Self-assessment questions

4 Select examples of adverts from the press or TV that give the impression that a product will make its user more 'popular', 'powerful', 'loved', 'younger', 'free', 'a real man', 'a loving mum', 'safe and secure', 'with it'. Do they have the desired effect?

5 Which do you think benefits most from advertising: a truly superior product, a product no better or worse than its competition, or an inferior product?

Answers to questions

(i)   No.

(ii) You can point out politely that faulty goods are the retailer's responsibility. If this fails to resolve the problem, you should go to your Citizen's Advice Bureau or Consumer Advice Centre.

(iii) This depends upon whether or not the retailer advised you that the shoe would stretch. If the assistant said that the shoe might not stretch, or didn't know whether it would, and you still insisted on buying a pair of shoes that hurt, then you can hardly blame the shop for your blisters.

(iv) No, your only legal right is to your money back.

(v)   Yes, unless you want a lot of trouble (for example being sued by the garage). An estimate is only a guide to the price the trader will charge. A quotation, on the other hand, once agreed is generally binding on both sides.

(vi) £1280

(vii) No, you are liable to accept the bike and pay the full price even if you haven't paid a deposit or signed an HP form. There is a cooling off period for people who change their minds about credit agreements they sign at home, but this doesn't apply to shops or showrooms. The retailer may be prepared to let you off but you could still be liable for any loss suffered by the showroom (for example if the bike is resold for less). If you signed an HP or personal loan agreement you may even have to pay up to half of the total price.

(viii) (a) The Kitemark appears on goods that have been made to comply with standards laid down by the British Standards Institution (BSI). Tests have shown they are fit for their purpose.

(b) The Safety Mark is awarded by the BSI to goods that are shown in tests to comply with its safety standards.

(c) The Design Council has selected these products as well-made, pleasant to look at and practical in use.

(d) Washing instruction – do not use chlorine bleach.

(e) Warm iron temperature.

(f) Dry cleanable.

7 Technology

The aim of this section is to outline the development of technology. You will be encouraged to consider the role of human ingenuity in this process and the accelerating rate of technological change.

What is technology?

Ever since man first discovered that he could make useful cutting tools by breaking pieces of flint, technology has been an essential part of everyday life. This section is designed to help you understand more about technology and its relationship with people and the environment.

You already know a lot about technology: you have been surrounded by its results since birth and you are probably working in an industry that has been (or will be) greatly affected by modern technological innovations. Without looking at a dictionary, *write a definition of TECHNOLOGY* in your own words.

What do other students think about your definition? How might it be improved? Here are a few questions that may help you to clarify your ideas.

Self-assessment questions

1 List at least 20 different examples of technology. Think of the hundreds of examples that you encounter during an average day: tools, machines, equipment, processes, inventions, goods and structures. If you are stuck for ideas, here are a few to start you off: lathe, motorcycle, pocket calculator, motorway.
   If *all* your listed items are examples of technology, it follows that they must *all* have *some* features in common (even if your list contains such varied items as calculators and motorways). If you can find out what these *common features* are, then you will have discovered the features of technology.

2 Write down any feature that all the listed items seem to have in common. For instance, you will realize that many of your listed items are *man-made*. Can you find any examples that are not produced by human labour? If not, assume that it is a characteristic of all technology. How many other common features can you find?

3 Now write a new definition of technology, making use of some of the ideas in your list of features.

Compare this new definition with your original attempt. If it is an improvement, then you have gained something from this exercise. You also have a list of the features of technology that you have worked out for yourself, without referring to a textbook. Look up the definition of technology in a dictionary. Buckminster Fuller said that technology is 'Getting more out of less'. Do you think that this is a good definition? If not, how can you improve it?

Some features of technology

While science is concerned with *finding out*, technology is about *making things work*.

(i)   Technology involves things that humans:
      Invent
      Design
      Make
      Use

(ii) It involves the discovery and transformation of natural resources, such as minerals and energy.

(iii) It helps to change our way of life, for better or worse.

(iv) It gives mankind some control over the environment.

The whole history of mankind has involved the increasing importance of technology in our relationship with nature (the physical environment).

Self-assessment question

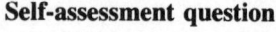

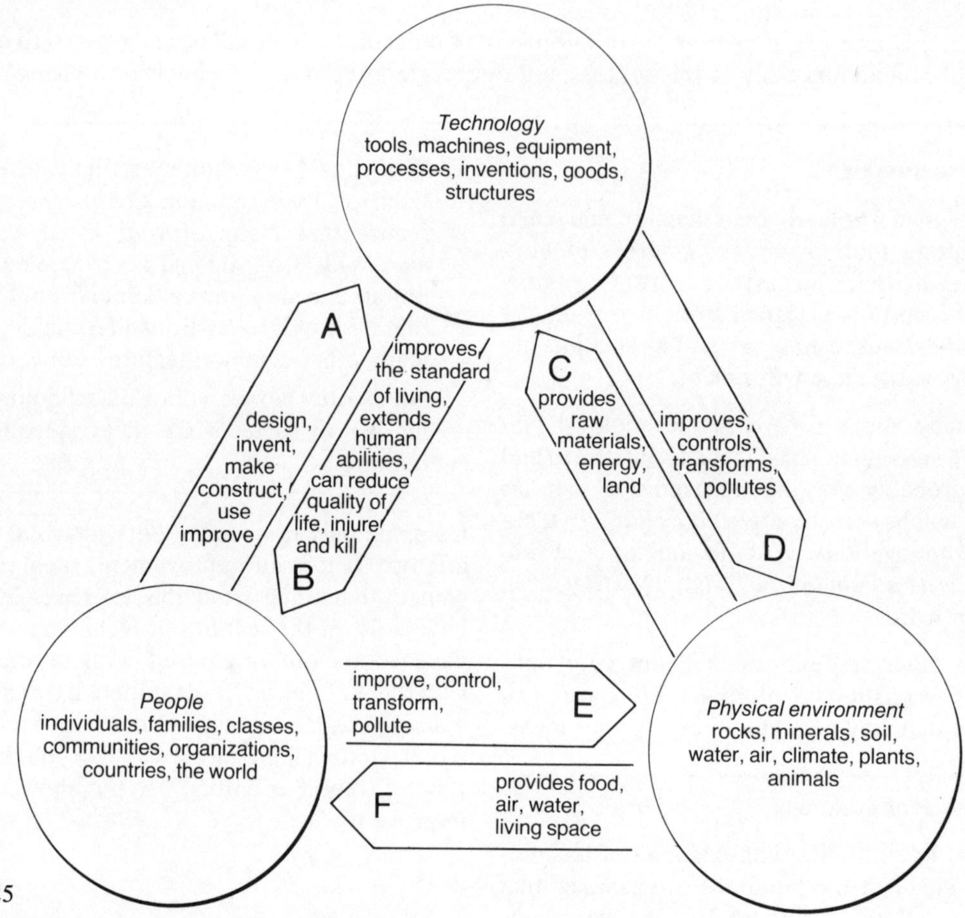

Technology
tools, machines, equipment, processes, inventions, goods, structures

A

improves the standard of living, extends human abilities, can reduce quality of life, injure and kill

design, invent, make construct, use improve

B

C

provides raw materials, energy, land

improves, controls, transforms, pollutes

D

People
individuals, families, classes, communities, organizations, countries, the world

improve, control, transform, pollute

E

Physical environment
rocks, minerals, soil, water, air, climate, plants, animals

F

provides food, air, water, living space

Figure 25

4 (i) Study Figure 25 which outlines the relationship between people, technology and the physical environment.

(ii) Select an example of technology (for example motor vehicles) and use the diagram to help you classify the relationships between the three factors: people, technology and environment. Concentrate on categories A–D which all involve technology directly. Here are some points to start you off.

A People → Technology
   1 Engineers design motor vehicles.
   2 Production line workers assemble automobiles.

B Technology → People
   1 Vehicles provide transport for people and materials.
   2 Employment in, and income from, the motor industry.

C Environment → Technology
 1 Iron ore required for the production of steel parts.
 2 Land for car plants, roads, garages, car parks.
D Technology → Environment
 1 Tractors help to improve soil fertility.
 2 Exhaust fumes pollute the atmosphere.

The development of early technology

A few writers, notably Erich von Daniken, have claimed that technology might have been brought to earth by members of an advanced technological civilization from another planet. While these ideas make interesting reading, there is a severe shortage of reliable evidence to support them. The facts actually confirm a far more fascinating conclusion:

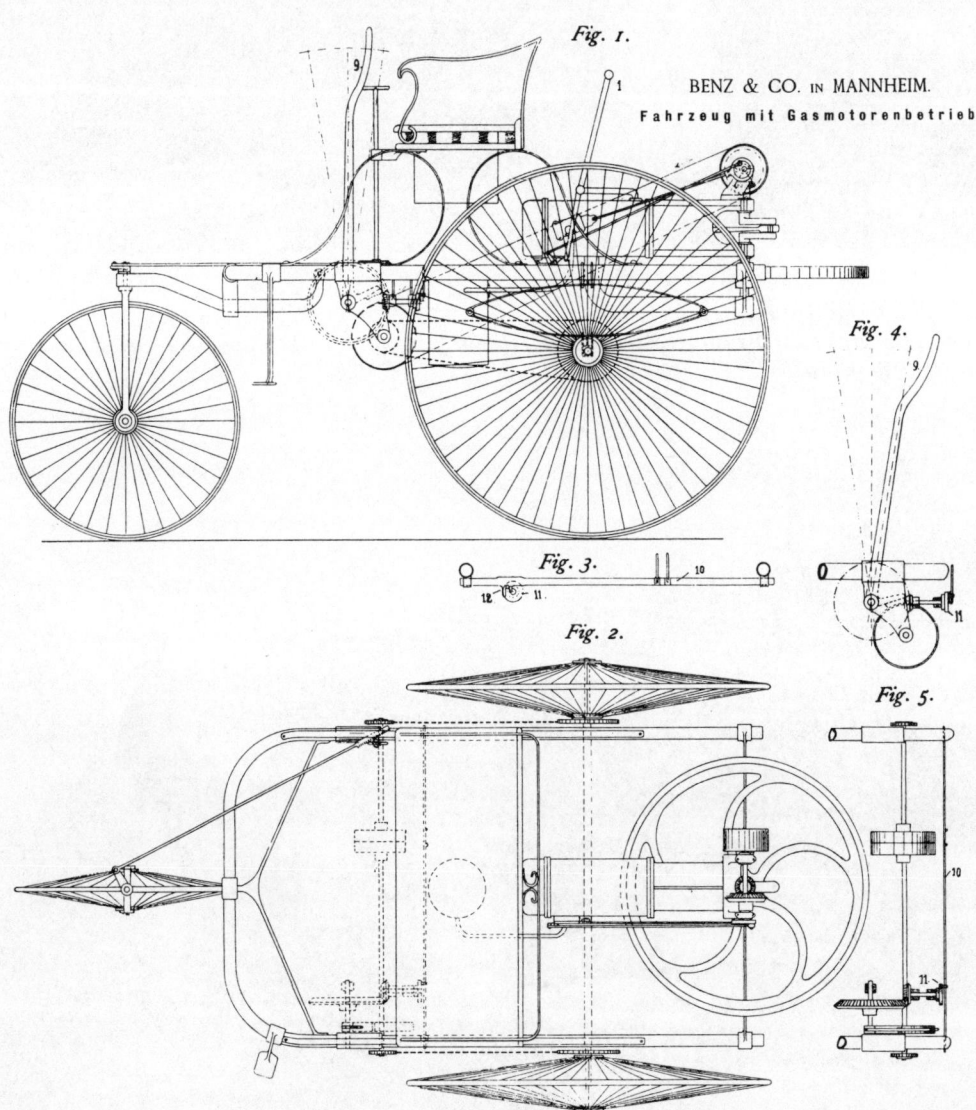

Figure 26

Figure 27
(a) Mass-production of Morris motors
(b) Competition in the British car industry led to thousands of cars being produced cheaply. This enabled more and more people to take to the roads

that man alone has been able to create and develop all the technology on earth.

The first humans two or three million years ago had enough intelligence and manual skill to find uses for the resources that nature provided: pebbles, sticks and bones were used as tools and weapons. There was a period of tool *using* before there was any tool *making*. Some of the first examples of tool making – cutting tools shaped from broken flint – have been unearthed by archaeologists and are on display in museums. These simple stone tools were used to transform other natural materials: for example, to shape tree branches into spears and to cut animal skins for thongs and clothing.

Development to the level of the spear thrower, bow and arrow, bow-drill and fire-bow could be achieved merely by applying mankind's skill and ingenuity to only three natural resources (trees, stones, and animals).

Self-assessment question

5   (i) Extend the diagram in Figure 28 yourself by adding some other natural resources (for example clay, copper ore, tin ore and iron ore) and developing a series of new inventions.

    (ii) What kind of processes now become possible?

  (iii) How will technology develop?

Technology in a difficult environment with few natural resources

Human beings are resourceful enough to create and develop technology for themselves, without outside assistance, even under very difficult conditions. Our ancient ancestors had to survive four long Ice Ages during which a third of the planet's surface was permanently covered with ice and snow. The following exercise is set within the

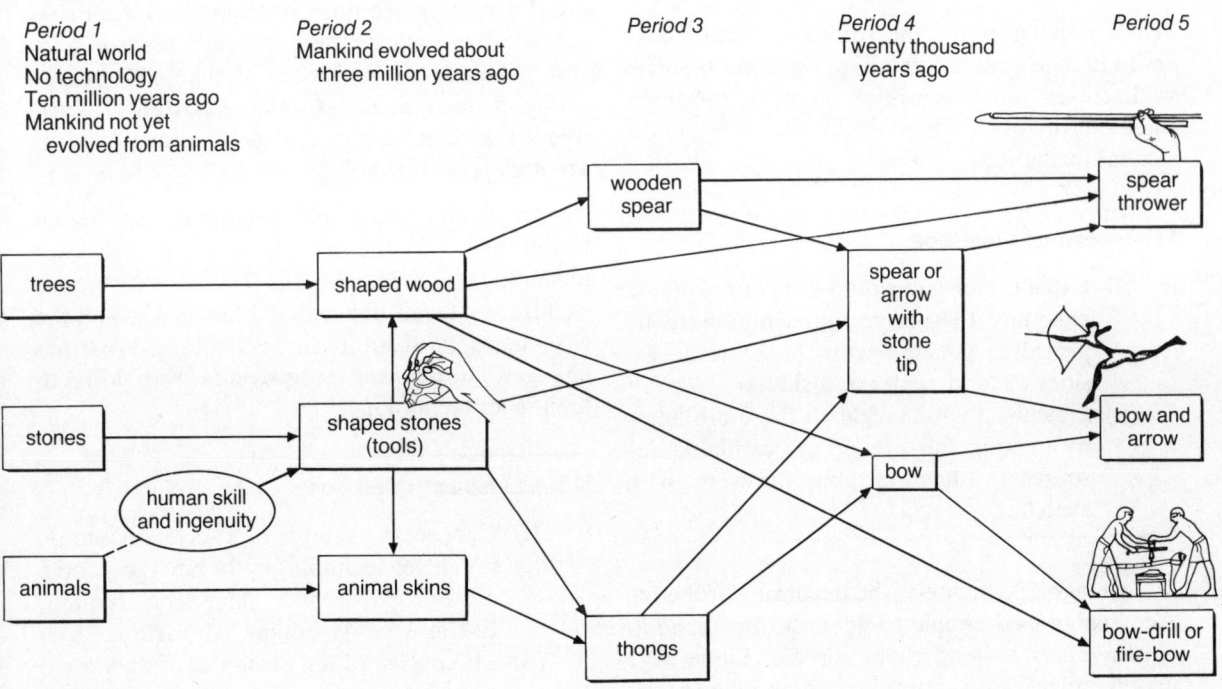

Period 1
Natural world
No technology
Ten million years ago
Mankind not yet
    evolved from animals

Period 2
Mankind evolved about
    three million years ago

Period 3

Period 4
Twenty thousand
    years ago

Period 5

Figure 28

Arctic Circle, where conditions today are similar to those in northern Britain during the last Ice Age.

Imagine that you have been shipwrecked, with a friend, on the coast of northern Canada when your boat collided with an iceberg. The long winter is approaching, and most of the ground is already covered with hard snow to a depth of about 30 cm. There are no plants or trees in the area, and all the animals have migrated south for the winter. The average winter temperature is −45°C (−30°F) and the sea is beneath a layer of ice.

You have two dogs that have survived the shipwreck, and they lead you to the carcass of a Caribou deer that appears to have died of old age before the winter migration. Exploring the frozen ground, you find various types of stones: some are hard but others can be broken easily. Among the rocks of a frozen river bed you find a few lumps of copper metal. There are also some pieces of driftwood, up to three metres long, the remains of tree branches that were carried by the river from woodlands further south during the summer.

While walking across the frozen sea, your dogs sniff out a hole in the ice, about three centimetres in diameter, which you think might be the breathing hole of a seal. There might also be fish in the sea below the ice.

Self-assessment question

6   (i) Explain how you would use your skill and ingenuity to survive the winter here by providing yourself with the basic necessities of food, water and shelter.
   (ii) How would you tackle all these problems by making full use of the available resources? Illustrate your answers with sketches.

The changes of climate at the beginning of the Ice Age encouraged people to develop new technology in order to help them survive. Stone Age people might have improved their chances by inventing and making tools and equipment similar to those that you 'invented' for yourself in this exercise. We can attempt to reconstruct their way of life by studying the remains of their tools, but a more complete picture is gained from the lives of present-day 'Stone Age' peoples. Until a few decades ago, for instance, Eskimos were living quite successfully in the far north of Canada with a technology that would have been familiar to our own ancestors of 20,000 years ago.

Self-assessment question

7   Find out more about the way of life of the Eskimo people. A film, *Eskimo – Fight for Life* may be borrowed from the Canadian High Commission, Canada House, Trafalgar Square, London SW1.

Levels of technology

A lot of technology has been around for a long time and we now take it for granted: we can call it *low-level* technology. On the other hand, there are areas where the frontiers of technology are being extended and where the impossible is made only just possible. The advances of the 1980s, especially in such fields as microelectronics, aeronautics, pharmaceutics and genetic engineering, are *high-level* technology.

These classifications are not fixed: the steam locomotive and the telephone were high-level technology for the Victorians. There is a vast range of different levels between the Stone Age and the Massachusetts Institute of Technology. What has changed during our progression from low- to high-level technology?

Self-assessment questions

8   (i)   Choose an example of a society based on low-level technology: Stone Age people of Europe, North American Indians, Eskimos or Australian Aborigines.
   (ii) Make a list of ten examples of their technology (tools, weapons, structure, etc.).
   (iii) Then analyse each one as follows:

(a) What is it used for?

(b) What materials are involved in its manufacture and use?

(c) What forms of energy are involved in its manufacture and use?

(d) How does it affect the environment?

> Here is an example: *The Eskimo harpoon*
>
> For killing seals and Caribou, in order to provide food and materials.
> Wood, bone, seal skin.
>
> Human energy.
>
> No effect, apart from a reduction in the population of seals and Caribou.

9 (i) Now make a similar analysis of ten examples of high-level technology (for example Concorde, nuclear power plant, video-cassette recorder, high-rise building.

(ii) What conclusions can you draw about the basic differences between low- and high-level technology?

Different levels of technology often exist side by side. The modern Eskimo now lives in a world of Coca Cola and transistor radios: his harpoon has given way to a rifle with telescopic sights and his huskies have been replaced by a motorized sledge.

In Britain, carpenter's and bricklayer's hand-tools have not changed much over the centuries. Computer-controlled tractors can plough the fields, but hill farmers still depend on dogs to round up sheep.

Self-assessment question

10 Why does low-level technology survive?

Table 13 *Time scale for the development of technology*

Period A Before technology	
Formation of the earth 4,700,000,000 years ago	
Life on earth	
The first humans	
Period B Prehistoric technology	
Tool making 3,000,000 years ago	
Flint and stone axes	
Fire for cooking	
Bow and arrow 20,000 years ago	
Fishing	
Agriculture	
Period C Technology from early civilization onwards	
Pottery	
Use of metals	

The first cities	3500 BC (*in Middle East*)
Wheels for transport	
Writing	
Metal coins	
Magnetic compass	
Iron casting (cannon)	{ AD 1390 (*in Germany*)
Printing press	{ AD 1540 (*in Britain*)
Period D Recent technology	
Iron smelting with coke	AD 1709 (*in Britain by Darby*)
Mechanical power from burning fuel	
Rotary steam engine	
Railway locomotive	
Electric telegraph	
Production of cheap steel on a large scale	

Carbon-filament lamp
Internal combustion engine
Steam turbine   1884 *(in Britain by*
                                    Parsons)

Petrol-driven automobile
First synthetic fibre
Aeroplane   1903 *(in USA by*
Radio   *Wright Brothers)*
Television
Jet aircraft engine
Atomic bomb
Transistors   1948 *(in USA by*
Electronic computer   *Shockley and others)*
Nuclear power plant
Artificial satellite
Hovercraft
Laser
Man on the moon
Microprocessors   1971 *(in USA by*
                                    Noyce, and others)

11 Find the approximate date when, and location where, each of these developments first occurred (a few have already been supplied for you).

12 Table 13 lists some of the most significant events in the development of technology from three million years ago to the present day. The list is very selective: what other developments do you think are important enough to be included?

13 (i) Select from the list the development that you think is most important.

  (ii) Find out as much as possible about it: the events that led up to its invention; the circumstances in which it occurred; its direct and indirect effects on other technological developments, on people and on the environment.

  (iii) Arrange a discussion to try to persuade other students that your chosen development is the most significant.

14 Prepare time charts for Periods B, C and D as follows:
Draw three straight lines, each to represent the time from the beginning of the period to the present day.
Suggested scale:
Period B – line 300 mm long with 10 mm representing 100,000 years.
Period C – line 200 mm long with 10 mm representing 500 years.
Period D – line 300 mm long with 10 mm representing 10 years.

The first line represents the time from the origin of simple tool making, about three million years ago, to the present. Beside this time scale, plot all the events listed in Period B. Also indicate the beginning of the last Ice Age (120,000 years ago) and its end (15,000 years ago). Repeat this operation for Periods C and D.

Extrapolation

While working on the time charts you will have realized that new developments in technology are now appearing much more rapidly than ever before. There is, unfortunately, no obvious way of measuring levels of technology but we can make a crude and approximate assessment by simply counting the number of developments that have taken place by a particular time. Derry and Williams in their book *A Short History of Technology* supply a series of tables showing the time relations of selected events in technological history. If we simply count the number of separate events mentioned in these tables, we can plot them on a graph as can be seen in Figure 29.

Derry and Williams's table of events extends from earliest times to AD 1900. We have continued the graph up to the year 2000 (the broken line). This technique of predicting future developments by assuming that past trends will continue is known as *extrapolation*. Can we assume that technological change will continue to follow the same pattern to AD 3000? What does your prediction imply?

In trying to measure technological change, we

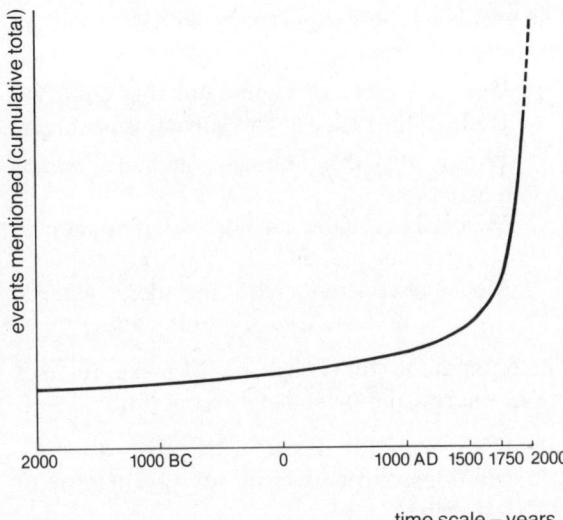

Figure 29 *The acceleration of technological changes*

have simply counted events, as if they were all equally important. How could we have allowed for the fact that some of the developments are more important than others? Does the fact that our list was obviously incomplete make the graph meaningless? Are there any other ways to measure the progress of technology?

Self-assessment question

15 Use encyclopaedias and other reference books to find out about some of the following spheres of technology. Present the data in the form of a graph: show how quantity has changed over time.

  (i) The power of prime movers (amount of power available for operating a machine) – for example humans, animals, water-wheel, windmill, steam power, internal combustion engine, steam turbine.

 (ii) Speed of human travel – for example foot, horse, railway, motor vehicle, aircraft.

(iii) Speed of communication (of information over a long distance) – for example

messenger, letter post, telegraph, telephone.

 (iv) Range (or lethal power) of weapons – for example bow, sword, ballista, cannon, rifle, machine gun, tank, bomber plane, missile.

  (v) Production (or use) of iron and steel/coal/petroleum/electricity in Britain or the world.

 (vi) Human life expectation/world population. How is technology involved here?

Your graph, like ours shown in Figure 29, will almost certainly be *exponential* rather than *linear*. We have a system of technology that has been accelerating rapidly for the last 250 years, and now the speed of change has become so fast that many people find it increasingly difficult to adjust. But why is the rate of technological change accelerating?

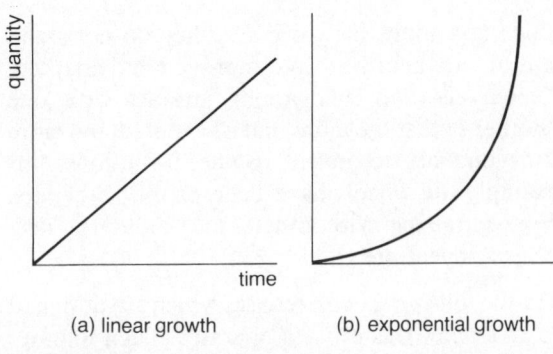

Figure 30

The increasing pace of technological change

Inventions breed inventions

New technology does not just appear from nowhere in a flash of inspiration: it usually emerges by combining two or more existing inventions in an original way. The development of some of mankind's earliest inventions in this manner was described in Figure 28 on page 91. Similarly, the sixteenth-century blast furnace resulted from the

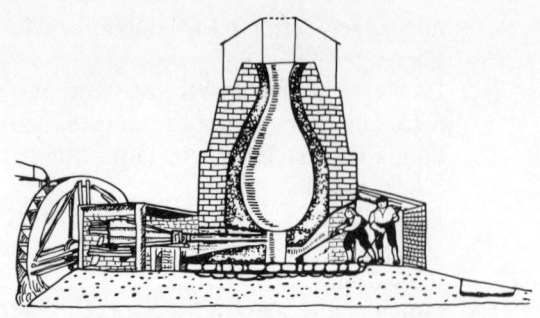

Figure 31   *A sixteenth-century blast furnace*

combination of three familiar elements of technology: the iron furnace, the water-wheel and the bellows. By directing a blast of air through an enlarged furnace, a sufficiently high temperature was achieved to produce molten iron continuously.

The invention of television was not a single event but rather the culmination of a complex series of developments in electricity, telegraphy, photography, motion pictures and radio.

Once inventions have arrived, they do not stand still but are nearly always improved and adapted. Techniques and innovations interact with one another so that the more that is invented, the more it is possible to invent. Some inventions (for example the wheel) have been prolific breeders, cross-fertilizing with others to produce a host of new inventions.

Try the following two exercises which are designed to show how this process operates. Then find out about other inventions that have been made by combining existing knowledge in new ways.

Invention – two problem solving exercises

A

The year is 1550. You own a number of smelting furnaces for the production of copper and other metals. The raw materials, metallic ores, have previously been quarried near the furnaces but these deposits are now almost exhausted. You have excavated a vertical shaft and discovered a thick seam of ore 17 metres underground.

The problem is how to get the broken lumps of ore up to ground level.

(i)   Design a piece of equipment that could be made in the year 1550 to solve this problem.

Power available: human, animals, water, wind.

Materials available include: wood, rope, iron and other metals.

Mechanical equipment includes: wheels, gears, pulleys, levers, crank, cams.

The equipment you design should make efficient use of energy and be reliable in operation.

(ii)   Compare your design with other students' solutions, and assess your solution in terms of following:

(a)   Could you make better use of the energy driving the equipment?

(b)   Could you reduce the number of people needed to operate it?

(c)   Does it involve heavy or boring work?

Do you think that your 'invention' is a realistic one that might actually have been used if this were a real situation? Check your invention by obtaining a copy of *De Re Metallica* by G. Agricola (first published in 1556). This book contains dozens of illustrations of machinery that was used in mining in Europe in the sixteenth century. You may find that your design is similar to one used at the time.

Four different ways of driving millstones in 1550 are shown in Figure 32. The millstones were used to grind metallic ores ready for smelting. How would you adapt these machines for raising ore from a mine?

B

The year is 1700. You are an engineer at a tin mine in Cornwall. You want to exploit a new seam of ore, but there is a serious problem of flooding. To overcome this problem you must lift water from the bottom of a 17 metre shaft.

(i)   Design a machine to solve the problem using coal to generate steam, either with or without using a piston and cylinder.

Figure 32 *Four different ways of driving millstones*

A—First mill. B—Wheel turned by goats. C—Second mill. D—Disc of upright axle. E—Its toothed drum. F—Third mill. G—Shape of lower millstone. H—Small upright axle of the same. I—Its opening. K—Lever of the upper millstone. L—Its opening.

You are aware of the following:

Air pressure, acting against a vacuum: supports a column of water 10 metres high; collapses a sphere; moves a piston, lifting a weight.

Steam pressure: causes rotation by jet effect; forces water out of a closed tank.

Condensation of steam creates a vacuum that allows air pressure to: force water into an evacuated container; move a piston into the evacuated cylinder, thereby lifting a weight.

Try to combine two or more principles known to engineers at the end of the seventeenth century in order to arrive at your own 'invention'. Check your invention using reference books to see how engineers of that period really did solve the problem of mine drainage.

Availability of resources

Technological development may be delayed if a serious technical problem cannot be solved or if necessary resources are unavailable.

Leonardo da Vinci designed flying machines but did not have access to suitable materials for putting his ideas into practice. With twentieth-century materials combining lightness and strength, his invention would almost certainly have flown successfully.

The natural world provides the resources (energy and raw materials) for all our technology. The development of technology has led not only to the discovery of new resources, but also each resource has tended to become more abundant. At the start of the Industrial Revolution supplies of charcoal were running out, but new uses were found for coal and its increasing availability made possible the rapid development of steam power and iron production. These advances led in turn to a wide range of innovations in manufacturing and transport.

During the twentieth century petroleum has become available in vast quantities and oil-dependent technology has expanded accordingly.

Now, however, we are coming to realize that some of the earth's resources are *finite*, and we cannot use them at an exponential rate indefinitely.

Self-assessment question

16   (i) Which key resources are likely to be in short supply in the future?
      (ii) Is this situation likely to speed-up or slow-down the rate of technological change?

Scientific research

Until the end of the nineteenth century, scientific research was a haphazard and inefficient process. There were few specialist inventors and most innovations were the result of chance discoveries.

Over 7000 years ago it was noticed that certain, brightly coloured stones were transformed into metallic copper by the action of fire. This chance observation led eventually to the smelting of metals from their ores.

Similarly, medieval glass-makers did not know why sand and soda/potash behaved as they did when heated in the fire, but they were able to make wonderful transparent objects from the malleable material that they obtained.

In contrast, the modern development of new metal alloys or toughened glass is a highly scientific process and little is left to chance. Technologists today know the properties of materials in advance, and work systematically until the desired result is obtained.

There has been a massive increase in the sums spent on research and development. The number of industrial research laboratories in the USA grew from fewer than 100 in 1914 to 220 in 1920 and over 5000 in 1960. Huge amounts of money have been invested to develop new projects, especially in industries concerned with aircraft, drugs, synthetic fibres, computers and oil extraction. In 1953, for example, the Rolls-Royce Dart engine sold for £7000. Its technological successor, the Spey, cost £65,000 in 1964. By 1970 each engine

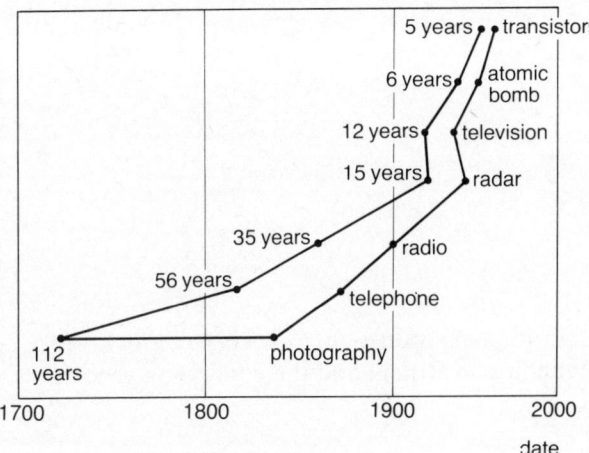

Figure 33   *The time between the invention of a product and its entry into the market place*
Source: New Scientist, April 1980

for the RB211 cost about £350,000 to produce. The escalating sums involved are due almost entirely to cost of additional research and development.

It is often said that the majority of scientists who ever lived are still alive and working today. There has been a similar growth in the number of scientific and technical journals, so that a discovery in any part of the world is soon known generally thanks to modern methods of communication. Contrast this to the estimated rate at which the use of printing machinery spread across Europe: only 12 kilometres per year during the fifteenth century. The diffusion rate for the introduction of pottery during the Stone Age was even slower, at a quarter of a kilometre per year.

The needs of society

So far we have looked at technology in a very one-sided way, suggesting that it developed in isolation from society and that it merely provided people with materials and means to achieve a new way of life. New technology is, however, developed with specific purposes and practices in mind: 'necessity is the mother of invention'.

Scientific research may reveal a wide range of technical possibilities, but they are only realized in practice if they are selected for investment and development. This decision will depend upon the needs of society, or at least powerful groups within it, at the time.

The principles of television were understood in the 1880s. There were, however, not only immense technical problems to overcome before these ideas could be transformed into a mass TV broadcasting system. During the nineteenth century, conditions were not right for the successful *commercial* development of television. By the 1920s radio and cinema had demonstrated the potential of new forms of social communication and further research was undertaken. Yet it was not until the 1940s and 1950s that TV broadcasting became established, in a period of greater prosperity and mass consumption of consumer goods. Similar stages may be identified in the development of the motor car.

War and military needs are often a spur to certain kinds of technology, and since the Second World War large amounts of money have been devoted to research into new generations of weaponry, with resulting 'spin-offs' for civilian industries. On the other hand, when labour is comparatively cheap and readily available, as it was under the systems of slavery and serfdom, there is little incentive to develop labour-saving technology.

In Britain today the incentive for technological change is generally economic competition between separate business enterprises. Firms must relentlessly take advantage of every new technique to increase their efficiency, to produce better products, to reduce their costs, and to hold on to or increase their share of the market.

8 Industrial change

The aim of this section is to look at changes in the organization of production. You will be encouraged to consider the origins and impact of the Industrial Revolution in Britain and the continuing process of industrial change.

Industrialization

Look at the graph in Figure 29 on page 95. Find the point where the gradual accumulation of technological innovations appears to suddenly 'take off'. That was the beginning of *industrialization*: a period of inter-related economic, technical, social and political changes that have shaped the modern world.

It took man three million years to learn how to grow crops and domesticate livestock. The resulting increased food supply made possible a substantial growth in population, urban settlement with specialization of labour, and immense intellectual development. It took another ten thousand years to make the next advance of equal importance: the breakthrough that we call the Industrial Revolution. Thanks to this progress it has taken us less than 200 years to leap from the steam engine to atomic power.

The British Industrial Revolution occurred approximately between the years 1760 and 1840, although the forces that were to create the new society had been maturing for centuries. A comparison of pre- and post-industrial society reveals the main features of this process.

Urbanization

A rural way of life centred on the village was replaced by an urban society where most people lived and worked in towns.

Agriculture

Under the *feudal system* almost everyone worked on the land. Farmers were required to work laboriously for two or three days in the lord of the manor's fields in exchange for the right to cultivate their own small plots. By the fifteenth century feudalism was virtually dead, compulsory labour duties converted into money rents, and workers hired for wages to work on the bigger farms. The Industrial Revolution was associated with improvements in agricultural production and a great reduction in the numbers employed on the land (less than one worker in twenty-five in modern Britain). Displaced workers were eventually absorbed into the new industrial and service occupations.

Manufacturing

A wide range of handicrafts using simple methods flourished before industrialization, carried out either as domestic production in the villages or under the *guild system* in the towns. These trades were completely transformed when workmen and new machinery were concentrated inside factories, thereby achieving a massive increase in the productivity of labour.

The market economy

During the Middle Ages even a powerful lord did not own his land (that is, he could not sell it). Nor

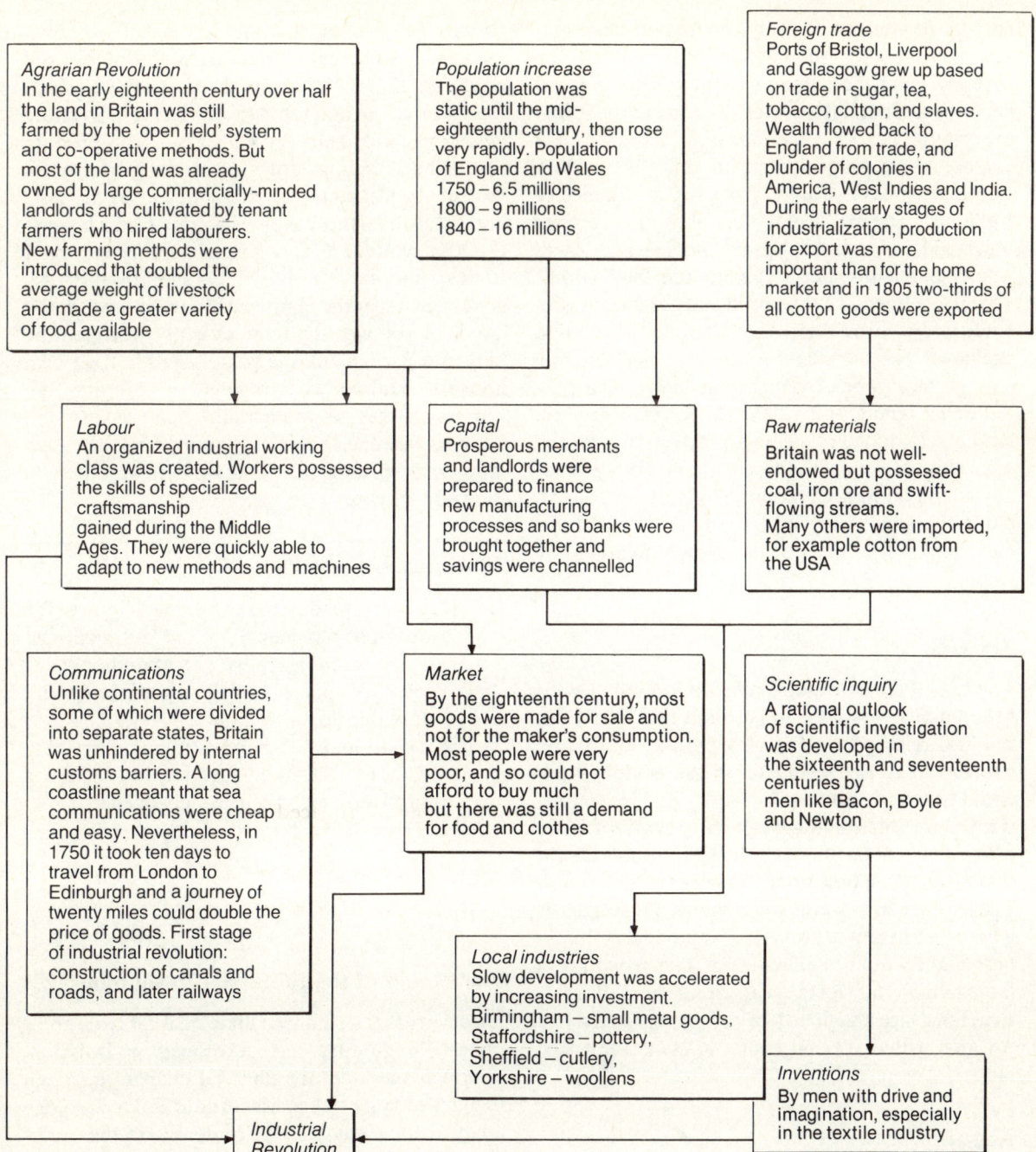

Agrarian Revolution
In the early eighteenth century over half the land in Britain was still farmed by the 'open field' system and co-operative methods. But most of the land was already owned by large commercially-minded landlords and cultivated by tenant farmers who hired labourers. New farming methods were introduced that doubled the average weight of livestock and made a greater variety of food available

Population increase
The population was static until the mid-eighteenth century, then rose very rapidly. Population of England and Wales
1750 – 6.5 millions
1800 – 9 millions
1840 – 16 millions

Foreign trade
Ports of Bristol, Liverpool and Glasgow grew up based on trade in sugar, tea, tobacco, cotton, and slaves. Wealth flowed back to England from trade, and plunder of colonies in America, West Indies and India. During the early stages of industrialization, production for export was more important than for the home market and in 1805 two-thirds of all cotton goods were exported

Labour
An organized industrial working class was created. Workers possessed the skills of specialized craftsmanship gained during the Middle Ages. They were quickly able to adapt to new methods and machines

Capital
Prosperous merchants and landlords were prepared to finance new manufacturing processes and so banks were brought together and savings were channelled

Raw materials
Britain was not well-endowed but possessed coal, iron ore and swift-flowing streams. Many others were imported, for example cotton from the USA

Communications
Unlike continental countries, some of which were divided into separate states, Britain was unhindered by internal customs barriers. A long coastline meant that sea communications were cheap and easy. Nevertheless, in 1750 it took ten days to travel from London to Edinburgh and a journey of twenty miles could double the price of goods. First stage of industrial revolution: construction of canals and roads, and later railways

Market
By the eighteenth century, most goods were made for sale and not for the maker's consumption. Most people were very poor, and so could not afford to buy much but there was still a demand for food and clothes

Scientific inquiry
A rational outlook of scientific investigation was developed in the sixteenth and seventeenth centuries by men like Bacon, Boyle and Newton

Local industries
Slow development was accelerated by increasing investment.
Birmingham – small metal goods,
Staffordshire – pottery,
Sheffield – cutlery,
Yorkshire – woollens

Inventions
By men with drive and imagination, especially in the textile industry

Industrial Revolution

Figure 34 *The Industrial Revolution in Britain*

could a person practise any occupation he chose: serfs were 'tied' to the land and were liable to be severely punished if they left the village without permission. In today's society we tend to think that everything 'has its price' and that a person may dispose of his property and his skills as he likes. These ideas have resulted from the resurgence of trade in Europe from the eleventh century onwards. Towns grew up around market places where merchants met and exhibited their goods. Townsfolk needed to buy food and the farmer who could grow more food than he required could exchange the surplus for money, and so buy strange new goods from distant lands. The pre-industrial family and village, however, were still largely self-sufficient. Factory production is for the market, not the needs of the workers. Today virtually all our household requirements – from food to entertainment – may be bought as commodities and the remotest parts of the planet are linked by trade.

New ideas

The rise of the protestant religion not only established a new relationship between man and God, but also released a spirit of scientific inquiry and enterprise. A rich man during the Middle Ages could not make his wealth 'work' for him to produce more wealth. Although the growth of trade offered new opportunities, the Church still taught that 'usury' (lending money at interest) was sinful. These objections were overcome as old standards gave way to a new attitude of commercial ruthlessness and economic self-interest. The growth of a large middle class fostered an atmosphere of (relative) tolerance and liberty in which there was scope for men with drive and ability to climb the social ladder.

Politics

While land was the major source of wealth and power, the lords were the real power in the country. The new urban middle class saw the king as bringing order and security, and as an ally in their struggle to win independence for their towns. So they helped the king to establish his authority over the barons and create a 'nation state'. But they did not forget that the king was also part of a system of feudal privilege and regulations that held back the development of a new, capitalist system of production. The resulting struggle was long and often violent. In England, the ruling power of the king was finally overthrown by Parliament in a civil war (1640s), while in France the aristocrats were sent to the guillotine after the 1789 revolution. British governments of the eighteenth century were in the hands of 200 wealthy families who controlled the king and Parliament and passed laws in their own interest. During the nineteenth century the representatives of industrialists, merchants and bankers became the ruling group, while the new industrial working class and women were denied the right to vote.

Self-assessment question

1   (i) Use the resources in your local library (for example old maps) to find out what the areas where you live (or attend college) were like before and during the Industrial Revolution.
    (ii) Try to find first-hand accounts describing what life was like. Have any old buildings survived? Has their use changed?

The spread of the Industrial Revolution

On a world scale, industrialization is far from complete. No country has developed in isolation, although the rate of industrial change has been uneven and piecemeal. Since industrial technology enabled the early starters to dominate the undeveloped world and ensure a market for the goods of their new factories, industrialization became a race for wealth and power. Britain was the first leader and the rest of the world pursuers. But it is a race without a finishing line and the pace is constantly becoming faster.

Table 14 *Uneven industrial development*

Country	(1) Non-agricultural population	(2) Energy	(3) Passenger cars	(4) Gross national product	(5) Doctors	(6) Diet	(7) Infantile mortality	(8) Annual rate of population growth
Britain	97	5780	236	2600	1110	3190	18	3
USA	96	11,960	461	5590	1590	3330	18	9
Argentina	85	1910	70	1290	2060	3060	60	13
Czechoslovakia	84	6690	72	1120	2150	3180	21	6
Japan	79	3600	117	2320	1140	2510	17	13
USSR	68	4930	30	1400	2540	3280	26	10
Iran	54	1090	13	490	320	2300	139	30
South Korea	42	910	2	310	500	2520	60	20
China	33	590	0	160	260	2170	55	17
Nigeria	33	70	2	130	40	2270	180	27
India	32	190	1	110	200	2070	139	24
Afghanistan	18	30	2	80	50	1970	182	25

Key to variables (All figures, except (8), for 1973)
(1) Percentage of economically active population in occupations other than agriculture.
(2) Consumption of all forms of energy in kilograms of coal equivalent per inhabitant.
(3) Passenger cars in use per 1000 inhabitants.
(4) Gross national product in US dollars per inhabitant.
(5) Doctors per million inhabitants.
(6) Dietary energy supply in kilocalories per inhabitant per day.
(7) Infantile mortality rate: deaths of infants under the age of one year per 1000 live births.
(8) Annual rate of population growth 1970–5 per 1000 inhabitants.
Source: Various (quoted in J. P. Cole *Geography of World Affairs*, Penguin 1979).

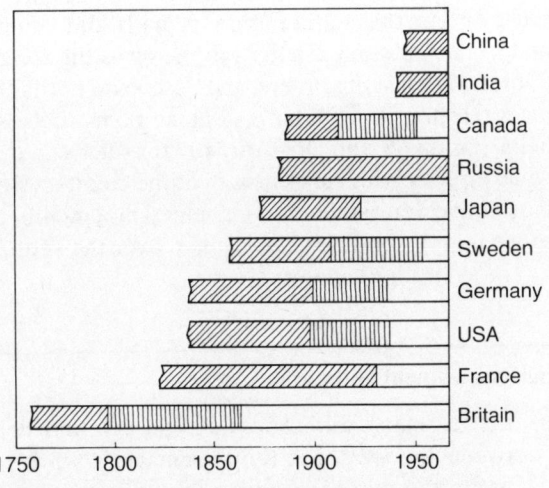

The beginnings of industrialization

40 to 20 per cent of active population employed in agriculture

Less than 20 per cent of active population employed in agriculture

Figure 35 *The spread of the Industrial Revolution*

Self-assessment questions

2 Which of the variables in Table 14 is the best measure of a country's level of industrialization?

3 What do these figures tell you about the way people live in each country?

4 What additional information would be helpful?

The late starters in the development race, once they have overcome the forces that held them back, have been able to leap over stages and move ahead quickly by using the experience of other nations. A country beginning to industrialize today would not start with the steam engine but adopt the latest equipment and the most advanced techniques. One authority has argued that the more backward a country, the greater the necessity for the state to play a role in promoting industrial growth (rather than leaving the initiative to private individuals).

Particular industries and regions have developed rapidly at certain times, only to experience periods of stagnation and eventual decline. Some writers have explained this in terms of a second and third 'technological revolutions'.

One measure of the 'maturity' of an economy is the proportion of workers employed in each of the main sectors:

Primary: agriculture, mining, fishing.
Secondary: manufacturing.
Tertiary: services (banking, hairdressing, teaching, etc.).

Although there was a substantial service sector (household servants) in existence at the beginning of the Industrial Revolution, the numbers who work in offices or handle goods that others produce have increased steadily since the late nineteenth century. Meanwhile, though the output of industry has greatly expanded, employment in manufacturing has stagnated and then fallen to a point where some authorities speak of a 'post-industrial society' and even the 'de-industrialization of Britain'.

Table 15

First technological revolution (c. 1750) Leading industries: cotton, textiles, railways.	Machines to do the work that was previously performed by human hands, for example spinning machines. Energy source: steam engine
Second technological revolution (c. 1850) Leading industries: engineering, steel, oil.	Machines that can make other machines, for example universal milling machine. Energy source: electricity, internal combustion engine.
Third technological revolution (c. 1950) Leading industries: electronic, chemicals	Machines that control production automatically to produce new goods, for example synthetic fibres, robots. Energy source: nuclear power.

Self-assessment question

5 It has been said that Britain was the first country to industrialize but the last to modernize. Explain this statement.

The guild system of production

Do you have a traditional cobbler's shop in your town? Think about how this craftsman works: he must obtain the leather, thread, nails and other materials necessary for the job; he owns the tools of his trade (last, hammers, awls, etc.) and perhaps his workshop as well; he may make items such as belts, handbags and clogs directly for sale; and he deals directly with customers over the counter. He may employ an assistant or be helped by a member of his family and he may even live over the shop.

Self-assessment question

6 List as many differences as you can find between the way that the shoemaker's work is organized and your own work.

Six centuries ago all manufacturing work was carried on in a way similar to our shoemaker. Craftsmen were organized into powerful trade associations called 'guilds' that also controlled municipal affairs. Craftsmen had two kinds of helpers:

(i) *Apprentices* Youngsters who lived and worked with the master craftsman and learned the trade. Apprenticeship, which might last from two to seven years, meant a formal agreement between a boy's parents and the master craftsman. In return for a fee and the promise to be hard-working and obedient, the apprentice was taught the secrets of the trade and lodged in the master's home.

(ii) *Journeymen* A worker who had served his time as an apprentice and passed the examination was called a journeyman. If he had insufficient funds to set up his own business, he would continue to work for the master for wages. In those days not much capital was needed and most workers expected to progress from apprentice to journeyman to master.

Self-assessment question

7 What do you think are the main differences and similarities between medieval and modern apprenticeship systems?

Why did the guilds disappear?

(i) Gradually the gap between masters and journeyman widened and it became more difficult to rise from worker to boss. It became harder to climb the ladder: the test to become a master was made stricter; larger sums had to be paid to the guild; and new rules were introduced restricting progress only to the sons of masters. Journeymen formed their own guilds and tried to get higher wages from their masters.

(ii) The guilds became increasingly conservative and opposed new methods and techniques.

Their main concern was to prevent outside competition: Glasgow Corporation of Mechanics tried to prohibit James Watt from work on his steam engine because he was not a guild member. Merchants who wanted to expand production set up new workshops in the countryside where there were no guild restrictions.

(iii) The medieval craftsman needed to be proficient in every aspect of his work. Writing at the start of the Industrial Revolution in 1776, Adam Smith commented: 'The greatest improvement in the productive powers of labour . . . seems to have been the effects of the *division of labour*'. By this he meant *specialization*: keeping a worker at a single job until he becomes expert at it. This saves time and so speeds up production. As a seventeenth-century economist wrote: 'Cloth must be cheaper made when one cards, another spins, another weaves, another draws, another dresses, another presses and packs, than when all the operations above mentioned were clumsily performed by the same hand'. All-round craftsmen working separately could not compete with semi-skilled workers co-operating together, especially when the latter were assisted by the introduction of machinery.

Self-assessment question

8 Describe the extent of the division of labour in your workplace or industry. What are the advantages and disadvantages of specialization?

The changing organization of production

Not all industry passed through these four successive stages: new industries arose that started in stage three and others skipped over one or more stages.

The time periods indicated are rough approximations. Always, when one stage was widely prevalent, signs of its decay were already there and

Table 16 *The changing organization of production*

System	Unit of production	Raw materials	Tools	Product	Market	Period
Domestic	Family. Simple division of labour.	Produced or obtained by the worker himself.	Worker's own.	Worker's own, for personal use.	Almost non-existent.	Early Middle Ages (until eleventh century).
Guild	Independent craftsmen (masters) usually employing two or three others. Home-based or small workshop.	Self-produced or obtained by master through trade.	Worker's own.	Master's own, produced for sale.	Small and stable.	Throughout Middle Ages (especially twelfth to sixteenth centuries).
Putting-out	Master craftsmen and helpers. Home or workshop.	Supplied by merchant.	Worker's own.	Owned by merchant who paid producers on piecework basis.	Growing.	Sixteenth to eighteenth centuries.
Factory	Workers collected together into employer's building, work under supervision. Complex division of labour.	Supplied by factory owner.	Owned by employer. Increasing use of machinery.	Owned by employer who pays producers' wage	Wider but fluctuating.	Nineteenth century to present day.

the seeds of the next stage were pushing upward. Thus, in the thirteenth century when the guilds were at their height, instances of the putting-out system had already appeared in Northern Italy. Examples of early factories were already working in England in the sixteenth century. The guilds did not lose their legal privileges until the early nineteenth century and aspects of the putting-out system survive in the British clothing industry to this day.

The Industrial Revolution is often seen merely as the sudden appearance of a series of inventions that led directly to the growth of towns, a massive improvement in our standard of living and the modern way of life. This is too simple a picture. The new technology increased the productivity of workers and greatly reduced the time required to manufacture the necessities of life. Paradoxically, the early factory system represented a clear deterioration in working conditions compared with cottage industry.

The life of the domestic handicraft worker was hard and poor and should not be romanticized. Nevertheless, such workers had to be driven into the alien environment of the factory by economic

Figure 36 *Cottage industry: the yeoman clothier and his family at work in the loom-chamber, eighteenth century*
Source: Phyllis Bentley, *The Pennine Weaver* (Firecrest Press 1970)

Figure 37 *Child labour in a South American village today*

Figure 38   *The factory system*

necessity. At the time, factory work was frequently compared unfavourably with the system of slavery, then a central concern of social reformers.

The negro slave in the West Indies, if he works under a scorching sun, has probably a little breeze of air sometimes to fan him: he has space of ground, and time allowed to cultivate it. The English spinner slave has no enjoyment of the open atmosphere and breezes of heaven. Locked up in factories eight stories high, he has no relaxation till the ponderous engine stops, and then goes home to get refreshed for the next day; no time for sweet association with his family; they are all alike fatigued and exhausted.

E. P. Thompson, *The Making of the English Working Class* (Pelican Books 1970)

Self-assessment question

9   If you were born in the early nineteenth century, would you rather have been a child employed in a Lancashire spinning-mill or a slave worker on a plantation? Why?

One protest movement, the Luddites, smashed the machines and attacked the mills that they thought threatened their livelihood and caused their misery. What should have been their response to the new technology?

RULES & REGULATIONS

TO BE OBSERVED IN THE

KERSHAW WOOD MILLS

1 No swearing, improper behaviour or conversation will be allowed on the premises.

2 Any person introducing or in possession of intoxicating liquors during work hours, or smoking in any part of these mills, will be fined 5s. for each offence.

3 Any one spoiling work, wasting or destroying property, or damaging machinery, will be either fined or immediately discharged, in which case the amount of the loss sustained will be deducted from his or her wages.

4 Any one employed in these Mills, and not on the premises when the hours for working commence, will not only be subject to a fine of from 2d. to 6d. for each offence, but to the loss of his her or employment, in which case all wages previously due will be forfeited.

5 All hands neglecting their employment, leaving their place, going into any other room, or introducing any individual into these Mills, without leave, will be fined 1s. for each offence.

6 Any person staying at home, or quitting the premises during work hours, without permission from his or her overlooker, will either be fined double the value of the time lost, or immediately discharged, in which case all wages previously due will be forfeited.

7 No one under 18 years of age will be allowed to remain in these Mills during meal times, on any pretence whatsoever.

8 Any offence against the factory act, will be entirely at the risk of the overlookers or the parents of any child who may be informed against. Every overlooker or spinner allowing an infringement upon the factory act, *shall be responsible* for any penalty or penalties which may be inflicted.

9 A fortnight's notice is required from every one leaving their employment; and should any trangress this rule, they will forfeit all wages previously due to them.

In addition to the above Rules, all persons employed in these Mills must conform and will be subject to the Rules and Regulations belonging to the room and department in which they work.

D. CUNNINGHAM, PRINTER, STALYBRIDGE.

Figure 39

Table 17 *Cottage industry* versus *the factory system*

System	Cottage industry	Factory system: early nineteenth century	Factory system: today Complete this column yourself
Employment	Husbands, wives and children work together.	Families divided: mill-owners preferred to employ women, juveniles and children who could more easily be compelled to accept industrial conditions.	
Hours of work	Decided himself when he would work: frequently took days off for agricultural jobs and holidays.	Regular and strict time-keeping (symbolized by the hooter and bell) took no account of ill-health or domestic arrangements. The introduction of gas-lighting allowed the working day to be extended (usually 6 a.m. to 8 p.m.).	

System	Cottage industry	Factory system: early nineteenth century	Factory system: today Complete this column yourself
Factory discipline	Personal control over conditions of work.	Factory discipline and systematic work enforced by brutal overlookers and a system of fines.	
Working conditions	Primitive conditions in workshop but could go outside for fresh air and relaxation. 'My work was at the loom side, and when not winding, my father taught me reading, writing and arithmetic.'	Unhealthy: noisy, stifling atmosphere. Workers often not permitted to sing, open windows or even drink water. Violent accidents – children cleaned unfenced machinery while in motion. Factories believed to be places of foul language and sexual immorality.	
Skill	Lifelong speciality in handling the same tool that serves the worker as a means of expressing his skill.	Machines encompass many of the traditional skills: worker's role is now to serve and supervise the machine.	

The new technology

The first wave of industrialization destroyed a wide range of traditional craft skills. Many survived, however, and new skills arose based on the higher-level industrial technology. Now a new wave of technological change threatens to make many of our existing trades as redundant as hand-loom weaving.

De-skilling

The pre-industrial craftsman generally designed the product himself as well as making it. Even when he merely followed a long-established design, there was still scope to introduce minor modifications of his own. Twentieth-century changes have taken the division of labour to the stage where there is now a separation between the 'thinking' and 'doing' stages of a particular task. The mental tasks associated with work processes are increasingly hived off to separate planning and design departments and the remaining jobs are so subdivided and specialized that the individual worker never sees the final product. The result is a significant reduction on the level of skill required by the worker.

New machines

The microprocessor revolution has substantially reduced the cost of certain types of advanced technology. The initial impact was the mechanization of office work: the industrial revolution has finally caught up with the white-collar employee. A word processor, for example, may be bought or hired for less than the cost of a secretary's wage but it enables one typist to do the work of two or three others. New methods of information storage and transfer are replacing many traditional clerical skills. In manufacturing, the changes have been slower but, in the long run, are likely to be no less dramatic:

Industrial robots Many workers do repetitive jobs (for example assembly work), and there is massive scope for their complete automation. On the British Leyland Mini Metro production line, welding operations that previously required eighty workers are now supervised by one man.

Computer-control Computers have been used for some time to control continuous process operations in chemical manufacture, breweries, paper making and oil refineries. More recently computers have been linked to individual machines (for example numerically controlled lathes and automatic milling machines). About 70 per cent of the engineering industry's output is batch, rather than mass production. Previously it was too expensive to automate this kind of work. As a result, inefficient general purpose machines were used, requiring long setting-up times and low machining rates. A lot of work in progress spends its time piled up on the shop floor waiting to get on the machine. To automate this work allows machines to be run at their full capacity.

It is now possible to programme a computer to design a new product and for that instruction to be fed directly into a computer-controlled machine that will fabricate it. In the process the craftsman is squeezed out, to be replaced by a small number of machine minders and maintenance staff.

Self-assessment questions

10 What new technology has been introduced into your workplace during the last few years?

11 Did an older generation of workers require more or less skill to do your kind of work?

12 What do you think your job will be like in ten years time? Is it 'a job for life'? Remember, the workers who shoed horses at the beginning of this century probably thought that they had a steady job for life.

9 Industry today

The aim of this section is to help you to understand the organization of modern industry and appreciate some important recent trends. You will be encouraged to consider the organization of your own firm, the concentration of industrial ownership, ideas about scientific management techniques, attempts to increase job satisfaction, moves towards industrial democracy and some aspects of health and safety.

Your firm

The best starting point for an investigation of modern industry is a thorough knowledge of the company that you work for. Try to find the answers to these questions about your firm. Information may be obtained from:

  (i) Company representatives (for example training officer).
 (ii) Written material that the firm produces for its owners and customers (for example catalogues, prospectus, annual report and accounts).
(iii) Reference books in a library (for example *Britain's Top 1000 Companies*, *Stock Exchange Yearbook*, *Kompass Directory*, *Who Owns Whom*, *Who's Who*, Extel and Moodies Cards).

Origins

When, where and by whom was the firm started?
In what circumstances?
Who put up the original capital?
What is the relationship of the founder(s) to the present owners and managers?
What were the early achievements of the firm?
How has it grown?
What factors have affected its performance (for example new products, dedicated work, external changes)?
What were the firm's turnover and profits last year?

What happened to the profits?
How does the firm obtain finance for new investment?

Production

What capital/consumer goods does your firm produce, or what services does it supply?
Is production labour-intensive or capital-intensive?
What methods are used (for example one-off, small batch, assembly line, continuous process)?
What raw material and energy inputs are required?
From where are they obtained?
How would you describe the level of technology used by the firm? (For example what are the newest/oldest machines? What is the most advanced technology available?)
How is the work process subdivided into separate departments and specialized jobs?
Draw a sketch map of the premises to show the location of various operations.

Market

What is it? How has it changed?
Does your firm have direct links with customers or trade through distributors?
Does it provide an after-sales service?
Who are your competitors?
How strong are they?

What part has been played by emblems, trade marks and advertising in creating a company image?

Labour

How many employees? Has the number increased/decreased in recent years?

What are their job descriptions and skills?

How are workers recruited and trained?

What distinctions exist between 'works' and 'staff'?

What are the wage-rates/average earnings of different crafts or groups?

How would you describe relations between employers and workers?

Organization

Is your firm a partnership, limited company, nationalized industry or a workers' co-operative?

Is there a parent-company with subsidiaries?

Is it a multi-national?

What channels of communication exist (for example company newspaper, notice board)?

Draw a chart to show the formal structure of your firm: that is the 'chain of command' (indicate those of equal importance in the firm's hierarchy by placing them on the same level in the organization diagram).

Decision-making

What kinds of decision are usually taken by directors, managers, office staff, foremen/supervisors and shop-floor workers?

Do any committees or other bodies exist for the purpose of consultation between management and workers?

Who are the directors? Are they on the board of any other companies?

What are the names and titles of managers?

What are their qualifications for the job?

Future

What are the aims of your firm?

What are its strengths and weaknesses?

What problems is it likely to face in the future?

What changes do you expect to occur?

How do you think your firm will be affected by the general economic situation?

What sort of firm do you work for?

Firms differ a great deal in terms of size, organization and objectives. Some small businesses may be founded with relatively little capital (for example plumbers), while other operations require massive investments (for example nuclear energy). Firms can either:

(i) Produce *consumer goods*, such as chocolate bars and washing machines, that are sold to the public; or

(ii) Produce *capital goods*, such as steel girders and machine tools, for other branches of industry; or

(iii) Provide *services*, such as garage repairs, banking facilities and computer soft-wear.

Sole traders

Many small businesses (for example decorators) were established by a single individual. He put up the capital, makes the decisions, takes the risks and enjoys all the profits. Sole traders often rely on their families for assistance, for example to lend money or help out in the shop. As the business grows, he may employ additional workers.

Partnerships

The trader may take on one or more partners in order to bring more resources into the business. This means losing some of his independence because the acts of one partner are legally binding upon the others. While a partner is entitled to share any profits that the firm makes, he is also personally liable for its debts up to the limit of his possessions (which means that he could end up being forced to sell his house and car). A *sleeping partner* is a person who contributes capital, but does not participate in the management of the firm.

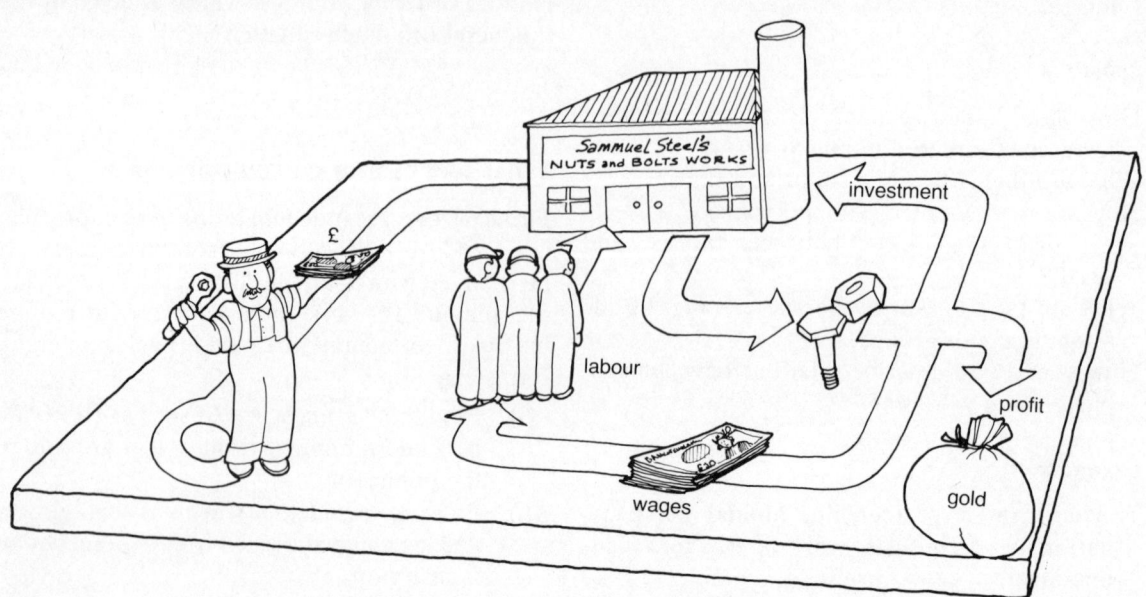

Figure 40

Figure 41

Partnership is the typical form of organization for small firms because:

(i)   There are few formal rules to restrict its activities.

(ii) Partners are regarded as 'self-employed' and so can claim business expenses against their tax liability.

(iii) The firm's affairs are confidential and there is no legal obligation to disclose its accounts.

On the other hand, membership of a partnership is generally limited by law to twenty people and obtaining fresh capital for expansion may be difficult when this number is reached. It is also difficult to leave a partnership: you must find someone who is willing to buy your share.

Limited companies

In order to overcome the problems involved with partnerships, businessmen form registered companies by issuing *shares*. Each share represents ownership of a part of the firm's assets and a right to the profits produced, which are distributed as *dividends*. About 90 per cent of all employees in private industry work for limited companies, which must contain the word or 'Ltd.' in their name. The advantages of this form of organization are that:

(i)   Ownership may be transferred easily by the sale of shares.

(ii) Whereas partners can only borrow money *as individuals*, a company may obtain a loan or buy materials on credit *as an organization*.

(iii) The liability of the owners is restricted to the amount of money that they have invested (that is, the value of their shares).

To protect the firm's suppliers, creditors and shareholders, a limited company must produce an annual report and properly audited accounts to show that its affairs are in order.

Small family businesses that wish to expand without the founders losing control are usually organized as *private companies*. Here shares are not

Figure 42

made available to the general public (only to specific individuals) and may not be sold without the permission of the directors. The shares of *public companies* are generally on sale to anyone who wishes to buy them and their price is quoted on the Stock Exchange. The main reason for 'going public' used to be to raise new capital, but today only about 10 per cent of investment is financed in this way. Most Stock Exchange dealing is in second-hand shares: ownership is transferred but the firm does not acquire additional funds.

The shareholders vote, in proportion to the size of their investment, for a board of directors who decide company policy. Directors are usually major shareholders in the firm and they may decide to pay themselves a fee for their efforts. At an annual meeting, they must report on the state of the firm and submit themselves for re-election. The large scale of modern industry means that individual shareholders usually have little say in determining company policy.

While some directors may take an active part in the day to day running of their company, it is more common in large firms for the board to appoint professional managers. Within complex organizations, there are greater possibilities for a conflict of interest. For example, shareholders want big dividends and for the value of their shares to rise; directors may be more interested in growth; while the manager's main concern may be a quiet life and avoiding risks.

Public sector

Nearly one employee in three works for local and central government or the state industries. The original *nationalized industries* were established by the post-war Labour Government that believed essential services should:

(i)   Be owned by and accountable to the public.
(ii) Carry out socially responsible policies (for example low prices).
(iii) Avoid waste and duplication by integrating parallel services.
(iv) Act as an instrument for planning the economy.

In practice, the nationalized industries have been run in much the same way as other companies with a board of directors appointed by a government minister. Since they were expected to serve the public interest as well as be efficient, their financial objective was to break even rather than make a profit. More recently they have been required to make sufficient profits to cover their investment programmes. Despite their popular image as loss-making enterprises, some consistently make a profit, others have a mixed record and only a few are regular losers.

One reason for this reputation is that substantial investments are necessary to overcome their inherited legacy of under-investment and obsolete technology. The state monopolies were created from branches of the energy and transport industries that had great difficulty in operating at a profit while in private hands, but which supplied essential services for the rest of the economy. Since they cannot raise money by issuing shares, they must borrow it. If a nationalized industry does not make sufficient profit to cover interest and repayment on these loans, the deficit appears on the balance sheet as a 'loss'. Losses are difficult to hide for state industries: a private company would merely pay its shareholders a reduced dividend or none at all.

The 1974 Labour Government believed that many of the problems associated with nationalization arose from the fact that only declining industries had been taken into public ownership. It therefore set up the National Enterprise Board (NEB) to acquire and run potentially profitable areas of manufacturing industry. In practice the NEB has provided a 'nursery' for new industries (for example computers) by lending money to high-risk enterprises and a 'hospital for lame ducks' (for example British Leyland). Ferranti and ICL were turned from loss-making into profitable companies and sold back to the private sector in 1978–9.

The distinction between the public and private sectors is no longer so obvious. Aircraft and missile production, for example, is a high-technology industry which is greatly reliant on government aid for research, development, sales promotions and contracts. The precarious state of the industry, however, was highlighted by the dramatic bankruptcy of Rolls-Royce in 1971: the firm was rescued by a government take-over. In 1977 British Aerospace was formed by the forced merger of the British Aircraft Corporation, Hawker Siddeley Aviation and two other companies into a single national industry. Thus, it became large enough to compete successfully with the US aerospace giants. Its trading profits rose from £44 millions in 1975 to £92 millions in 1980 with expectations of £150 millions in 1983. The Government recently sold half of the firm's assets to individual investors so that it is now a partnership with the private sector.

Mergers and take-overs

What do these companies have in common?

Ross Foods
Smedley HP Foods
Golden Wonder
John Player
Courage
John Smith's Brewery (Tadcaster)

They are all part of the Imperial Group.

The traditional theory of the 'market economy' assumes that there are a large number of small firms competing for the custom of the consumer. In reality, however, in many industries a few firms have grown so large that they dominate the market. On average, the five largest companies account for three-quarters of the total output of each major industry in Britain. In 1910 the 100 largest industrial companies produced 15 per cent of total manufacturing output. By 1950 this figure had risen to 20 per cent, 46 per cent in 1970, and is now about two-thirds of the total.

Market share

Firms may expand by the merger of enterprises producing the same product (for example Leyland and British Motor Holdings to form British Leyland). Many keep their 'old identities' in order

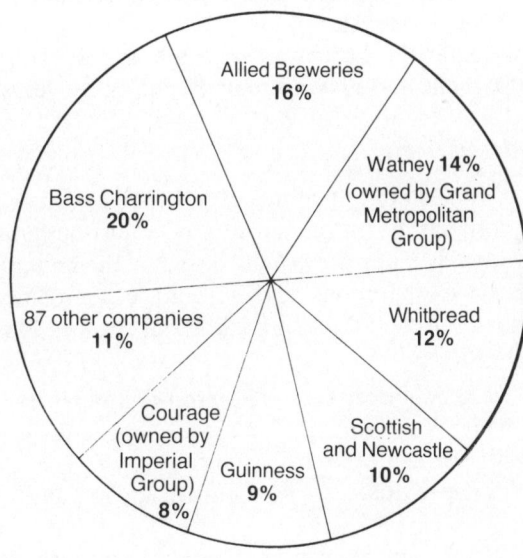

Figure 43   *Concentration in the brewing industry: market share 1977*

to retain traditional loyalties of the customers. Stork, Summer County, and Blue Band margarines appear to be in competition but they are actually produced by the same company.

More frequently concentration comes through a 'take-over bid' when a large firm swallows up a small or less successful company. Take-overs increasingly cut across traditional industry boundaries. The *Express* group of newspapers was acquired by Trafalgar House (shipping, hotels, property, construction).

Larger units enjoy enormous advantages over small competitors: they can reduce costs through larger production runs and other 'economies of scale'. A 15 ton lorry costs only slightly more than a ten-tonner, but requires the same number of men to operate it. Big firms have greater funds at their disposal so that they can:

(i)   Invest in more advanced technology and advertising;

(ii) Attempt operations that are so expensive or massive that they can only be successfully carried out on a large scale (for example oil exploration);

(iii) Bear the burden of research and development that may not pay off for many years.

Multi-nationals

The outstanding feature of economic concentration has been the growth of multi-national companies. They are usually based in one country but have operations and subsidiary companies abroad. Of the 30 leading industrial corporations in 1976:

15 were American	13 were oil companies
5 were West German	6 motor vehicle producers
1 was British (and 2 Anglo-Dutch)	4 chemical companies

The scale of their operations can be judged from this table:

Table 18

Gross national product of selected countries (early 1970s)		Sales of selected large companies (1972)	
Denmark	28	General Motors	28
Yugoslavia	21	Standard Oil	21
Venezuela	18	Ford	16
South Korea	12	British Petroleum	8
Portugal	10	British American Tobacco	5
Bangladesh	5	Unilever NV	4

Unit: Thousands of millions of dollars

Project Erika: a case study in multi-national organization

In spring 1977 Ford Europe decided it needed a new engine plant in addition to those at Dagenham (Britain), Cologne (West Germany) and Valencia (Spain). The company already had major operations in twelve European countries. The decision to expand was based on forward planning: a forecast that European car sales would rise from 9.8 million in 1977 to 11 million in 1982 (especially in the small car market). A 'new generation' of engines was therefore required.

The decision was taken by a ten man Policy Committee chaired by Henry 'Red' Poling. This committee oversees the national production companies (for example Ford UK) and is responsible for overall European strategy, product planning, investment and finance, and government relations.

However, investment decisions over $25 million (roughly £11 million) must be confirmed by the global HQ in Dearborn, Detroit, which has the ultimate power. The decision was to build the most technically advanced plant in Europe, if not the world, with a production capacity of 420,000 engines per year. Production and quality control would be totally automated and the factory would

only require highly skilled workers. It was considered that this would preclude employing workers as 'disruptive' as those at Ford assembly plants such as Halewood.

The new factory could be built anywhere. The company has a 'Doomsday Book' which is a collection of information – much of it secret – about different countries (for example political persuasion of government ministers, labour relations). The initial consideration of where to build was secret and most governments didn't know about the Ford decision until May or June. The countries involved in negotiation saw this new plant as a potential boost for their economies which were just recovering from a period of recession and high unemployment.

West Germany

When the German government heard of Ford's intention, the Minister of Economics informed the Berlin local government. The Mayor of Berlin selected two alternative sites for the factory and offered Ford a generous package: tax rebates and investment grants; long term tax concessions; an offer to train the workforce.

However, Ford had told the Germans that engines could be produced at £200 each (that is, £50 cheaper) in Britain or Spain because of lower labour costs. The Germans established other channels for pressure. Influential German–American businessmen contacted the main board in Detroit. In late June the German government appealed to President Carter (to put pressure on Ford), arguing that an economically strong Germany was essential for a free Europe. Early on in the negotiations, however, Ford told the Germans that they had no chance.

Ireland

Meanwhile, Ireland knew nothing of Ford's intentions. The government was not informed until after Jack Lynch became Prime Minister in June. He immediately went flat out to make a bid and by the end of July offered: a site in Cork; £50 million in investment grants; tax free profits until 1990. He also offered to give Britain a chance to help build the factory.

Spain

About this time Ford executives went to Spain on a 'courtesy visit'. The Spanish Minister of Industry was told he had a week to submit a bid. In that time the Spaniards not only had to match the German, Irish and British offers – which Ford revealed – but had to offer an extra percentage to overcome transport problems. Faced with this hard line, the Spanish just gave up the idea.

Britain

In spring 1977 Ford negotiated for a small spark plug factory to be built in Wales. Although these negotiations broke down, Ford inquired whether the incentives they had been offered would apply to a large factory and let it be known they were looking at a number of European sites.

Henry Ford II, the chairman and chief executive of the company, visited his Swansea factory during June. In contrast to the conflict-prone factories at Dagenham and Halewood, Ford admired labour relations at the Welsh plant. He said after speaking to two shop stewards at Swansea: 'Wales has the most intelligent and articulate labour force in the world'.

The Secretary of State for Wales quickly found a site at Miskin within easy reach of the docks and M4 motorway. It was in a special development area and so qualified for a maximum Industrial Investment Grant of 22 per cent. The deal was designed to be very competitive with the Irish. The Secretary of State for Industry, Eric Varley, contacted the head of Ford UK to offer every assistance and Red Poling was given a guided tour of Chequers.

On 25 August the Prime Minister, James Callaghan, met Henry Ford at Number Ten. He knew Ford loved Britain: he owns two houses over here. Callaghan is reported to have said, 'Henry, we are turning this country round. And you, if you choose, can help us do it.'

Callaghan later set up a secret meeting. We do not know where or when it took place, but it was between Ford and two trade union leaders: Jack Jones of the Transport and General Workers' Union and Hugh Scanlon of the Amalgamated Union of Engineering Workers. Nor do we know exactly what was said, but one notable newspaper commented that the two meetings 'effectively set the seal on the biggest industrial coup achieved by a British government in years'.

At the last minute Ford changed his mind. He didn't want Miskin but a site at Bridgend. It was larger and needed less preparatory work. However, this site only qualified for a 20 per cent investment grant. Ford gave an ultimatum to the Department of Industry: 22 per cent or no deal. They had until noon the next day to provide an equivalent package for Bridgend.

Conclusion

The capital cost of the Bridgend plant is £185 million. Total government aid came to £70 million (roughly 26 per cent). Given that the plant will only employ 2500 workers, the government has spent some £31,500 per job.

The irony is that Ford didn't take their decision to build in Wales on the 'money off' offer. It was based on the fact that Wales has good communications; low wage costs; a good labour relations record; instantly available skilled labour.

The Ford Europe Policy Committee recommended Wales to Detroit on 17 July. An executive from Ford Detroit later commented, 'There was no question, Wales was signed, sealed and delivered before 1 August.'

Adapted from *The Battle for Henry's Ear* by Stephen Aris (*Sunday Times* October 1977)

Scientific management

Management is concerned with producing goods as profitably as possible. This requires the most efficient combination of capital, raw materials, technology and labour. Labour is often seen as the most unpredictable element in this equation. It used to be widely believed that workers could be motivated by 'the carrot and the stick' (that is wages and fear of unemployment). These incentives have not always proved effective and management has been faced with problems that result from lack of motivation: strikes, absenteeism, sabotage, high labour turnover, low productivity.

The work of Frederick W. Taylor

'Speedy' Taylor is the father of work study and scientific management techniques. He was obsessed by efficiency. As chief engineer in a steel company he increased output by 60 per cent through time and motion studies. As a result of his research, he came to the conclusion that:

(i)   Management should systematically study work and gather together knowledge about the skills that workers already possess.
(ii) Management should use this information to devise the most efficient methods and workers should be required to follow them.
(iii) The work process should be controlled through the selection of the 'best men' and the use of incentives (that is, more money).

The work of Elton Mayo

Mayo conducted experiments at the GEC Hawthorne factory in Chicago during the 1920s. One by one, he varied certain conditions in the factory to see what were the effects. One test was to improve the lighting in a workshop on the assumption that the better the lighting, the better the work. Production increased. He then reduced the illumination, and output went up again! It also rose for a control group whose lighting stayed the same throughout. Productivity did not depend upon lighting, but upon the fact that the workers were being studied. During the experiment the observers paid attention to the workers, kept them informed, asked for information and listened to their complaints. Mayo concluded:

(i)   Workers' complaints are not necessarily objective statements of fact but may express their feelings of frustration and a sense that they are being ignored.
(ii) Frustration will increase the probability that workers become aggressive, apathetic, or fatigued.
(iii) Workers like to feel important: security and belonging mean more than improvements in physical working conditions. Morale is improved when workers are consulted (even if their complaints are not acted upon).
(iv) Informal work groups arise naturally which exercise a strong control over their members to conform to the behaviour of the group (for example students on vacation jobs are invariably warned 'not to work too hard').

Status

We often rely on external signs as an indication of a person's position. In industry there are many clues to status: clothing, separate canteens and toilets, size of desk, car parking space, working hours. Formal status is allocated by management. 'Staff' generally have longer holidays and time off with pay for personal reasons. 'Works' usually need to clock on, have pay deducted for lateness and are subjected to pilferage checks.

Problems can arise if management fails to realize that workers also have opinions about the proper relationship between groups of employees. Stacker-truck operators and cleaners may both be classed as labourers and so both are paid the same wage. The drivers, however, may consider themselves superior as a group. It then seems illogical to the management that a driver refuses to clean the lavatory when the attendant is sick.

Authority

Formal leaders in industry, like status, are also imposed from above: chargehands, foremen, supervisors, managers. At the same time, all groups produce natural leaders – the best person to take charge in a specific situation (football captain, shop steward, gang leader). The ideal person to promote – loyal and hardworking – may be alienated from his workmates and his promotion may be the cause of further antagonism and isolation.

Self-assessment question

1 What do you think might be the consequences of:
  (i) Making the workshop 'agitator' into a foreman?
  (ii) Recruiting specialists from university into management?

Foremen are often under pressure from all directions. Efforts to meet management's production targets may bring the foremen into conflict with workers (over safety or line-speeds or bonus rates, etc.) and other departmental foremen (over shortages of components, machine breakdowns, etc.).

There are essentially three kinds of 'bosses'.

Autocratic

An autocrat gives orders which he insists must be obeyed; takes decisions without consultation; and simply tells people what immediate jobs to do rather than briefing them about his general aims. He remains aloof from the group, and he alone decides who will receive praise or criticism.

Democratic

A democrat explains aims and obtains the acceptance of the group before giving instructions. He participates as a group member and makes it clear that the group as a whole will assess the performance of members.

Anarchic

An anarchist does not assume control over the group but leaves it to get on by itself.

A particular boss may display features from all three approaches from time to time.

Self-assessment questions

2 Which kind of boss would you prefer to work for?

3 Which do you think will produce the best results?

Try this experiment
Divide the class into three groups. Select three students and brief them *in confidence*. Assign the roles of autocratic, democratic and anarchic leader. Explain that the objective of each group is to construct a model from pins and straws and that the completed models will be judged in terms of their stability and artistic merit. Which group do you think will produce the best results?

Studies have shown that production is actually highest where:

  (i) There is less direct supervision and the leader takes an advisory role.
  (ii) Management is less concerned with production and places more emphasis on employees' interests.
  (iii) Workers participate in decision-making.
  (iv) There is less criticism and more praise. Foremen are far more inclined to reprimand

workers than to praise them. Praise is, nevertheless, many times more effective in improving a situation. A reprimand on the other hand, can make the problem even worse, especially public reprimands which tend only to harden attitudes.

Carrot versus stick

It is possible to make a person want to do something by offering suitable rewards. No amount of punishment, however, will make a person do it other than unwillingly. Attempts to solve problems by threats and punishments lead to resentment. This is especially the case where supervisors are inconsistent, turning a blind eye one week and clamping down the next.

Self-assessment question

4   You are employed at a bakery where smoking on the premises is not allowed. You have just been promoted to the position of foreman. You find a group of workers smoking in a room adjoining the bakery and threaten to report those concerned. Previous to your promotion, however, you have been a member of this group yourself and are therefore told in no uncertain terms to mind your own business. Explain how you would solve this situation to ensure your success as a foreman.

That Monday morning feeling

Why do workers absent themselves from work or knock-off early? Is it because they are lazy and want to escape from work? At the same time they pour their energy into allotments, cars, DIY, etc., during their leisure time. It appears that people need and want to work, but find their work unsatisfying. Why?

Powerlessness

You'd be working. Get into a bit of a system and just about keeping the job under control and then you'd find that you'd lost control, like. You'd be working that bit harder again. The bastards had altered the line speed. They'd swear blind they hadn't but they had. . . . You're just counted as a number here. Treated like a lot of robots. You could be in desperate trouble and they wouldn't help you.

Hew Benyon, *Working for Ford* (Penguin 1973)

Isolation

I place the car off the hoist, I've been doing that for three years now. With the line you've got to adapt yourself to the speed. Some rush and get a break. I used to try and do that but the job used to get out of hand. I just amble along now. . . . Some jobs you're on you just can't talk or you'll lose concentration. When I came here first I couldn't talk at all. Now I can manage a few words with the man opposite me. . . . I bring books and crossword puzzles to work. This gives me something to think about when I'm doing the job. You walk out of here in a dream.

Hew Benyon, *Working for Ford*

Meaninglessness

My working day starts with the time-honoured ritual known as 'clocking-in'. In a job such as mine this is one of the more constructive acts of the day. . . . After clocking-in one starts work. Starts work that is, if the lavatories are full. . . . After the visit to the lavatory there is the tea-break to look forward to; after the tea-break, the dinner-break; after the dinner-break, the 'knocking-off' time. Work is done between the breaks, but is done from habit and is hardly given a passing thought. Nothing is gained from the work itself – it has nothing to offer. The criterion is not to do the job well, but to get it over quickly. Trouble is, one never does get it over with. Either one job is followed by another which is equally boring, or the same job goes on for ever and ever: particles of production that stretch into an age of inconsequence.

Ronald Frazer, *Work: twenty personal accounts* (Pelican 1968)

Self-estrangement

I help make cigarettes. I also smoke them – I'm smoking one now. Each employee of the firm for which I work receives from the age of 18 a free issue of cigarettes weekly. Personally I'd prefer the money to the fringe-benefit, but it's the cigarettes or nothing. So I smoke; even though I agree with the medical profession about the relationship between smoking and lung-cancer. Sometimes I feel as if I'm working in an arsenal, an arsenal full of noisy machines painted green – the colour of grass – attended by green overalled women. My workmates know little and care less about the lung-cancer side of smoking. It's a long way from the tobacco factory to the coffin, so we keep churning them out, millions a day, converting the rather attractive raw material, parchment-like tobacco leaf, into unattractive cigarettes. We make a pittance, the company makes a fortune. Other drug pedlars go to prison.

Ronald Frazer, *Work: twenty personal accounts*

So why do people work?

You don't achieve anything here. A robot could do it. The line here is made for morons. It doesn't need any thought. They tell you that. 'We don't pay you for thinking,' they say. Everyone comes to realize that they're not doing a worthwhile job. They're just on the line. For the money. Nobody likes to think that they're a failure. It's bad when you *know* that you're just a little cog. You just look at your pay packet – you look at what it does for your wife and kids. That's the only answer.

Hew Benyon, *Working for Ford*

Some recent experiments

Problems of frustration, monotony and alienation are usually most closely associated with assembly work and short job cycles (time taken to complete a task). When the Ford Motor Company was founded in 1903, cars were still individually built by craftsmen who planned and organized work as well as carrying it out. The introduction of the assembly line ten years later was accompanied by the transfer of part of this work to management. As F. W. Taylor recommended: 'All possible brain work should be removed from the shop floor and centred in the planning or layout department'. Attempts to increase job satisfaction have started by trying to reverse this process of specialization and give back to the 'doers' some of the 'thinking' that has passed to design, work study and quality control departments. Various schemes have been devised.

Job rotation

People exchange jobs, usually at regular intervals.

Job enlargement

Several tasks are amalgamated into a single job and the work-cycle increased. One person might assemble a whole product. There is, however, little improvement in performing five boring and fragmented jobs instead of one.

Job enrichment

A person takes greater responsibility for planning, organizing and checking work.

Autonomous work groups

This process taken a stage further: groups of workers decide how work is to be divided up; the order in which tasks are completed; the methods for doing each task; and the amount of time they should take. The management still sets the targets but the workers decide how to achieve them. Obviously they are limited by the design of the factory, but in new plants workers can be involved in planning this too.

In Britain schemes of this kind are still quite rare. Although management benefits from the increased flexibility and interchangeability of labour, it will want to see immediate benefits (for example increased productivity) to offset any additional costs. Trade unions have also been reluctant to co-operate because craftsmen are unwilling to allow others to encroach upon their traditional skills.

Workers on the board?

In 1977 the report of the Bullock Committee recommended that the law should be changed to give workers a right to representation on the board of large private companies. The arguments for this proposal were that it would:

(i)   Make private companies accountable to workers as well as shareholders.
(ii) Give workers greater access to information about major policy decisions (for example investment, redundancies).
(iii) Allow workers greater opportunity to influence decisions.

Bullock recommended that company boards should have:

(i)   An equal number of directors nominated by shareholders and trade unions.
(ii) A small group of 'independents' acceptable to both sides.

The employers' representatives on the Bullock Committee rejected this proposal and produced their own 'minority report' advocating that workers should only be represented on a 'supervisory board' which would appoint and control a separate policy-making management board.

Workers' participation has also been criticized by some trade unionists because it would:

Involve worker-directors taking responsibility for collective decisions of the board that they might oppose (since they would be in a minority and could be out-voted by the other directors).

Put them under pressure to see management's point of view.

Commit them to promoting the capitalist system.

Britain lags behind most of Western Europe in the development of participation schemes: some form of workers' representation is already established in Scandinavia, Germany, Holland and France. Although the Bullock proposals have been shelved for the moment, it is likely that they will be revived in the future as a result of pressures from the EEC.

Worker co-operatives

The 1970s witnessed the appearance of several worker co-operatives, generally in response to growing unemployment. The larger co-operatives – Triumph Meriden, KME in Kirby, the Scottish Daily News – were established after major companies decided to close down particular plants and declare employees redundant. Although they received some financial aid from the Labour Government, they never had the injections of cash that were required to overcome the basic problems that caused the business to be unprofitable in the first place.

On a more modest scale, isolated worker 'collectives' have sprung up around the country. These often see their role as fulfilling needs ignored by the big firms or encouraging a more socially-responsible way of life. Thus there are whole-food shops, community printing operations, 'alternative' bookshops, stores selling craftmade pottery, wood and leather goods (both from local work-shops and the Third World), schemes to assist the disabled and provide useful services, such as home insulation and bicycle repairs.

Despite their different sizes, activities and situations, these co-operatives have certain features in common. There is some degree of common owner-ship, accountability of management to the workers and industrial democracy. In most co-operatives the workers *are* the management, reaching deci-sions and regulating work conditions by consensus.

At Triumph Meriden all workers, whether skilled or semi-skilled, men or women, blue or white-collar, were paid the same flat rate wage. The one exception to this rule was a professional company secretary and accountant employed by the direc-tors. The shareholders in the company were trustees for the workers in the co-operative and were legally bound to vote as directed by the majority of the workers in general meeting. The first board of directors was composed of the senior shop stewards and two part-time outside advisers.

The workers held regular monthly meetings on Saturday mornings to hear a report from the direc-tors and raise questions and problems. Special meetings of the whole workforce in working time were organized when larger issues required urgent attention. There was also an elected Grievance Committee to deal with minor disagreements that arose from time to time.

One of the first things that they decided was that super-visors and foremen would be a superfluous and irritating anomaly and that they would not employ anybody for this function but would have organisers and co-ordinators only, appointed by the shop steward direc-tors. Job enlargement and rotation have become quite commonplace and flexibility of labour means that bottle-necks can be overcome quickly. These achieve-ments are the envy of many employers who have taken a close interest in Meriden for this very reason, wondering whether they can replicate this situation in their own factories. Unfortunately for them, this happy state of affairs can only be achieved where employers are abolished and men and women are convinced they are 'working for themselves' as are the Meriden workers.

Ken Coates, *The New Worker Co-operatives* (Spokes-man Books 1976)

What form should participation take in companies?

	Managers	Shop stewards	Full-time trade union officers
More consultation with employees	62%	24%	9%
Worker directors elected by all employees	26%	10%	0%
Worker directors elected through union machinery	2%	26%	30%
An extension of workplace bargaining	6%	24%	39%
Worker ownership and control of companies	4%	12%	22%

Table 19

Source: D. Farnham and J. Pimlott, *Who wants Bullock?* (*New Society* March 1977)

Self-assessment questions

5 Is the writer correct in saying that 'this happy state of affairs can only be achieved where employers are abolished'?

6 The wages at Meriden were lower than those for similar jobs in the area, so what other rewards did the workers receive?

7 What factors work against the commercial suc-cess of worker co-operatives?

Health and safety at work

The Health and Safety Executive announced that in 1979 there were 318,765 accidents at work, 639 of which were fatal (the construction industry accounting for a quarter of these deaths).

Patrick Kinnersly in *The Hazards of Work* argues that the official figures under-estimate the toll of life and health because employers do not report all accidents to the Health and Safety·Executive and there is no legal responsibility to notify the authorities about certain industrial diseases.

According to Kinnersly, every year in British industry:

(i)　About 2000 workers die from accidents.

(ii)　About 1000 are killed by recognized industrial diseases.

(iii)　Nearly one million are off work for at least three days because of an injury or industrial disease.

(iv)　About ten million need some form of first aid.

Table 20

Hazards	Possible effects	Workers at risk
Noise Depends on: noise level; period of exposure; your own susceptibility. Most damage is caused by long exposure to noise that is loud, but not so loud that you can't get used to it. Most factories: 90 dB Many machines: 100+ dB. Also low-frequency and ultra sound.	Complete and partial deafness, nausea, headaches, fatigue. Not hearing warnings in emergencies.	About one million workers in a wide range of industries. One in ten people are prone to hearing damage after exposure to noise at levels below 85 dB and we are all susceptible above this level. The recommended 'safe level' at 90 dB is *twice* as loud.
Vibration Level of risk depends upon: frequency (Hz); amplitude (how far surface moves); duration (length of exposure).	Whitefinger, abdominal, spinal and bone damage, tiredness and irritability.	Power tool operators. Lorry and tractor drivers.
Temperature Extremes of heat and cold.	Accidents, heat-stroke, frost-bite, rheumatism, heart disease, arthritis.	One million outdoor workers, especially foundry workers, miners, construction workers, cold store and farm workers.
Radiation Microwaves. Infrared radiation. Ultraviolet radiation (for example welder's flash). Ionizing radiation (for example X-ray machines).	Burns, cataracts, cancers, sterility, genetic defects.	Construction, hospital and nuclear energy industry workers. All people employed in ionizing radiation areas must wear a dose-meter (usually a film badge).

Hazards	Possible effects	Workers at risk
Chemicals There are approximately half a million chemical substances being manufactured. A new, potentially harmful chemical enters industrial use every 20 minutes. Poisons. Oils. Corrosives (for example acids). Dust. Gas and fumes. Asbestos – especially lagging and insulation industries.	Poisoning, dermatitis, skin or scrotal cancer, burning and blinding, explosions, fires, bronchitis, silicosis.	Virtually everyone. Especially engineering and manufacturing industries, mines and potteries, and transport workers.
Germs Bacteria and spores.	Weil's disease, brucellosis, anthrax.	Workers in rat infested premises. Farm workers, some textile workers.
Patterns of work Pace too fast. Excessive overtime. Boring and meaningless work. Isolation from workmates.	Fatigue, ulcers, indigestion, high blood pressure, depression, migraine, accidents.	Assembly line workers. Anyone who works a shift system or regular overtime.

Hazards at work

David and the foam on the floor

The operator was away at lunch when foam was found leaking from a pipe beneath the insulation plant at the Frigidaire factory in North London.

The foreman gave David Adair a paint scraper and told him to go in and scrape it off the floor before it hardened. He had to go right in under the machinery. The smell was so strong that the foreman went off to look for a respirator. He came back with one from the paint shop; it was covered in paint and the air came in round the edge. David wore it for the rest of the job which took him an hour and a half in all.

A few days later he began to feel chesty, wheezed a lot and had great difficulty in breathing.

The works doctor said his throat was infected. In the middle of the following night he had to get up and go outside to get enough air to breathe. The doctor said he had a cold but when his 'cold' got no better it was finally realised that he was suffering from severe asthma.

His condition was caused entirely by exposure to toluene di-isocyanate (TDI), one of the chemicals used in making the polyurethane foam he scraped off the floor. Even if it had been brand-new the respirator he wore would not have stopped the vapour. It was not the right type.

TDI is so powerful that one teaspoonful of vapour mixed into the air of a large room would make the air very dangerous to breathe. Under the machine where David worked the vapour was so concentrated that he could hardly stand it. By the time the respirator arrived, 20 minutes after he started, it probably didn't matter what type it was: irreversible damage had already been done to his lungs.

The specialist who later tested his lungs concluded that he was 30 per cent disabled, could never be cured and might get worse as he got older.

David had already got older. The damage to his lungs had turned him into an old man at the age of 36.

Labouring was out of the question: the best job he could get was as a lavatory attendant. Light sweeping was about all he could manage and that left him too exhausted at the end of the day to do anything but sit watching TV. His nights were often a gasping agony.

David sued Frigidaire for negligence. They denied that the accident had even happened and resisted all attempts to uncover the truth. When he had told his story in the High Court, Frigidaire finally admitted their negligence. David was awarded just over £4,000 for his ruined life.

Patrick Kinnersly, *The Hazards of Work: How to Fight Them* (Pluto Press 1973)

This kind of 'accident' could happen to any worker. In theory many safeguards stood between David and the TDI. One by one they failed him:

(i) *The employer*
Frigidaire is a division of General Motors, the largest company in the world. It knew all about the dangers of TDI: the makers had issued a warning and other workers had fallen victim of it. The firm was negligent and David was not told of the danger.

(ii) *The foreman*
He did not understand the danger.

(iii) *The works medical officer*
He should have alerted management to the risks. Instead he diagnosed a throat infection in a man who had been handling a substance which was a well-known cause of industrial asthma.

(iv) *The safety officer*
Again, he ought to have been in the front line in publicizing the dangers and insisting on safe working practices. Instead, he was more concerned to cover up the incident.

(v) *The plant*
The leak need not have developed into a tragedy if it had triggered an automatic shut-down or alarm, and if there had been adequate warning notices.

(vi) *Protection*
A suitable, well-labelled respirator was not located close to the plant.

(vii) *The law*
The law lays down minimum safety conditions in workplaces and requires that everything possible must be done to protect employees from 'injurious or offensive substances'.

(viii) *The unions*
You should be able to rely on your shop steward to warn you of hazards known to have affected other workers.

When David took the paint scraper he was down to his last safeguard – his own knowledge of the hazards of his workplace.

Would you have known?

10 Trade unions

The aim of this section is to help you to understand the role of trade unions in society today. You will be encouraged to consider the functions and structure of trade unions, and some aspects of industrial relations and conflict.

Trade unions

The role of trade unions is probably the most contentious issue of contemporary British politics. They are condemned as the main cause of the country's economic ills, and defended as indispensable safeguards against the worst aspects of capitalist exploitation.

Are they undemocratic groups of trouble-makers or genuine representatives of reasonable workers' interests?

Are there 'two sides of industry' or are management and workers really a team united by the common aim of industrial prosperity?

Why would you join a union?

Here are the reasons given in a survey of members who did not work in closed shops:

30 per cent – protection against the employer/solidarity and security.

26 per cent – better pay, hours, working conditions and other benefits.

17 per cent – believe in unions/always been a member.

14 per cent – was asked to join/pressure to join/had to join in previous job.

13 per cent – everyone else was a member.

Since the Second World War, the attitude of most large employers to trade unionism has changed from bitter hostility to begrudging acceptance. A few employers actually encourage their employees to join. On the other hand, some employers – mainly in small manufacturing and service trades – still do not recognize that unions have any role to play. There have been many bitter industrial disputes arising from employers' refusal to accept unions, even when a large group of employees are already members (for example Roberts–Arundel strike 1966–7, Fine Tubes 1970–3, Grunwick 1976–9).

You have a legal right to belong to a union and the Employment Protection Act (1975) entitles you to reasonable time off work to participate in certain trade union activities. The Employment Act (1980) stresses your right *not* to belong to a union and requires new closed shop agreements to be ratified by an 80 per cent majority of workers in a secret ballot. At the same time individuals were entitled to take legal action against unions for refusal to let them join.

Self-assessment questions

1 What proportion of employees at your workplace belong to a union?

2 Does your employer place obstacles in the way of membership or refuse to employ trade unionists?

3 Does your employer 'recognize' a union as the representative of the workers for bargaining purposes? If so, how was this recognition achieved?

Are trade unions too powerful?

How powerful should they be? Consider the situation in your own industry: who takes important decisions about the issues listed in Table 21 at your workplace? Complete the table.

Table 21

	Management	Trade unions	Both, by agreement
Basic pay and hours			
Bonus, shift and overtime pay			
Holidays			
Health and safety			
Overtime working			
Recruitment and dismissal			
Discipline			
Work allocation and manning			
Training			
Promotion			
Design of new plant and machinery			
Investment in new plant and machinery			
Pricing of the products you make			

Traditionally, employers have insisted on the right to manage; to determine what happens in the workplace without interference. Here control is all on the boss's side. Trade unions have maintained that employers should deal with their employees *as a group* rather than individually, and that issues should be *agreed* between management and workers. This situation, where matters are jointly regulated by negotiation and agreement, is known as *collective bargaining*.

At your workplace, some issues may be dealt with by collective bargaining while others remain the sole prerogative of your employer. Managers, who readily consult their employees and obtain agreement on some questions, often refuse to accept that unions have a right to dispute their decisions on others.

Disputes commonly arise when workers feel that management has taken a decision without ade-

quate consultation or agreement. Many firms have a clearly defined procedure for negotiation on specific matters: this process may result in formal (written) or informal ('custom and practice') agreements.

Self-assessment questions

4 What issues should be covered by collective bargaining?

5 Are there any matters that should be decided by management or workers alone?

6 What is the difference between consultation and negotiation?

7 What written agreements affect your conditions of employment?

8 Why does management often prefer informal to formal agreements?

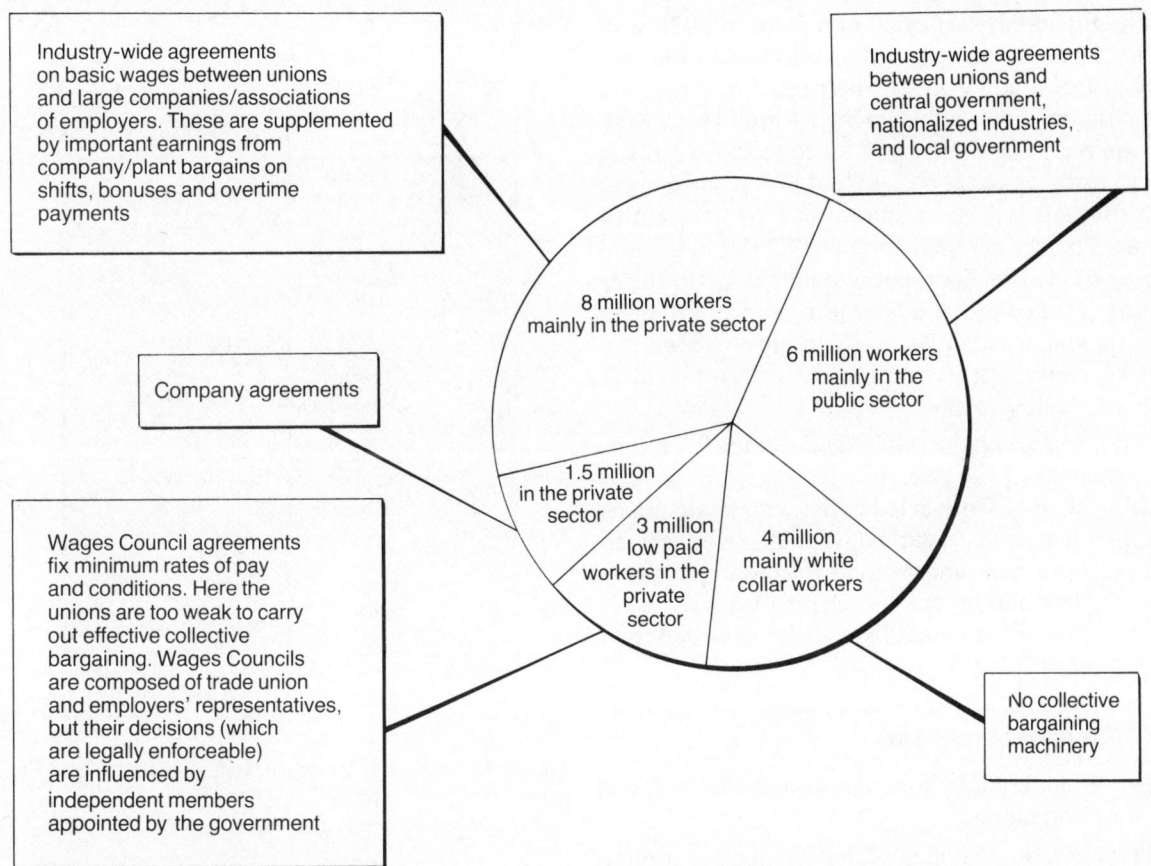

Industry-wide agreements on basic wages between unions and large companies/associations of employers. These are supplemented by important earnings from company/plant bargains on shifts, bonuses and overtime payments

Industry-wide agreements between unions and central government, nationalized industries, and local government

Company agreements

Wages Council agreements fix minimum rates of pay and conditions. Here the unions are too weak to carry out effective collective bargaining. Wages Councils are composed of trade union and employers' representatives, but their decisions (which are legally enforceable) are influenced by independent members appointed by the government

8 million workers mainly in the private sector

6 million workers mainly in the public sector

1.5 million in the private sector

3 million low paid workers in the private sector

4 million mainly white collar workers

No collective bargaining machinery

Figure 44

The pattern of wage bargaining: Where do you fit in?

Who is involved in fixing your pay?
You, your shop steward, national trade union leaders, Wages Council, employer, etc?

Different aspects of industrial relations

Pay

Since the Second World War, spells of free collective bargaining over pay have alternated with increasingly frequent periods of incomes policy or *wage restraint*. On a few, rare occasions, the Government has even imposed a complete wage freeze for a time. More commonly though, governments have aimed to reduce the *rate* of pay increases by setting a *maximum* for pay rises (for example £1 plus 4 per cent, £6, 10 per cent, 5 per cent were maximums at various times during the 1970s). The purpose of such policies was to prevent strong unions using their full bargaining strength to obtain greater increases.

Self-assessment questions

9 Do the major political parties have the same policies for incomes?

10 Why are the unions more prepared to agree to wage restraint under a Labour government than a Conservative government?

The Equal Pay Act came into force in 1976 with the intention of preventing discrimination between men and women with regard to terms and conditions of employment. Employers were required to give equal pay for the same work and for work of equal value. In 1973 women were getting on average no more than 64 per cent of men's hourly earnings and by 1982 this figure had only risen to 73.9 per cent. Women make up 40 per cent of the country's labour force and a third of all trade unionists. So why does the average woman still receive less than three-quarters of a male worker's hourly pay?

(i)   Some employers have avoided the full intentions of the Act.

(ii) Women work in industries with weak unions that have traditionally paid low wages to both men and women (for example retail distribution, textiles, clerical work).

(iii) Women are more likely to be unskilled than men.

Self-assessment questions

11 What kind of jobs do women do at your workplace?

12 How do the men's and women's earnings compare?

Overtime

Right from the start, unions have fought to reduce the length of the working week. In the process, they have obtained both government legislation and company agreements that fix the maximum hours that you are required to work. Nevertheless, over half of all male manual workers undertake overtime, each of them working on average an extra 10 hours per week. Overtime is particularly high in engineering, transport and communication, construction, printing and textile industries. Some manual workers, especially the lowest paid and those aged between 30 and 40, depend upon overtime payments to provide a quarter of their gross earnings.

Regular overtime – as distinct from occasional overtime to meet specific contingencies – is often a

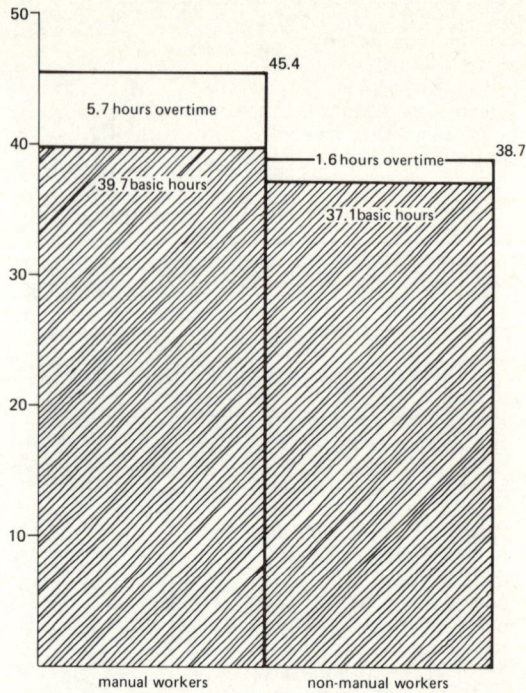

Figure 45   *Average hours worked by males over twenty-one-years old*
Source: Department of Employment, *New Earnings Survey* 1982

deliberate management policy. Why do you think that management may prefer overtime rather than employing additional workers?

Self-assessment questions

13 Do you work overtime? How much? How does this compare with the average for your workplace?

14 Is overtime entirely voluntary? Who decides who does the overtime that is available?

15 Is there a conflict between the aims of increasing your earnings with overtime and improving your quality of life?

16 How can the need for regular overtime be eliminated while maintaining earnings?

17 Should people work overtime when there are so many unemployed?

Table 22 *Survey of earnings for full-time workers (April 1982)*

	Men			Women		
	manual	non-manual	all	manual	non-manual	all
Average gross weekly earnings	£133.8	£178.9	£154.5	£80.1	£104.9	£99.0
Proportion arising from payments in addition to basic wage:						
Overtime	12.9%	3.0%	7.6%	3.6%	1.2%	1.7%
Payment by results	7.6%	2.2%	4.8%	6.9%	0.9%	2.1%
Shift premium	3.3%	0.7%	1.9%	2.4%	1.1%	1.4%
Total	23.8%	5.9%	14.3%	12.9%	3.2%	5.2%

Source: New Earnings Survey, Department of Employment, 1982

18 With reference to Table 22, why do you think that there are differences for men/women and manual/non-manual workers?

19 What are the consequences if a high proportion of your earnings arise from additional payments?

Employment

Control over hiring and firing is usually held to be the sole right of management. In practice, however, unions have obtained some influence over these decisions. In many cases, workers are able to exercise a veto over employment by rejecting some persons as unsuitable.

Apprenticeship Many craft jobs are only open to workers who have served a recognized period of training in the trade.

The closed shop Where a person must become a trade unionist as a condition of employment.

Demarcation Informal agreements about what sorts of worker may do a particular type of job within a workplace.

The ability of management to arbitrarily sack employees has been modified, in many cases, by agreements that require a series of warnings and lesser penalties before dismissal. Union representatives are generally entitled to accompany members before disciplinary and appeals hearings.

Self-assessment questions

20 What are the arguments for and against the closed shop?

21 Does individual freedom conflict with the aim of unions to protect and advance the interests of their members?

22 Do you have a right to refuse to work with certain other employees?

Self-assessment questions

23 What disciplinary procedure covers you at work (for example what happens if you are persistently late?).

24 Consider the case of any fellow workers who have been dismissed.

Reorganization

There are few industries unaffected by technological change or reorganization. Has new machinery (for example automatic or computer-controlled systems), or new work methods (for example flexibility of labour) been introduced in your workplace?

These may result in:

(i)   Better pay, shorter hours, more satisfying working conditions, easier work; or
(ii) Job losses, new health hazards, the replacement of skilled work by boring, tedious jobs.

For instance, productivity deals often involve unions giving up 'restrictive practices' (for example lorry drivers must be accompanied by another employee to assist with the unloading) in exchange for a share of the profit resulting from higher productivity.

Self-assessment questions

25   Are union controls over who does what at work best described as *restrictive* or *protective* practices?

26   Should unions sell their control of workshop practices for extra earnings?

Dealing with disputes

When disputes arise out of action taken by trade unions (for example to improve wages or conditions), situations stay the same until agreement is reached.

On the other hand, management tends to act as if it has a right to initiate changes without first obtaining agreement. Employers usually insist that they may take unilateral action to dismiss workers, promote employees or reorganize working arrangements. Workers who object must operate under the new conditions until the grievance is sorted out.

Self-assessment questions

27   What are the grievances of people at your workplace?

28   Do they arise from the actions of management or trade unions?

29   Should changes be agreed by both sides before they occur or by management alone?

Industrial action

By workers	By employers
Work to rule/go slow	Blacklisting
Overtime ban	Sacking
Strike	Employing other workers
Picketing	to break a strike
Blacking	Lock-out
Occupation/work-in and sit-in	

Workers who go on strike stop work and usually attempt to persuade others not to work either. They may try to make their action more effective by:

(i)   Picketing (to stop supplies entering or goods leaving their workplace).
(ii) Preventing their work being done elsewhere.
(iii) Appealing to other trade unionists for financial and moral support.
(iv) Appealing for sympathetic industrial action where appropriate.

During the 1970s there was a trend for strikes to last longer and involve more workers. With employers becoming more resistant to union demands, workers developed more aggressive tactics such as the 'flying' picket and factory occupation. Violent incidents became more common.

The law already stated that strikers could not deny other workers the right to cross a picket line (for example by linking arms), stop vehicles or demand the right to join a picket if the police believe that the number already there might lead to a breach of the peace. The 1979 Conservative Government resolved to 'restore the balance between unions and employers' by restricting picketing to the strikers' own workplace. The Employment Act makes it 'unlawful' to picket your employer's head office, other plants where work has been diverted, your firm's suppliers and customers, or to demonstrate solidarity with other trade unionists. The police can stop and turn back coach loads of supporters going to a mass picket and may restrict the total number of pickets in a picket line to six. Furthermore, any union action must be 'reasonably capable' of furthering the trade dispute in question: otherwise the employer can ask a court to order the union to stop the action and even to award damages against union members.

Self-assessment questions

30 What should be the role of the Government, courts and police in industrial disputes? Can the State act as a 'referee'?

31 What is the right balance between unions and employers?

32 What tactics used by unions/employers are acceptable and what are unacceptable?

The perfect strike?

In his article *A Perfect Strike*, Michael Frayn argues that, while the public unquestioningly conceded the right of workers in a free society to withdraw their labour, it draws the line at strikes.

He applies the methods of modern market research to design a strike that the public will accept. Thus the evidence shows that people do not agree with strikes that:

(i) Are motivated by desire for material gain (for example higher pay, shorter hours, better conditions). The public has an instinctive respect for uncomplaining poverty, often summed up by some such remark as 'Look how much worse off old age pensioners are, and you don't see them coming out on strike'.

(ii) Are called over some irrelevant side issue not connected with pay and conditions.

(iii) Cause any loss of production or affect the country's supply of goods and services.

(iv) Cause any loss or inconvenience to innocent victims (for example potential customers).

(v) Are launched at a time when the country is facing economic competition from overseas or when a rise in wages would tend to increase prices.

(vi) Occur under a Conservative government, when they might seem like political mischief-making.

(vii) Occur under a Labour government, when this could be represented as stabbing one's own side in the back.

(viii) Are unofficial since any justifiable strike would have been taken up by responsible union leaders.

(ix) Are official since this confirms the public's worst fears about irresponsible union leaders.

The perfect strike is therefore never likely to occur. The public might possibly be prepared to tolerate a small strike on a Sunday afternoon under a Liberal government in favour of lower wages for trade union officials, just as soon as America, Japan and our other principal economic competitors happen to sink into the sea!

Self-assessment questions

33 What do you think are the main objections to strikes? Look at press reports of strikes to check whether they present the same objections as those listed above.

34 Are any strikes justified?

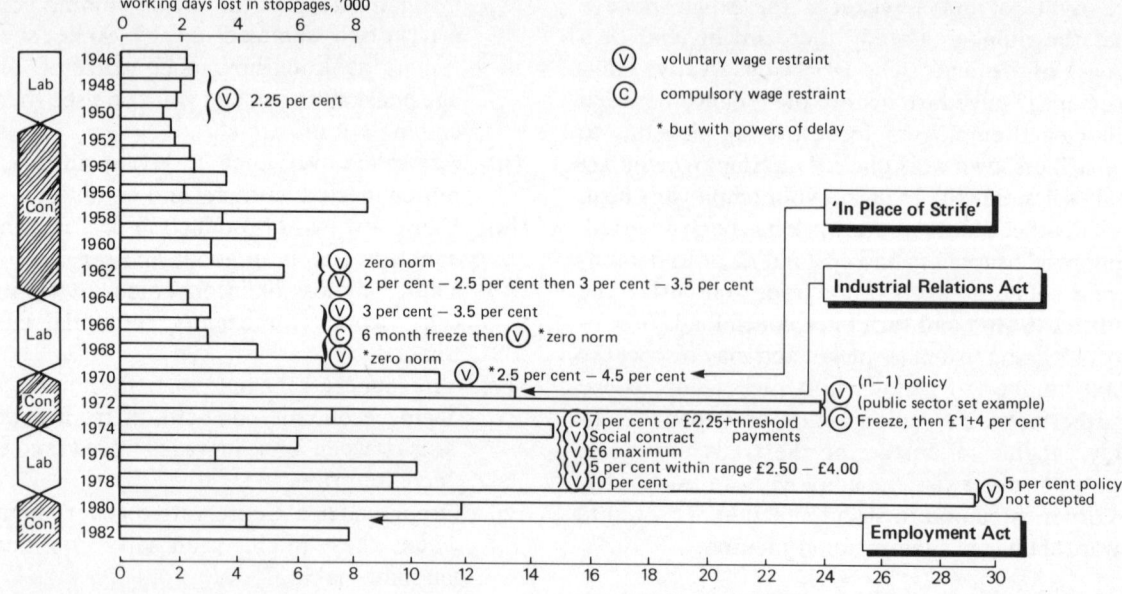

Figure 46 *Working days lost in stoppages*

An exercise in negotiations

This negotiation exercise is designed to illustrate the roles of management and trade union representatives, and to demonstrate the nature of collective bargaining. Below are the details of a fictitious company:

F. Furter & Co. is a long established family firm, justly famous for its range of traditionally made sausages. The firm has expanded rapidly over the past three years since its takeover by Mammoth Foods, the huge international combine that owns shipping companies, deep-sea trawlers, processing factories, farms, supermarkets and hotels. In particular, sales of the brands Tasty Bangers and Super Saveloys are doing extremely well and production needs to be increased. Profits have reached record levels and management can take credit for running an efficient firm and making the right decisions at the right time.

The firm has a labour force of 100 production workers: all members of the National Union of Sausage Makers (NUSM).

10 skin moulders, all men, earning a basic wage of	£130 per week
20 meat mixers, all men, earning a basic wage of	£80 per week
40 meat stuffers, all women, earning a basic wage of	£70 per week
40 packers, men and women, earning a basic wage of	£60 per week

Over the past few years wage increases have not quite kept up with inflation. The management has argued that the responsibility for this lies with the Government's incomes policy. Last year the union secured a £10 across-the-board increase on basic rates for all production workers. At present they get three weeks annual holiday in addition to bank holidays. Yesterday the press reported that the NUSM were likely to press for a substantial pay rise and longer holidays this year.

Two separate bonus schemes operate within the factory. The meat mixers work to an individual incentive bonus, giving them on average an extra

£20 per week, and the meat stuffers have a collective bonus averaging £10 per week. The skin moulders have recently been arguing that their traditional differential in pay rates compared to the semi-skilled meat mixers and stuffers and unskilled packers, has been eroded. In addition, the female workers want parity – equal pay – with the men. Trade union negotiators should attempt to obtain a settlement that is of maximum benefit to all their members.

As far as management is concerned, the current expansion can only be maintained if the bulk of present profits is used to finance new schemes and modernize the plant. It believes that if the union shows restraint now, the benefits to all workers in a few years time will be enormous. The management wants a settlement that will cost as little as possible. In addition, it needs to persuade the workers to accept a reduction in the labour force.

Now:

(i) Allocate the roles of workers and management.

(ii) Workers draw up their claim, taking into account inflation, the current level of wage claims and the existing differentials between various groups of workers in the factory.

(iii) Management decides what it is prepared to concede and agrees its initial bargaining position.

(iv) Workers choose representatives to negotiate with management.

(v) It is possible that the outcome of negotiations will fall short of the union's initial claim. The workers must decide whether to settle on this basis or to take industrial action in order to bring pressure on management.

(vi) For the purpose of this exercise, the side that obtains most points will have gained the most advantageous settlement.

Scoring

(i) *Pay rises*
Calculated as the total increase in the company wage bill (per week).

£		Management	Union
Less than	500	100	−75
	600	90	−70
	700	80	−65
	800	70	−60
	900	60	−55
	1000	50	−50
	1100	40	−45
	1200	30	−40
	1300	20	−35
	1400	10	−25
	1500	0	−20
	1600	−10	−15
	1700	−20	−10
	1800	−30	−5
	1900	−40	0
	2000	−50	20
	2100	−60	40
	2200	−70	60
	2300	−80	80
	2400	−90	100
	2500	−100	120
More than	2500	−150	150

(ii) *Holidays*
For each extra day's holiday obtained from settlement, workers gain 100 points and management loses 100 points.

(iii) *Redundancies*
For the purposes of this exercise, trade union agreement must first be obtained before a worker can be made redundant. By replacing workers with new machines, management can achieve an increase in productivity and reduce costs.

For each worker made redundant, management gains 20 points and union loses 20 points.

(iv) *Industrial dispute*
A majority vote of all workers is necessary before strike action may be taken. A strike will cause management some loss of profit, but workers will also suffer a loss in earnings, overtime and job security. Once declared, a

strike will continue until called off by the union or the expiry of a set time limit (we shall assume that at some stage the parent company, Mammoth Foods, will decide to cut its losses and close your firm completely, making everybody redundant).

Duration of strike	Management loses	Union loses
After 2 minutes	−10	10 points per
4 minutes	−20	minute
6 minutes	−40	
8 minutes	−80	
10 minutes	−150	
15 minutes	−300	

(v)   *Management tactics*

The management may also use various strategies to help them in negotiations.

(a) Commission a time and motion study: this may increase productivity at the expense of jobs or bonus earnings. This tactic can only be used once. Management gains 50 points.

(b) The sack: can only be used while workers are on strike. Managers may dismiss as many workers as they like (but remember, if all the workers are sacked, there will be no one to make sausages once the dispute is over). 10 bonus points for every worker sacked.

(c) Arbitration: if management can persuade the union to have the settlement decided by an independent arbitrator (say your teacher, who listens to both sides explain and justify their claims). 20 bonus points.

Conclusions

(i)   How realistic is this exercise?

(ii)   How could it be improved to make it closer to real life?

(iii)   Can both sides win? How?

(iv)   What other action could each side take to strengthen its bargaining position?

(v)   Were all the workers satisfied by the performance of their negotiators?

Who represents you?

At a workplace, trade unionists often choose one of their members to represent them all to the employer. These shop floor representatives are usually called *shop stewards* (of whom there are about a quarter of a million in Britain), and the majority were selected by their fellow workers in unopposed elections. Their leadership is based on persuasion and consent, rather than compulsion. Although he is often portrayed as a wrecker, a Royal Commission under Lord Donovan described the shop steward as 'more of a lubricant than an irritant' exerting a moderating influence and sorting out minor grievances that might otherwise blow up into major disputes. What is your experience?

In addition, unions employ professionals to administer the organization, conduct research and deal with important negotiations. These full-time officials may be either elected from the union's membership, or else they are appointed by the union's national leadership (usually called the executive). Some unions employ a system combining elements of both election and appointment.

Self-assessment questions

35   Are full-time officials in your union elected or appointed? By whom and for how long?

36   To whom are they responsible?

37   Which system is best, and why?

38   Why do union leaders sometimes act in a way that is contrary to the feelings of their members?

Union elections have traditionally been conducted by a show of hands at branch meetings. In recent years, however, several unions have adopted the postal ballot: voting papers are sent to a member's house and returned by post. These secret ballots reduce the pressure from other trade unionists and tend to increase the numbers that participate in elections. On the other hand, the voters may be less informed about the candidates and issues, and open to influence from outside interests such as the press.

Self-assessment questions

39 (i) Which system is best?

(ii) How are other decisions made in your union?

40 Study Figure 47. Is your union organized like this? How is it different?

Where do you get information about your trade union?

(i) Attendance at branch meetings.

(ii) Union notice board.

(iii) Talking to shop stewards or other trade unionists.

(iv) Union journal.

(v) From press, radio or TV.

Self-assessment question

41 (i) Which source do you think is most reliable?

(ii) How do you communicate your views and interests to other trade unionists?

Why should unions be democratic?

We generally do not expect management or other important organizations (for example the army, press, civil service, police, courts, colleges) to be run in a democratic way. Why should we apply different criteria to trade unions?

Unions must exert pressure to further workers' interests and for this they require the active involvement and support of their members. Collective organization needs discipline and members

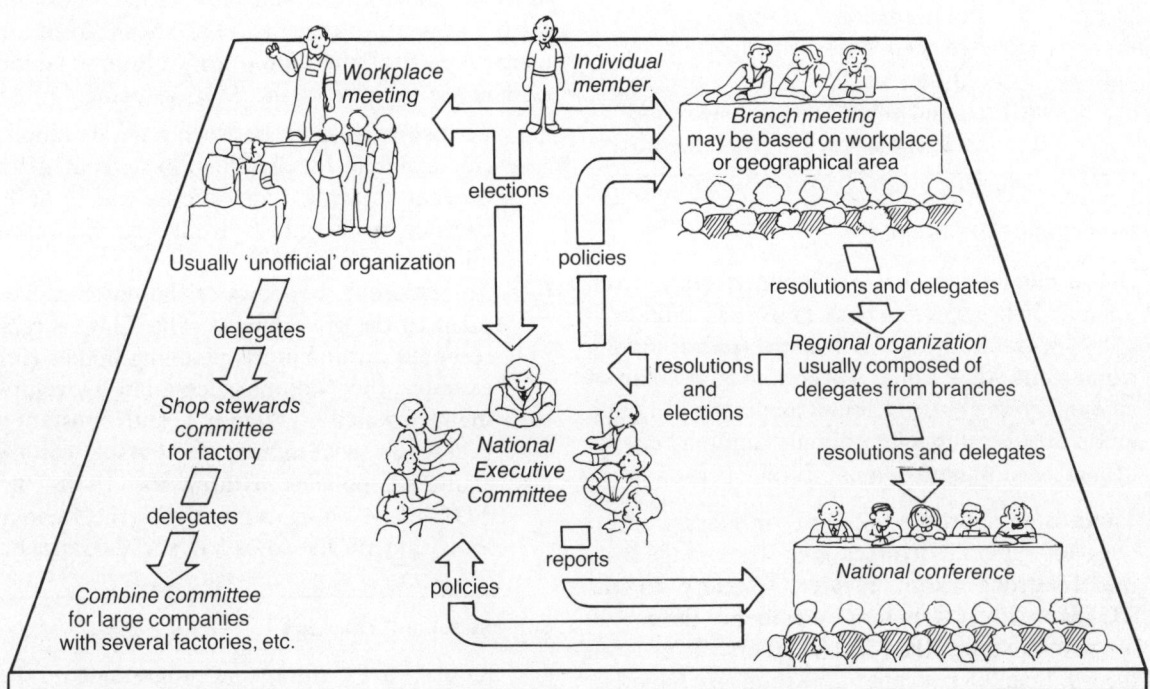

Figure 47

will only accept majority decisions if they have had a say in making them.

Self-assessment question

42   (i) Is your union democratic? Suppose you wanted your union to adopt a particular policy (say, longer holidays for apprentices), how would you go about it?

(ii) If this policy were adopted, how could you ensure that it is implemented?

Who leads the unions?

Self-assessment question

43   (i) Analyse the reports on trade union matters by the press, radio, or TV.

(ii) List the names of all trade unionists mentioned.

  (a) Which unions do they belong to?

  (b) What position do they hold? (General secretary, shop steward, rank and file member, etc.)

  (c) Are their statements quoted? What did they say?

  (d) Should union officials lead or merely act as spokesmen for their members?

Trade union membership

Union membership has expanded steadily, from 9.5 million in 1950 to a peak of over 12 million in 1980, with the rate of growth fastest among women and white-collar workers. About a half of all employees are trade union members, although union membership fell by about 1 million because of increased unemployment during 1980–3.

There is an appropriate union for every worker: over 400 separate organizations. They range from the 18-strong Cloth Pressers' Society to the TGWU with 1.8 million members. Over 200 unions have fewer than 500 members and account for less than 0.5 per cent of the total. On the other hand, 80 per cent of all trade unionists belong to one of the 24 largest organizations.

Because of the historical conditions in which they developed, unions organize workers:

(i)   By trade or craft.

(ii) By industry.

(iii) In general unions open to all employees.

Self-assessment question

44   Find examples of each type of union (see Figure 48).

The TUC

Among the best-known abbreviations are the initials of the Trades Union Congress. It was founded in 1868, and during times of widespread industrial and social conflict, the TUC has been pressed to provide leadership for the whole trade union movement (for example by organizing support for the miners during the 1926 General Strike). Individual unions, however, have always been jealous of their independence and show little enthusiasm for the suggestion that the TUC should form the 'general staff of the union army'. Rather, union leaders see the role of the TUC as being:

(i)   To resolve quarrels between separate unions (for example the Bridlington agreement to prevent poaching and ensure the orderly transfer of members from one union to another).

(ii) To represent the views of the union movement to the government. The TUC is represented on numerous planning bodies (for example the National Economic Development Council – 'Neddy') and constantly urges the government to pursue certain economic policies. During the 1970s the TUC made an agreement with the Labour Government, the so-called 'social contract'.

Self-assessment question

45   Simulate a TV discussion programme on the role of trade unions today.

The participants are: a Conservative MP

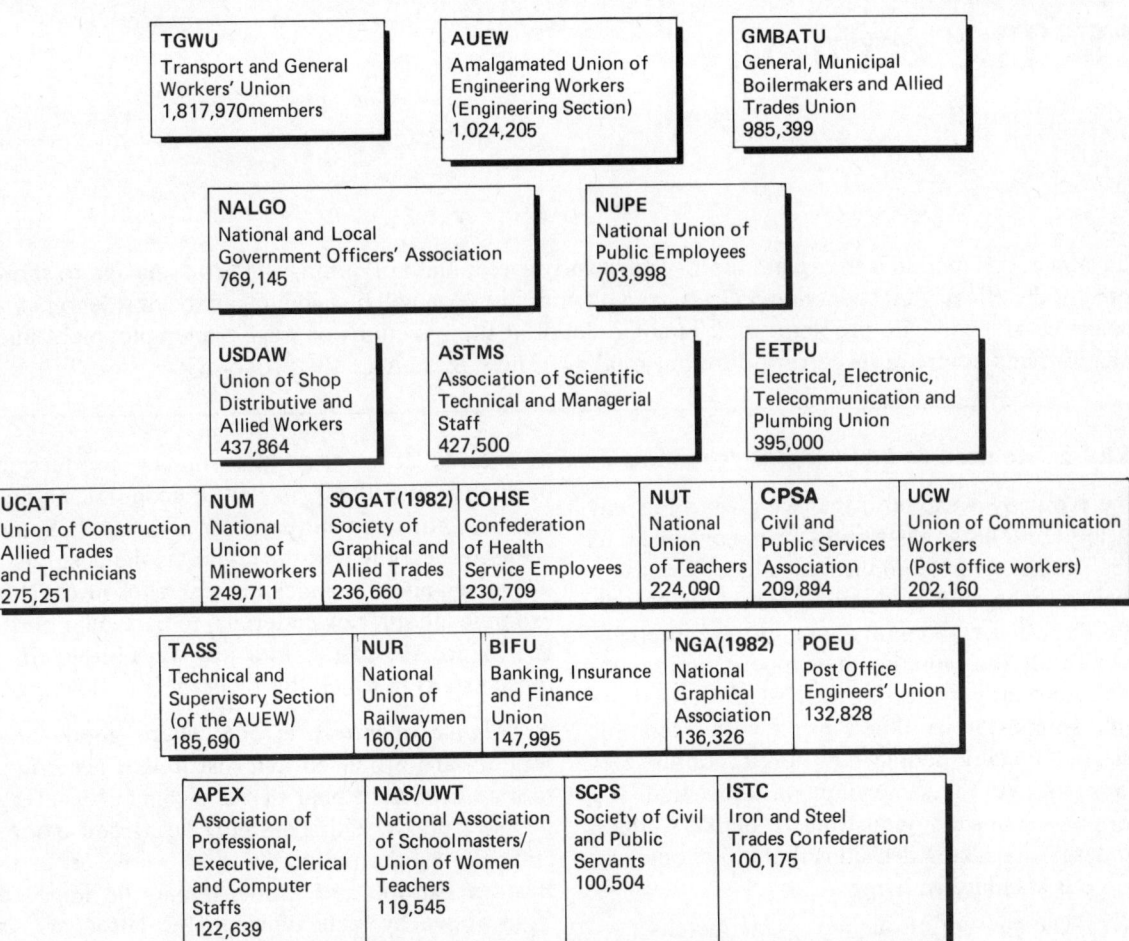

Figure 48   *Membership of the 24 largest unions in 1983*

a Labour MP
a company director
a trade union general
   secretary
a shop steward

Each has three minutes to make an opening statement.

(i) Make some notes summarizing the main points that each speaker might make.
(ii) Simulate the subsequent discussion.

11 The economy

The aim of this section is to explain the structure and development of our market economy and to show some of the effects that economic policies have on your life. You will be encouraged to consider what is meant by an economic problem; look in some detail at the questions of wages, unemployment and inflation; and compare three very different models of how to manage the economy.

Why do we need to know about economics?

The economy is the term that we give to the way society produces, distributes and consumes its wealth. It is a very complicated subject because it deals with the combined actions of millions of individuals, often with conflicting aims and interests. As a result, the economy may appear 'out of control', constantly frustrating the best efforts of those who administer it. When faced with economic questions, many people feel bored, confused or powerless. At the same time we know that 'top people' – ministers, industrialists, bankers, union leaders – are taking decisions that affect our lives and our standard of living:

(i)   The amount of our next wage increase.
(ii) Our chances of being made redundant.
(iii) The prices of goods in the shops.
(iv) The provision of public services (for example hospitals).

Types of economy

If we look around the world we see that industrial societies are ruled by a variety of different forms of government: parliamentary democracies, soviet republics, military dictatorships, etc. Similarly a country's economy may be organized in a number of different ways. Here are two 'models' of the best way to operate the system.

In a *market economy* goods and services are produced in response to *demand* from consumers. Demand means not only that people want a certain commodity, but also that they are able and willing to buy it at a price that makes production profitable. It follows, in purely economic terms, that the poor can never exert a demand. Some economists argue that the market is the best possible mechanism for allocating scarce resources (for example labour, raw materials) to particular ends. See Figure 49. Can you see any ways (other than those listed) in which this diagram is misleading?

A *planned economy* is one where goods and services are produced and distributed according to a co-ordinated plan that is designed to satisfy people's needs. This plan may be agreed democratically by the population as a whole or, as in Eastern Europe and China, it may be imposed from above by state officials (the latter case is usually referred to as 'command economies').

Self-assessment questions

1   Which type of economy is the British economy?

2   What is the best way to allocate the resources of society?

3   Would it be desirable to leave the provision of all goods and services to the market: defence, street lighting, fire fighting, etc.?

Making a profit

From the earliest times, man has worked to produce items for the simple reason that they are

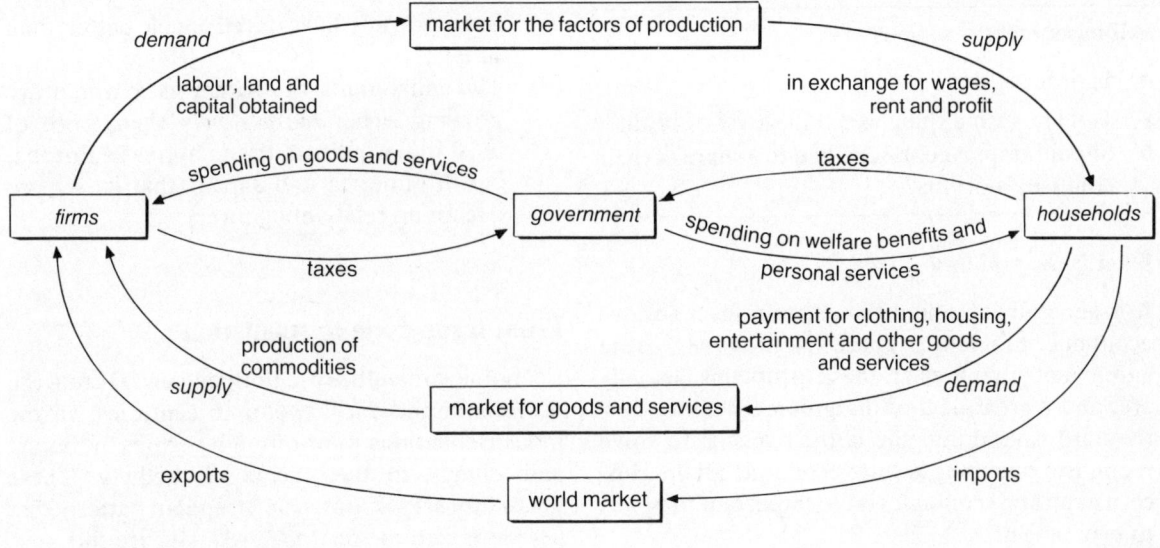

→ *direction of arrow indicates net flow of money*

This diagram is an over-simplification:
(i)   Firms import goods too (for example raw materials);
(ii) Money flows from households to firms via savings deposited in banks. However, much new
      investment now comes from 'retained profits';
(iii) Firms generally pay the rent for the land they occupy
      to other firms, not to households.

Figure 49

useful in some way. However, usefulness is not a good enough reason for modern industry to put a particular product into production. This is because the primary motive for economic activity within a market economy is to make the largest possible profit. Unless a product has a sufficiently high value as an item for sale, it will not be produced.

Wealth that is used to pay for the factors of production – machinery, raw materials, energy, etc. – and the labour necessary to transform these materials into finished goods is called *capital*. Obviously, businessmen will not *risk* their capital in an enterprise unless they expect the amount of money they end up with to be greater than the sum they started with. More precisely, they will want their capital to grow by a greater amount than the rate of return they could obtain by simply putting their money into a safe investment such as government bonds.

So where does profit come from? Depending on your point of view it is either:
(i)   A reward that the capitalist receives for the efficient organization of product; or
(ii) The result of paying his employees less in wages than the full value of their labour.

Whatever their origin, profits are essential for the survival of a capitalist enterprise, at least in the long term. This is because each firm is in competition with other companies for a share of the market. The firm that produces more efficiently than its rivals will be able to sell its goods more cheaply. So, for instance, if Ford installs a new assembly line with the most advanced technology, other car manufacturers must re-tool or risk going out of business. Those firms that draw upon the largest pool of profits have the greatest opportunity for investment.

Self-assessment questions

4   Is profit a 'dirty' word?

5   Is there such a thing as a 'fair' level of profit?

6   Should employees be entitled to a share of their company's profits?

What is the problem?

It is generally accepted that Britain faces serious economic problems. There is, however, little agreement about what these problems actually are, and a great deal of disagreement about how they are caused and the correct means to solve them. But one thing is sure: economic affairs concern us all and economics is too important to be left to economists.

Self-assessment question

7   The following have been put forward as the most serious problems facing the British economy. Which one(s) do you consider most important and should be tackled first, which are not really problems, and are there any other problems not listed?

cheap imports	low productivity
high interest rates	low profits
high taxation	poor management
inflation	strikes
lack of investment	strong pound
low pay	unemployment

Study newspapers and watch the television to find out what politicians, industrialists, union leaders, etc., believe are the main problems, and try to discover what reasons they give to support their views.

What is your *standard of living*? Is it merely the quantity of goods that you own? Or does it involve *quality of life*: freedom from stress, attractive surroundings, opportunities to enjoy leisure, etc.?

On the 'narrow' definition, most people in Britain have a higher standard of living than ten or twenty years ago. But:

(i)   Some groups have fared much better than others.

(ii) The inhabitants of Britain as a whole are growing richer *more slowly* than those of most other industrialized nations in Europe, North America and Japan (that is, we are becoming relatively poorer).

From trade cycle to stagflation

Economic difficulties are nothing new. During the nineteenth and early twentieth centuries, all the industrial nations went through periods of 'boom' and 'slump' in their economic activity. These fluctuations took on such a regular pattern that people talked of the *trade cycle* (Figure 50).

During the 1930s it appeared that the world economy had become stuck in the slump phase of the cycle. It took the stimulus of military demand during the Second World War to utilize spare industrial capacity, bringing jobs to unemployed workers and putting the rest into uniform.

The war involved massive public expenditure and established full employment. Another ruinous

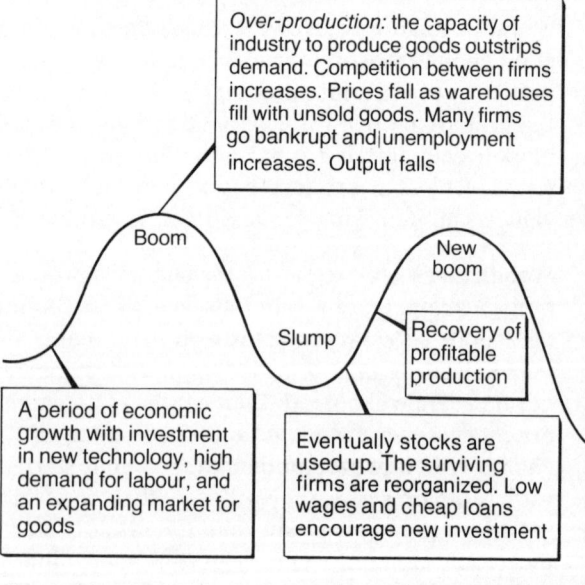

Over-production: the capacity of industry to produce goods outstrips demand. Competition between firms increases. Prices fall as warehouses fill with unsold goods. Many firms go bankrupt and|unemployment increases. Output falls

Boom

New boom

Slump

Recovery of profitable production

A period of economic growth with investment in new technology, high demand for labour, and an expanding market for goods

Eventually stocks are used up. The surviving firms are reorganized. Low wages and cheap loans encourage new investment

Figure 50

Table 23 *How well is the British economy doing?*

The following are important indicators of performance. Figures are for the second week in August 1981 and 1982. Beware: one month's or one year's figures for a particular country may be misleading. Find out the most recent figures.

Country	Industrial production		Earnings*		Consumer prices		Trade balance for last 12 months ($ millions)		Unemployment (percentage rate for latest month)		Exchange rate of currency (per US $)	
	(percentage change over previous 12 months)											
	1981	1982	1981	1982	1981	1982	1981	1982	1981	1982	1981	1982
France	−6.0	1.0	14.5	18.5	13.5	13.5	−12000	−12300	7.2	8.2	6.03	6.98
West Germany	−2.0	−1.0	5.0	3.5	6.0	5.5	5000	19600	5.6	7.7	2.54	2.51
Italy	−3.0	2.0	25.0	16.5	20.5	15.5	−22000	−14300	8.4	10.4	1250.00	1397.00
Japan	2.0	0.5	5.5	6.0	5.0	2.5	13000	20800	2.3	2.5	246.10	263.00
USA	8.0	−9.5	9.0	7.0	9.5	7.0	−32000	−41600	7.3	9.8	1.00	1.00
Britain	−8.0	3.5	13.0	10.5	11.5	9.0	6000	1400	10.7	12.3	0.56	0.59

* Earnings: hourly rates in manufacturing industries
Source: The Economist 1982

slump, however, was widely expected to follow when things returned to 'normal'. But the slump did not arrive. Instead the 1950s and 1960s were a period of unprecedented growth and rising prosperity for the world's industrial nations. The problems of over-production and slump appeared to have been solved permanently.

Then along came *stagflation*, the term given to a combination of inflation and no (or very slow) growth in output. In the past, the prices of goods, labour (wages) and interest rates had always risen during the up-swing in the trade cycle, and then fallen back during the down-turn. This had helped to re-establish the conditions necessary for profits to be made and a new boom. Since the Second World War, however, prices have continued to rise even during periods of recession. Inflation – previously considered a problem only for unfortunate Latin American countries – became a normal state of affairs among the great Western powers.

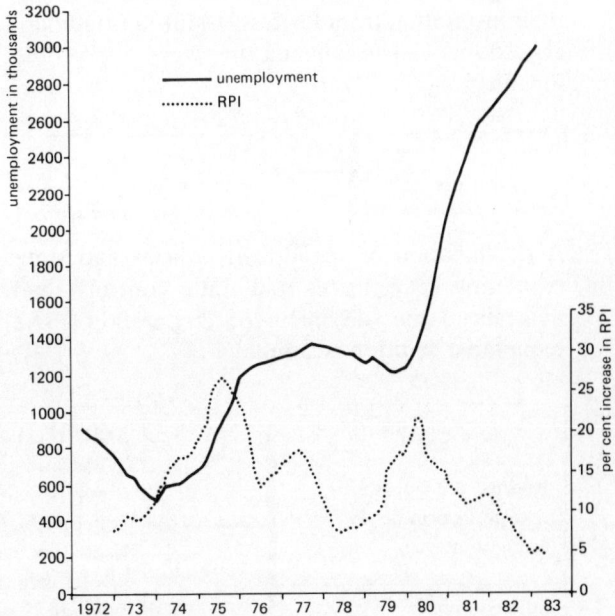

Figure 51 *RPI and unemployment in Britain*
Source: Employment Gazette, May 1983

How would you run the economy?

Economics is about choosing between various options. Is the government 'forced' to carry out certain policies? Or are policies only 'necessary' if you look at a problem in a particular way? We would like you to consider whether the options chosen by decision makers are inevitable.

Here are three contrasting views about how the economy should be managed. They are each based on a different idea about the nature of the problem to be solved.

Keynesianism

On the basis of a study of the 1930s recession, John Maynard Keynes concluded that the operation of the market alone could not ensure either full employment or economic stability. His ideas persuaded post-war governments to intervene in the running of the economy to a far greater extent than ever before.

Keynes argued that the government should adopt measures to smooth out the trade cycle and in particular to counter the tendency of the economy towards over-production by stimulating demand. These policies have included:

State spending to create a demand for the products of industry. The government may spend money directly (for example contracts to the defence and construction industries) or indirectly by giving cash benefits to poorer families who are likely to buy consumer goods.

Financial measures to increase or decrease the level of economic activity by manipulating the spending-power of consumers, for example tax cuts and cheap credit will encourage people to buy goods.

Aid to private industry to maintain jobs, assist research and development, promote exports and bail out firms in financial difficulties. (For example Development Grants.)

Monetarism

During the 1970s a group of economists, taking their inspiration from Professor Milton Friedman, argued that Keynesian measures were responsible for inflation.

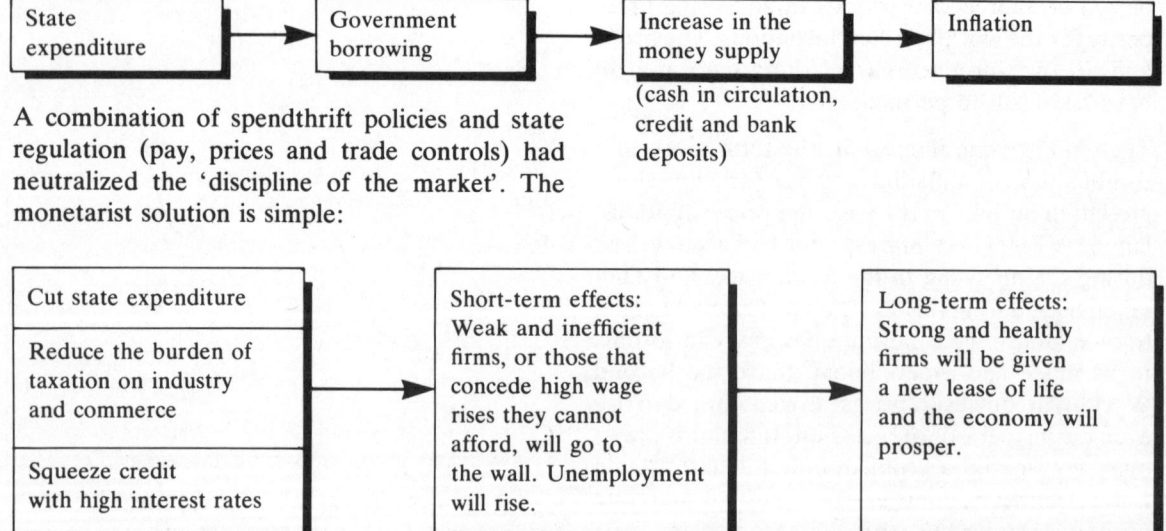

A combination of spendthrift policies and state regulation (pay, prices and trade controls) had neutralized the 'discipline of the market'. The monetarist solution is simple:

But the critics of monetarism argue that:

(i) Inflation is not caused simply by 'too much money' (alternative explanations include wage rises, higher oil prices, the activities of monopoly firms and the burden of arms spending).

(ii) Cutting state aid to industry has a much more damaging effect on the economy than inflation – the 'cure' is deadlier than the disease and is liable to kill the patient.

Socialist planning

Both Keynesian and monetarist policies have been followed by recent governments. However, despite their differences they represent fundamentally the same approach to economic issues because they remain within the framework of the market economy. A third more radical approach is also contending for public endorsement. It argues that:

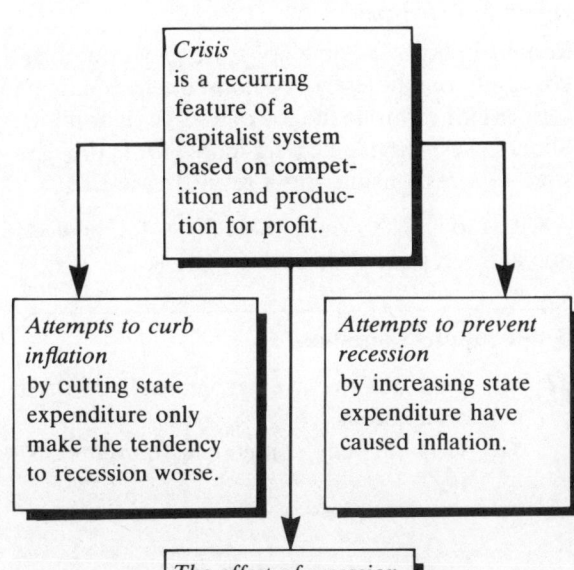

Crisis is a recurring feature of a capitalist system based on competition and production for profit.

Attempts to curb inflation by cutting state expenditure only make the tendency to recession worse.

Attempts to prevent recession by increasing state expenditure have caused inflation.

The effect of recession is to hasten the reorganization of industry with production being increasingly concentrated under the control of a few large firms.

This approach claims that capitalism is a system based on exploitation and over which workers have no real control. Therefore, they should refuse to accept any responsibility for its problems and resist any attempts to pass on to them the burden of the crisis through:

(i) Redundancies that create an 'industrial reserve army of the unemployed'.

(ii) Cuts in public services that hit hardest at the poorer and weaker sections of the population.

(iii) Incomes policies that are designed to reduce workers' living standards.

(iv) Harder work to increase employers' profits.

At the same time people should unite to achieve:

(a) The social ownership of industry, to be run by the workers themselves.

(b) The replacement of competition and instability by co-operation and planning.

But critics of this view argue that:

(i) It proposes conflict between classes whereas we should all be working together to solve the country's economic problems.

(ii) Capitalists would be replaced inevitably by a privileged state bureaucracy similar to that in Russia and we would all lose our freedom.

Are wages to blame?

Both Conservative and Labour governments have claimed that wage rises are a major cause of Britain's economic difficulties. Here are the comments of two Prime Ministers:

'One man's wage increase is another man's price increase.'

'If you pay yourselves more for producing less, there will be more unemployment.'

Governments have therefore been concerned to ensure that the average level of wage settlements is lower than rises in the cost of living and industrial productivity (output per worker).

We live in a society where there is a big differential in wealth and income. A Royal Commission found that the top 10 per cent of income earners get about a quarter of all total incomes and so do the bottom 50 per cent of income earners. The richest 0.1 per cent of the adult population own about one-eighth of all wealth, the top 1 per cent own a quarter and top 10 per cent own two-thirds.

Over recent years, trade unions have secured a small shift in the pattern of incomes for those on the lower half of the scale. The gap between women's and men's wages has marginally narrowed, as has that between young and old workers; manual and non-manual workers; and skilled and unskilled workers. Some older, male, skilled and non-manual workers have therefore felt 'worse off'.

Self-assessment questions

8 Should workers attempt to restore their traditional differentials?

9 Are these inequalities inevitable?

10 What is the difference between income and wealth?

What factors should determine incomes?

This is a question that produces argument in all societies. What factors determine the level of incomes in Britain: qualifications, age, union organization, the supply of and demand for labour, power, hard work?

Self-assessment questions

11 Can you think of any other factors?

12 Which do you think are most important?

Here are some factors you might consider when deciding how much people should be paid:

Skill Some people sacrifice a higher income for a period of time in order to do a poorly paid apprenticeship or go to college. Do the people who perform difficult and skilled jobs actually receive more?

Usefulness Some jobs fulfil basic human needs and contribute to the well-being of society. We can survive without garden-gnome makers but miners, nurses and firemen are essential. How do we decide who is essential?

Unpleasantness Some jobs involve a high degree of physical or mental strain (for example, deep-sea fishing). Other jobs are pleasant and satisfying (for example a musician's job and some teaching jobs). Given a free hand, hardly anyone would opt for an unpleasant job. Should workers who must perform unpleasant jobs be paid more as an incentive? Or should we all take turns, say three days a year emptying dustbins?

Need Everyone has to pay the same for the necessities of life. Does a bus conductor need two homes and a month's holiday in Bermuda more or less than a company director? Should a married man with three young children to support receive more than a single person or a married man whose wife has a well-paid job?

Responsibility If some jobs are performed inefficiently or carelessly, the consequences may be serious (for example the job of a surgeon or pilot). Should these people be paid more? Or is the prestige of a responsible job a reward in itself?

A list of jobs is shown in Table 24. Allot between one and ten points for each factor:

Self-assessment question

13 (i) Find out the average incomes of these occupations.
    (ii) How do they compare with your ranking?

How much money do you need?

Suppose that you are in your mid-twenties, just married and setting up home. Make a list of the things that you realistically expect to buy: what sort of home, furniture, vehicle, entertainment, etc.? Then estimate the amount of money that you will need to earn to pay for them.

Table 24

	Skill	Usefulness	Unpleasantness	Responsibility	Some other factor you consider important	Total
General studies teacher						
Face worker in coal-mine						
First Division footballer						
Car mechanic						
Hospital doctor						
Tool-maker						
Hospital porter						
Shorthand-typist						
Police constable						
Hairdresser						
Insurance salesman						
Shop assistant						
Princess Margaret						

	Total cash down-payment	Weekly payment
Mortgage		
Rates		
Gas and electricity		
HP (furniture, cooker, carpets, TV, etc.)		
Food (for two persons)		
Transport (second-hand car?)		
Clothing		
Entertainment		
Others		

Self-assessment question

14 (i) What is the take-home pay of a 25 year old worker in your job?

(ii) Are you likely to have sufficient savings and income to afford the life-style you expect?

(iii) Are your expectations realistic? If not, why?

International trade: who needs it?

The German alarm clock wakes me up at six-thirty and I turn on the Japanese radio. I step on to the Moroccan rug and pull an Irish dressing-gown over my pyjamas from Hong Kong. I go downstairs and switch on the South Korean kettle to make a cup of Indian tea. The milk I take from the Italian fridge comes from a British cow and is in a British bottle (with a foil top made in Britain from metal mined in Central America), but the sugar has been imported from Jamaica.

I drink a glass (French) of juice made from Israeli oranges while I scan the Australian-owned newspaper printed on Scandinavian newsprint. While the Danish bacon and Channel Island tomatoes sizzle under the grill of the British cooker, I spread New Zealand butter on a slice of bread made from Canadian wheat.

After shaving with my Austrian electric razor, I dress in a Portuguese shirt, American jeans and Italian shoes. Then I climb on my old British bike, with new East German tyres and tank full of petrol from Kuwait.

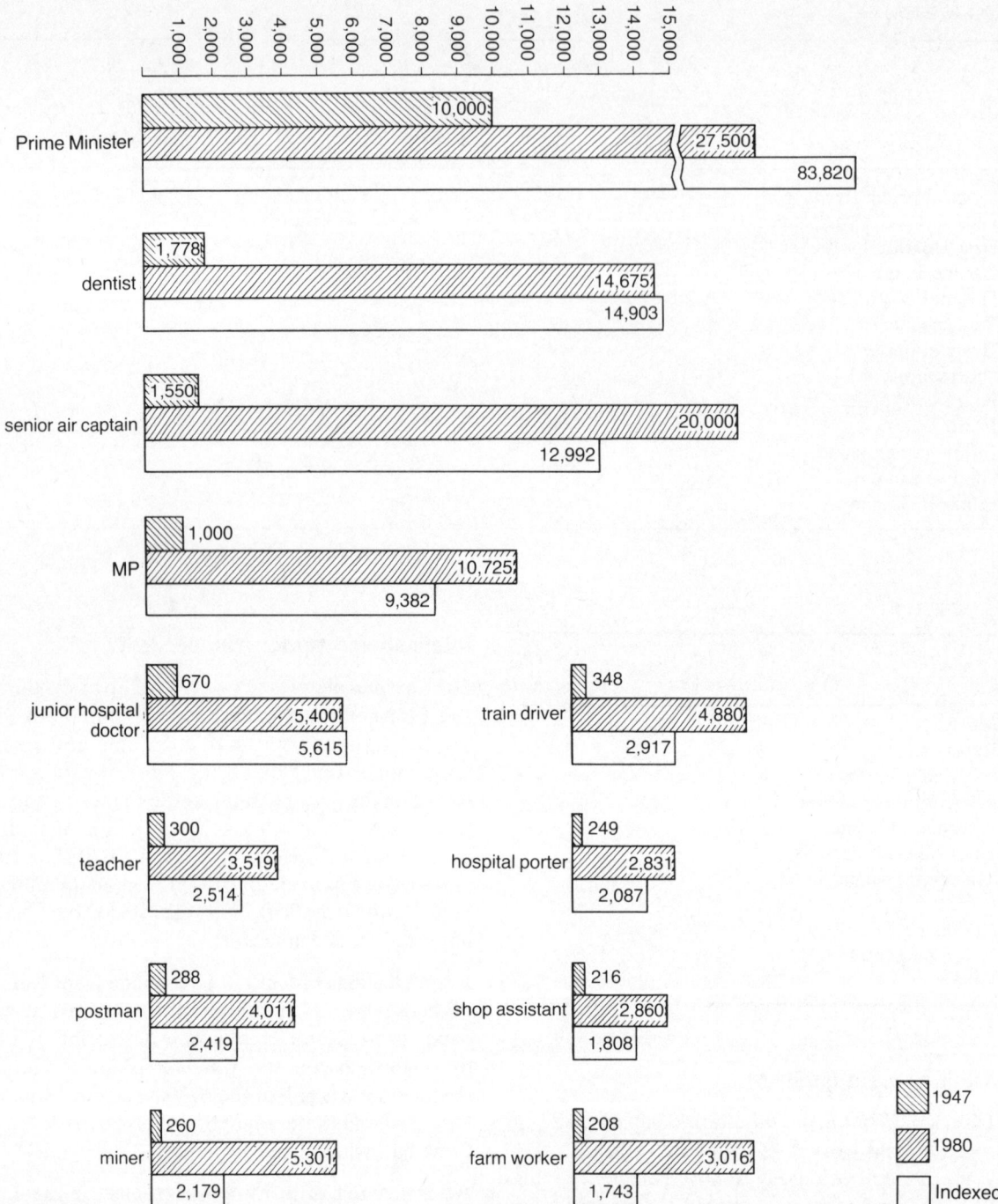

Figure 52 *Since the Second World War, the purchasing power of the pound has fallen considerably. This diagram shows the typical salary of selected occupations in 1947 and 1980. If incomes had been indexed-linked to keep up with inflation since 1947, they would have increased by a factor of 8.38 over the period. Which occupations are now better off and which are worse off than before?*

When I get to work I find a pile of steel made from Swedish iron ore, Australian coking coal and Derbyshire limestone. The American-owned firm I work for makes oil drilling equipment for export to Saudi Arabia.

Self-assessment questions

15 How is your own firm dependent on international trade?
16 Which goods and materials presently imported could Britain eventually provide for itself?
17 What would be the consequences for workers and consumers if a British government controlled imports in pursuit of such a policy of economic 'self-sufficiency'?

12 Government

The aim of this section is to interest you in politics. You will be encouraged to consider conflicting political standpoints; Parliament and the role of the State; voting behaviour; pressure groups; and the distribution of power in Britain.

Who rules Britain?

Politics is about power:

(i) To initiate and block changes.
(ii) To decide who gets what (how the wealth that society creates will be distributed).
(iii) To make the rules that regulate our lives.

Self-assessment question

1 (i) How much power do you think that each of the following institutions has to influence what happens in Britain? Rank them from one (very little) to five (a lot).

	Parliament
	Conservative Party
	Labour Party
	Liberal Party
	Civil Service
	Police
	The Royal Family
	Television
	National newspapers
	The City
	Private industry
	Trade unions
	The Professions
	The Church

(ii) Which institutions obtain an average score of four or more in your group?
(iii) How do you rate their performance?

(iv) Who are the top decision-makers in each of these institutions?
(v) Can you name any of the directors, major shareholders and senior managers of the hundred largest industrial firms, banks and nationalized industries in the country?
(vi) How do you become a 'top person'? How are judges, army generals, newspaper editors and peers recruited?
(vii) Are the elites who head these institutions separate and independent from one another, or are they united by common ties of family, class and education?

Some writers argue that in large and complex societies it is unrealistic for the mass of people to participate effectively in political decisions. The masses, however, are not completely powerless as long as there are regular elections in which they can choose between competing elites. This situation is called *representative democracy* to distinguish it from:

(i) *Totalitarianism*, where no alternative to the ruling elite is tolerated; and
(ii) *Direct democracy*, where the mass of people have an opportunity personally to play an active part in political decision-making.

Self-assessment questions

2 How responsive are British institutions to the wishes of the majority of citizens?

3 Are most people apathetic about politics? If so, why?

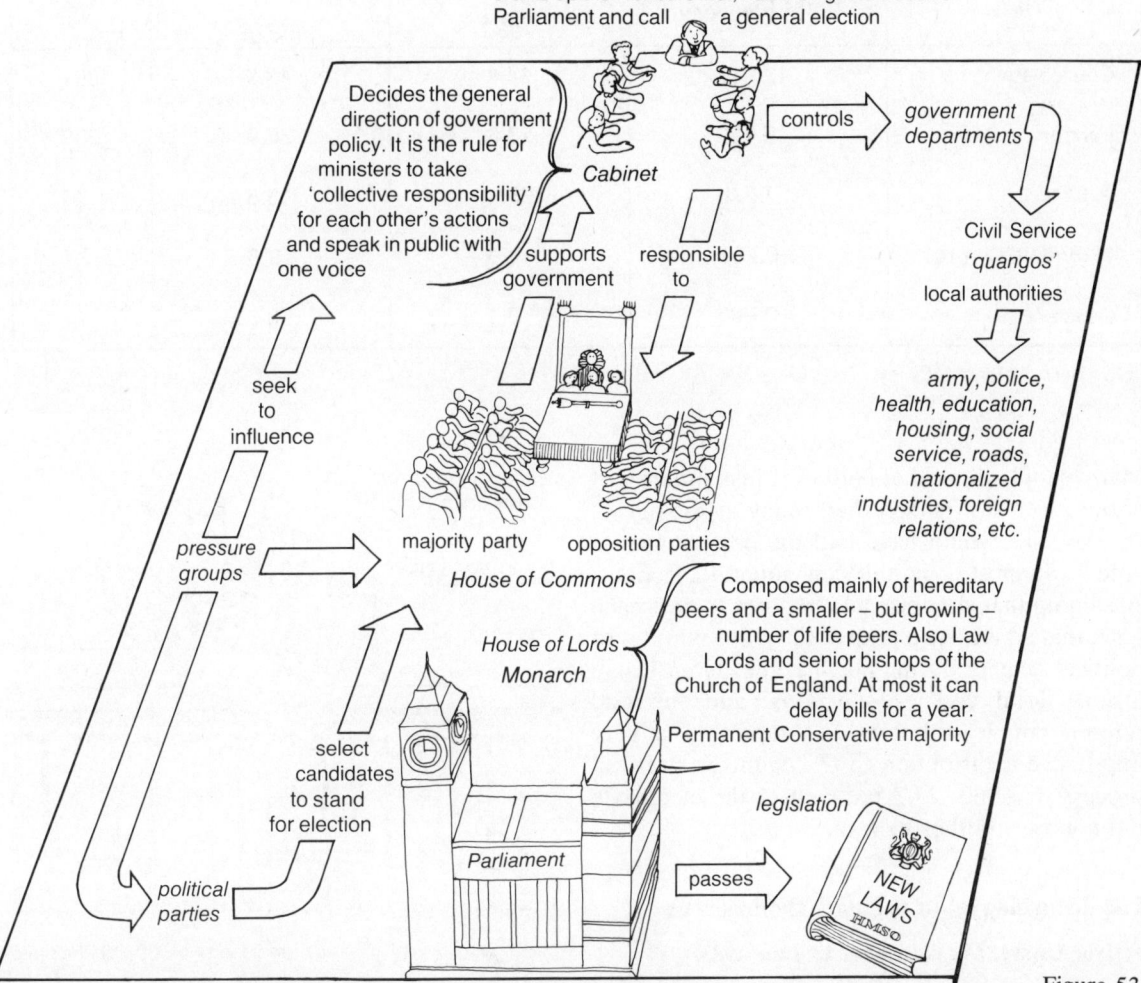

Prime Minister

Appoints and sacks members of the government, creates peers, controls appointment of top-rank civil servants and chairmen of nationalized industries, draws up the Honours List, has the right to dissolve Parliament and call a general election

Decides the general direction of government policy. It is the rule for ministers to take 'collective responsibility' for each other's actions and speak in public with one voice

Cabinet

controls

government departments

supports government

responsible to

Civil Service
'quangos'
local authorities

army, police, health, education, housing, social service, roads, nationalized industries, foreign relations, etc.

seek to influence

pressure groups

majority party   opposition parties

House of Commons

House of Lords
Monarch

Composed mainly of hereditary peers and a smaller – but growing – number of life peers. Also Law Lords and senior bishops of the Church of England. At most it can delay bills for a year. Permanent Conservative majority

select candidates to stand for election

legislation

political parties

Parliament

passes

NEW LAWS
HMSO

Figure 53

How does Parliament work?

To answer this question find out for yourself by doing the following exercise.

(i) Select:

   (a) A bill that is going through Parliament; and

   (b) An issue on which the Government's performance is being challenged.

(ii) Follow their progress and development.

(iii) What part is played by the Prime Minister, Cabinet Ministers, the Leader of the Opposition, Shadow spokesmen, the Speaker, backbench MPs and peers?

(iv) Do the archaic conventions of Parliament help or hinder the business of government?

Elections and voting

Table 25   *General Election results: June 1983*

Party	Votes (millions)	Percentage of votes		MPs
		1983	1979	
Conservative	13.013	42.4	43.9	397
Labour	8.462	27.6	36.9	209
Alliance	7.776	25.4	13.8	23
SNP/Plaid Cymru	0.457	1.5	2.0	4
Others	0.963	3.1	3.5	17*

*Northern Ireland MPs

Many people think that politics is just a matter of voting. Yet, if a person died today at the age of seventy, she would have had the opportunity to vote – at most – in thirteen general elections. Assuming that she took five minutes to cast each vote, that adds up to a total of sixty-five minutes of political activity during her lifetime. Even if you include local and bye-elections, and the odd referendum, it still does not represent a very impressive contribution to the country's political process. In 1983, 27.3 per cent of the electorate did not even bother to vote.

here's your ration of democracy . . .

. . . and don't walk off with the pencil

The disturbing truth behind Labour's rout

by Ivor Crewe, *The Guardian*, 13 June 1983

All election results are deceptive. They are judged by seats won, even though seats do not switch in exact tandem with votes. The Conservatives' net gain of 37 seats over their 1979 position produced a landslide majority of 144, but came from a modest 30.8 per cent of the total electorate. The Conservatives' vote share was actually higher when it lost narrowly to Mr Wilson in 1964.

The electorate did not embrace the Conservatives; it rebuffed Labour and flirted with the Alliance. At 25.4 per cent the Alliance's vote share was the best performance of the Centre for 60 years. The Labour vote was down by 9.3 per cent – the sharpest fall incurred by a major party at a single election since the war – and the poorest showing since the party was founded in 1900.

Until 1979 surveys consistently showed that, compared with the old, the young voted Labour in higher proportions and, in addition, swung more heavily against whichever party held office. In 1979, for the first time, new voters divided equally between Labour and the Conservatives. This time the swing to the right has gone further still. Labour came third among new voters, taking a mere 17 per cent of the vote, 3 per cent behind the Alliance and 11 per cent behind the Conservatives. *That*

Labour should fail so dismally among the young at a time of severe youth unemployment must seem a mystery. Among unemployed 18–22 year olds, almost half did not bother to vote at all.

A permanent feature of all elections until recently was the higher Conservative vote among women than men. The gap disappeared in 1979 and has now gone into reverse. For the first time, and under Britain's first woman Prime Minister, the Conservatives drew less support from women than men.

It is not age or sex, but social class that continues to structure party choice. Yet the class basis of party choice has steadily weakened over the last quarter century. In 1959 there was a 40 per cent gap between Labour's share of the non-manual as against the manual vote; by 1983 that gap had fallen to 21 per cent. In the middle classes there was barely a swing to the Conservatives at all. Among clerical and office workers the small Labour vote held up.

The pro-Conservative swing was confined to the working class. This was not because the working class Conservative vote rose, but because the working class Labour vote, which had already haemorrhaged badly in 1979, continued to bleed away – mainly to the Alliance. Support for the Alliance was remarkably even across the class spectrum.

In 1959, when the Conservatives' overall majority was 100, 62 per cent of manual workers still voted Labour; in 1983 the figure was 38 per cent. *The transformation of working class partisanship over the past quarter century must rank as the most significant post-war change in the social basis of British politics.*

To be sure, Labour remains the party of a segment of the working class – the traditional working class of the council estates, of the public sector, of Scotland and the North. Among these slowly dwindling groups Labour was still the first, if not always the majority, choice. But it has lost the new working class. Among manual workers owning their house, or living in the South, the Conservatives had a commanding lead and Labour came third behind the Alliance. The old working class is now too small to give Labour electoral victory; the new working class too big to be ignored.

Self-assessment question

4(i) Comment on the validity of the three sentences in italics in the newspaper article above.

  (ii) Study Figure 54. Explain the cartoon in your own words. Find and discuss current examples of political cartoons.

How political are you?

Do you:

  (i) Follow news reports about political affairs with interest?

  (ii) Take part in political discussions and arguments?

Figure 54   Eskimo Knell

(iii) Vote in elections?

(iv) Support a political party?

(v) Attend political meetings?

(vi) Belong to an organization with political aims (for example Motorcycle Action Group, Campaign for Nuclear Disarmament)?

(vii) Belong to a political party (you may be affiliated to the Labour Party through your trade union)?

How much do you know about politics?

Which political parties are in favour of the following policies?

Abolishing the House of Lords

A separate Parliament for Scotland

Cutting income tax

Cutting tax on company profits

Giving workers seats on the boards of major companies

Imposing import controls

Improving public transport services

Introducing a maximum 35-hour week

Introducing a minimum wage

Introducing a wealth tax

Introducing profit-sharing for employees

Nationalizing the banks

Outlawing the closed shop

Proportional voting in elections

Reducing defence spending

Restoring capital punishment

Restricting coloured immigration

Selling more council houses to occupants

Strengthening the powers of the police

Taking Britain out of the Common Market

For further information, look at copies of the parties' election manifestos (available in most libraries and printed in *The Times Guide to the House of Commons*, Times Books).

Which political parties do you associate with the following descriptions? Does their past performance confirm these party images?

reliable	untrustworthy
exciting	dull
modern and forward-looking	out of date and old fashioned
experienced	impractical
for individual freedom	for equality
united	split
moderate	extreme
peaceful	war-loving
strong leadership	weak leadership
for the nation	for own supporters

Why do about one in three working class people vote Conservative? Are they acting contrary to their 'class interests'?

One explanation is that working class Tories are people who:

(i) *either* are deferential to their social superiors, regarding Conservative leaders as 'born to rule';

(ii) *or* see themselves as middle class (or at least aspire to become so).

On the other hand, conservative ideas reflect prevailing political values such as patriotism and faith in our traditional institutions of authority. It is not therefore 'natural' to vote Labour: rather it is 'deviant' to support a party associated with socialism.

Self-assessment questions

5 Do people vote for the party and policies that they think are best for the country as a whole, or merely for what is in their own self-interest?

6 Which sectional interests appear to be the interests of the whole society?

Interest groups: putting on the pressure

As an individual it is unlikely that you can have much influence on what the Government does.

However, unity is strength and you will have more impact if you get together with like-minded people to form a *pressure group*. Many already exist: they may be seen as two distinct types with different aims.

Protectional interest groups have been formed to defend shared sectional interests. They are usually permanent organizations that unite people who have a common status (for example: motorists –

the Automobile Association; employees – trade unions).

Promotional interest groups exist to achieve a specific object or cause. They unite people who share the same attitudes towards an issue (for example Anti-Nazi League, Campaign for Nuclear Disarmament, Friends of the Earth, Shelter).

Some interest groups incorporate features of both types and often there are groups which represent opposite sides of a cause (for example anti-blood sports and pro-field sports).

These groups are most effective when they can influence government directly. The Government, for its part, is generally ready to talk to those groups whose active co-operation it needs to carry out its policies (for example: NFU – farmers; BMA – doctors). Formal consultative committees have been set up as channels of communication and so the Government can test reaction to possible new policies at an early stage. For instance, the National Advisory Council of the Motor Industry comprises representatives from government, manufacturers, traders and unions.

Groups also seek support from individual MPs who will take up their cause with ministers or ask questions in the House. They may do this by writing letters, lobbying, or through informal contacts. It is even possible for an organization to employ an MP as a 'parliamentary consultant' to keep an eye on their interests. Before he became a Labour minister in 1964, James Callaghan was receiving £3500 per year as an adviser to the Police Federation.

It is usually an indication of lack of success through direct channels when a group appeals to 'public opinion' for support to achieve its aims. Then its effectiveness will depend upon the skill of its leaders, its organizational support and the money at its disposal. The Campaign Against Building Industry Nationalization spent half a million pounds before the 1979 election, most of it on posters and leaflets in marginal Labour constituencies. Groups without funds must rely on their ingenuity to obtain free publicity from news and current affairs programmes, for example through public demonstrations.

Figure 55   *Protest marchers on their way to hand in a petition, in a bid to save the Triumph factory*

Self-assessment questions

7   (i)   Make a list of all the pressure groups that you can think of. There are several groups concerned with each of the following issues:

animals	minority groups with
civil liberties	particular problems
employment	peace
environment	poverty
housing	transport
	women

   (ii)   Which groups do you think are worth supporting?

 (iii)   Invite a speaker from one of these groups to come to your college to explain their aims to your class. (It may be difficult to find a contact address: try your local library, telephone directory and students' union notice-boards.)

 (iv)   What groups make use of the media to get publicity for their cause?

8   Write a letter to your local newspaper, explaining why and how a particular cause should be supported or opposed.

The local press is usually desperate for newsworthy items so it is relatively easy to exploit the media for your own purposes as long as your report is sufficiently sensational. You should try to link your story to some kind of controversy or activity, but, however, it will still need to be acceptable to the political bias of the newspaper. When you issue a press release you are more likely to be reported if you make the journalist's job as easy as possible. You will also have more control over what is eventually printed.

Self-assessment question

9   Invent your own press release. (Remember to make your report sensational.)

The State

Governments come and go, but the State remains. Until the early nineteenth century the State consisted simply of:

(i)   Those who handled the government's relations with foreign countries (for example ambassadors, armed forces).

(ii)   The bodies that kept social conflict within the bounds of law and order (for example police, prisons).

(iii)   Those who collected taxes.

Although seeming to 'stand above society', the State was really an instrument for defending the interests of the rulers. Today a much more complex State machine exists in all industrialized countries. In a democratic society, it is argued, the State cannot show any marked bias towards some interests and against others, but acts to reconcile conflicting pressure groups.

In addition to its traditional functions, the modern British State also administers the *public sector* of the economy and the *welfare state*.

The local state

As the activities of central government expanded, it became necessary to devolve more power and responsibility to local bodies. In each area the business of local government is carried out by elected councillors, assisted by their own 'civil service' at the town hall. Local authorities are responsible for education, housing, social services, recreation, planning, local highways, refuse collection and environmental health. They once controlled electricity, gas and water services, hospitals, police and poor relief in cash, but these functions have been taken over by non-elected boards.

Local authorities have a legal duty to provide certain services, and additional powers to provide others at their discretion. The scope of councils to pursue policies in opposition to central government is limited, however, because they depend upon Westminster for nearly half of their funds.

Self-assessment question

10 Arrange a visit to a meeting of your local council *or* invite a councillor to explain to your group how the local authority works.

Other bodies

What do these bodies have in common?

British Broadcasting Corporation
Countryside Commission
Horserace Betting Levy Board
National Coal Board
Sports Council
Technician Education Council

They are all *quangos*: quasi-autonomous non-governmental organizations. The State has set up hundreds of bodies to:

(i) Run publicly-owned commercial operations (for example British Airports Authority).
(ii) Promote causes that are considered important for society (for example English Tourist Board).
(iii) Regulate certain activities (for example Office of Fair Trading).

Self-assessment questions

11 Do you think that the State does too much?
12 Which are the areas where the State should interfere less (or more) in our lives and the running of society?

It is often said that Britain is over-taxed and that the State spends too much. Yet the proportion of gross national product (the value of goods and services produced) devoted to general government expenditure in Britain is similar to that in West Germany and France, and much lower than in the Netherlands and Sweden. And the burden of taxes and social security contributions is actually smaller than in these Continental countries.

State income and expenditure

The pie charts in Figures 56 and 57 show the different types of income central and local government receive. This revenue is spent on public expenditure. Figure 58 shows the total expenditure for 1982–3.

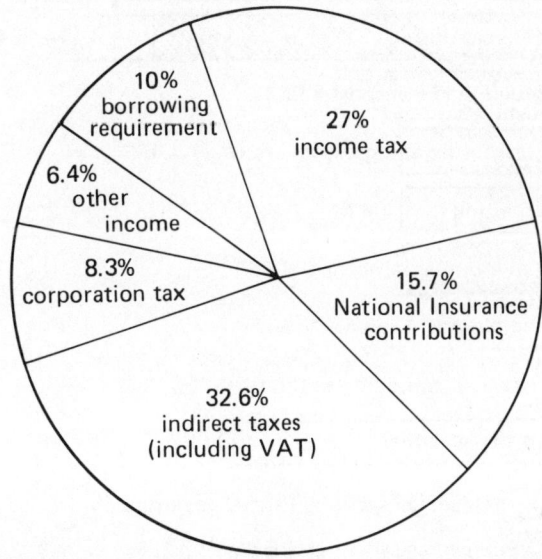

Figure 56 *Central government income 1981: total £101,769 million*

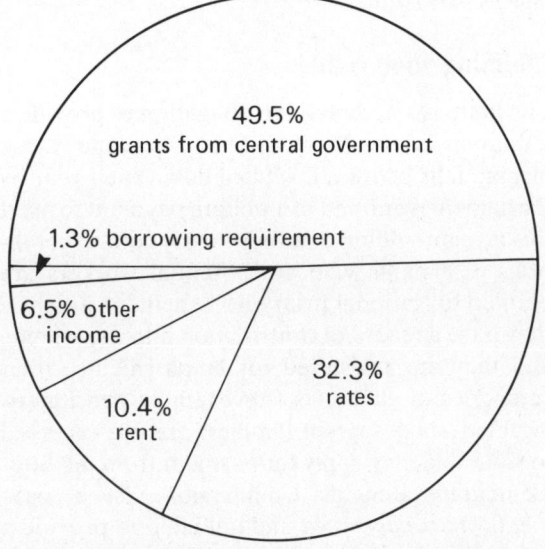

Figure 57 *Local government income 1981: total £32,102 million*

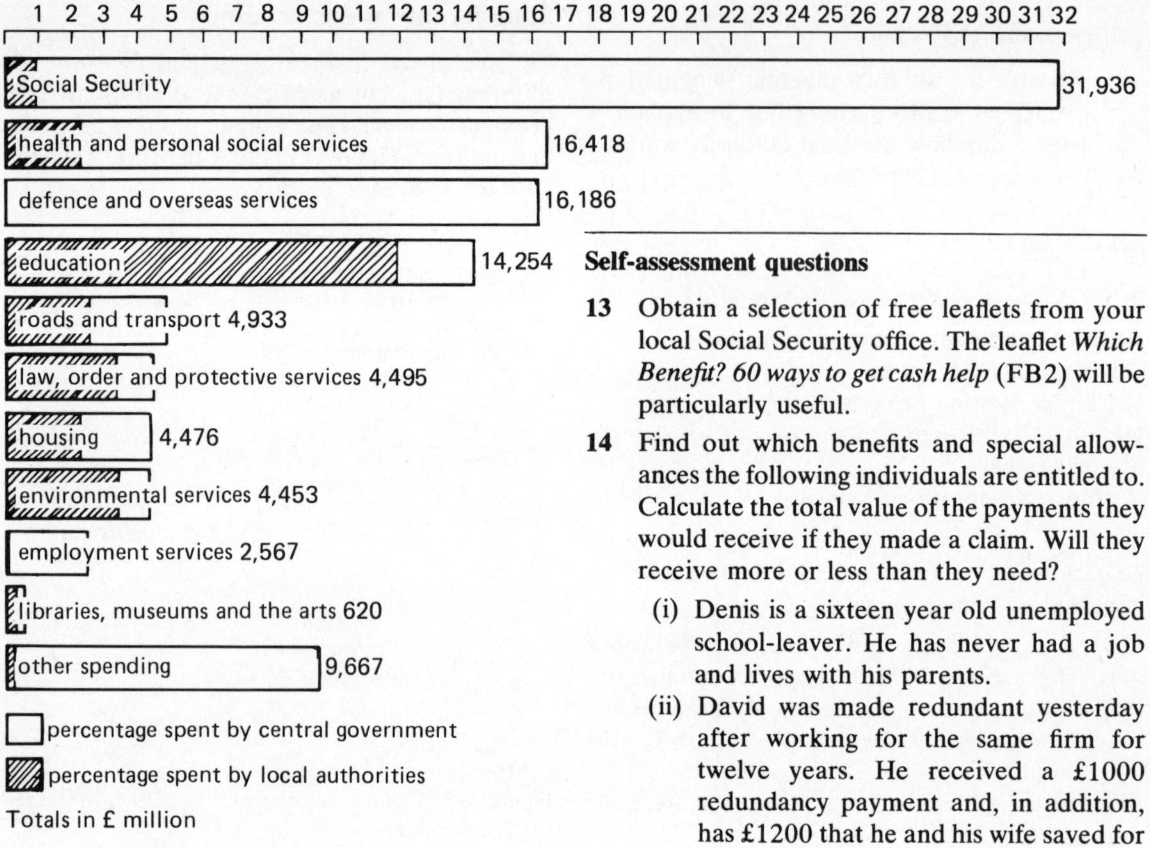

1 2 3 4 5 6 7 8 9 10 11 12 13 14 15 16 17 18 19 20 21 22 23 24 25 26 27 28 29 30 31 32

Social Security — 31,936

health and personal social services — 16,418

defence and overseas services — 16,186

education — 14,254

roads and transport 4,933

law, order and protective services 4,495

housing 4,476

environmental services 4,453

employment services 2,567

libraries, museums and the arts 620

other spending 9,667

☐ percentage spent by central government

▨ percentage spent by local authorities

Totals in £ million

Figure 58 *Public expenditure 1982–3 (Treasury estimates, March 1982)*

Claiming your rights

The State has accepted the obligation to provide a minimum income to all citizens. Everyone whose income falls below a level laid down each year by Parliament is entitled to a welfare payment to meet this level providing that they satisfy certain conditions. Claimants who are potential workers are entitled to National Insurance benefits as a right if they have a record of contribution into the scheme and they are registered for employment. Other categories of claimants (for example pensioners, disabled, single-parent families) are not expected to work and may apply for payment from the Supplementary Benefits Commission. These payments are *means tested* and intended to provide a safety-net for the 'losers' in our society (currently nearly one in ten of the population).

Self-assessment questions

13 Obtain a selection of free leaflets from your local Social Security office. The leaflet *Which Benefit? 60 ways to get cash help* (FB2) will be particularly useful.

14 Find out which benefits and special allowances the following individuals are entitled to. Calculate the total value of the payments they would receive if they made a claim. Will they receive more or less than they need?

 (i) Denis is a sixteen year old unemployed school-leaver. He has never had a job and lives with his parents.

 (ii) David was made redundant yesterday after working for the same firm for twelve years. He received a £1000 redundancy payment and, in addition, has £1200 that he and his wife saved for the deposit on a house. He used to earn £100 per week. At the moment they live in a flat (rent and rates £18 per week), have no children. David's wife earns £45 per week.

 (iii) Doreen is twenty years old. She does not work because she needs to look after her two year old baby. She has a rent-free room in a friend's house. She doesn't have any savings.

 (iv) Duncan earns £70 per week from his job in a garage. He has three children, aged five, eight and eleven. His wife does not work and he lives in a council house costing £15 per week.

 (v) Doris is seventy-three years old. She has lived alone in her own house since her husband was killed during the D-Day landings. Although she has never worked, she has £300 in savings.

The development of the welfare state

The Elizabethan *Poor Law* (1601) recognized that something should be done to assist paupers, but feared that generous handouts would encourage idleness. The principle was established that benefits should be lower than the lowest wages.

The 1834 'new' Poor Law aimed to reduce the cost of poor relief by limiting assistance to those able-bodied paupers who were prepared to accept the humiliation of the workhouse.

In 1931 the *means test* was introduced to ensure that only unemployed workers with a bare minimum of resources received financial assistance.

Post-war policy makers have taken into account the legacy of bitterness produced by these attitudes to the poor.

During the nineteenth century it was slowly recognized that government intervention was needed to remedy the worst aspects of unplanned industrial growth.

The *Factory Acts* (1833 and 1842) introduced regulations to limit the exploitation of children and women.

Following a series of cholera epidemics, *Public Health Acts* aimed to improve sanitation and slum housing, and stop the adulteration of food.

When the working class gained the vote, Parliament accepted that it was time to 'educate our masters'. Industry also needed more skilled workers. In 1870 school boards were empowered to provide premises and compel school attendance.

With the growth of trade unions and the birth of the *Labour Party*, popular agitation increased for better living standards for working people. The Liberal Party, in competition with the Conservatives for workers' votes, evolved a policy of social reform.

1897 compensation for injury at work.
1905 local authorities were given the power to set up labour exchanges.
1906 school meals for children were introduced.
1908 old age pensions were introduced.
1911 sickness and unemployment insurance for the lower paid.
1919 first Council Houses Act.

In 1942 the *Beveridge Report* contained detailed proposals for a new and comprehensive system of social security to meet basic needs, financed by contributions which everyone would pay. This system was to be based upon government policies to maintain full employment and was put into effect by the post-war Labour Government.

1944 free secondary education up to the age of fifteen.
1946 National Health Service provided free medical attention and treatment.
1949 Youth Employment Service was set up and the Legal Aid and Advice Act made legal action possible for the poor.
1961 graduated pensions, related to previous earnings, were introduced.
1970 special provisions were made for the chronically sick and disabled (sheltered accommodation, aids, home helps, day centres).
1971 Social Services Departments were created by merging local authority, children's and hospital welfare departments.

How should a government spend our money?

When a new government takes office, it usually modifies its predecessor's spending plans in the light of its own priorities. Thus, the 1979 Conservative Government announced its intention to:

(i)   Reduce spending on education, housing and industry;

(ii) Increase spending on law and order, defence and social security.

Self-assessment question

15   What do you think of this decision?

Since the mid-1970s the general expansion of the welfare state has been halted and provisions even cut. This policy has been justified on the grounds that:

(i)   In a period of economic difficulty, all sections of the population must make sacrifices.

(ii) Excessive public spending fuels inflation and diverts resources from productive investment.

(iii) The welfare state equals 'creeping socialism' and saps the nation's initiative.

At the same time there has been a trend towards:

(i)   Greater selectivity in the provision of services, restricting them to 'those in need' rather than making them freely available to people in general.

(ii) The commercial provision of services: pay-beds, private education, sale of council houses, etc.

Self-assessment questions

16   What has been the effect of cuts in public spending in your area?

17   (i) Suppose that the Cabinet decides to cut its budget by £20 million. Should it axe plans for:
    (a) a small hospital;
    (b) two Tornado aircraft;
    (c) eight advanced passenger trains;
    (d) 1600 council houses?
   (ii) Are there any other alternatives?

13 The law

The aim of this section is to look at the process of law-making and enforcement. You will be encouraged to consider the definition of crime, the image of the criminal, the work of the police, punishments that the courts may impose, and civil liberties.

Legal and moral rules

All societies have rules that govern the actions of individuals and the relationships between them. Etiquette, for instance, is a set of informal rules that regulates such everyday matters as the way we use cutlery, introduce strangers or blow our nose. Breaches of etiquette are likely to be amusing or embarrassing. At worst they can permanently damage our relationships with others. Figure 59 compares these rules with others of a more general application.

Self-assessment question

1 How is the public reaction to crime different when a moral rule as well as a legal rule is broken?

We do not all hold the same moral standards although there are many widely-held sentiments that virtually everybody shares, for example that we should not be cruel to children. Since the law reflects morality, there are few laws that are accepted by the population as a whole. Particular laws are opposed by minorities, not only because they want to break them, but because they believe they are 'wrong'. Thus there is a continual struggle taking place over what is, and what should be, considered as *crime*.

Ideas about which actions are crimes vary from time to time and place to place. During the Middle Ages heretics and witches were savagely punished, while today most dissenting spiritual beliefs are

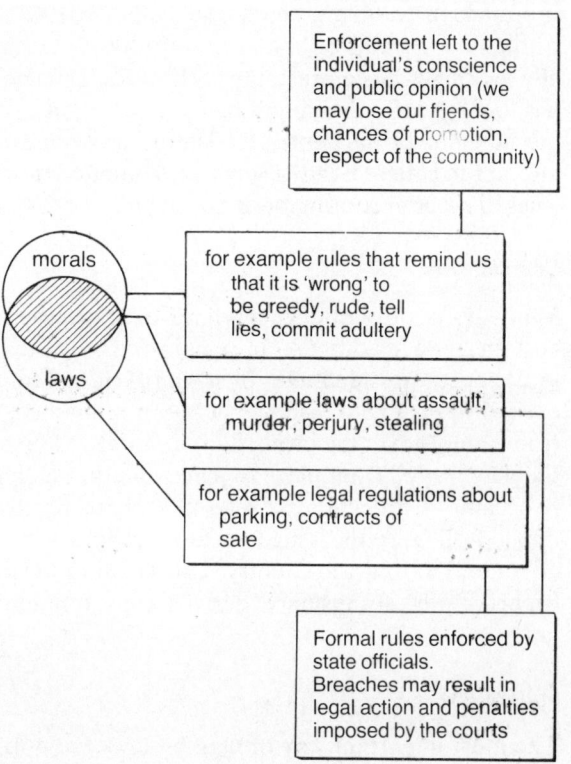

Figure 59

tolerated. In Moslem countries a man may have several wives at the same time, but in Britain he would be prosecuted as a bigamist. In South Africa marriage between people of different races is illegal.

Self-assessment question

2 Can you think of examples of:

  (i) Actions that were previously illegal in Britain but are now permissible?

  (ii) New crimes that have been created?

  (iii) Actions that are legal in Britain but are crimes in another country?

  (iv) Crimes in this country that are legal activities abroad?

How the law is made

In France in 1804, and the Soviet Union in 1936, whole new systems of law were introduced virtually overnight. In contrast, the body of English law has been accumulated gradually and amended piecemeal over the centuries. There has been no attempt to collect it into a single, systematic set of rules. The origins of modern law are:

Common law

Many of our present day laws have their origin in customs and traditions. In Anglo-Saxon times local courts, presided over by a sheriff or bishop, existed to deal with disputes between individuals (for example over the ownership of cattle). At first the 'law' varied from place to place, but gradually it became a collection of rules that were firmly applied all over the kingdom after judges were appointed to tour the country. Our claim to local 'rights of way', for instance, derives from common law.

Statute law

The most important way of making laws today is through legislation in Parliament. Since the nineteenth century there has been a tendency for Parliament to revise common law into statutes (for example the old contract of sale rules became the Sale of Goods Act in 1893). Because Parliament now has insufficient time to consider all the legal changes it thinks necessary, modern Acts often empower someone (usually a minister) to make specific regulations.

Case law

Judges try to ensure that the law is consistent over a period of time by following the decisions taken by other judges in similar cases. Once a precedent is established, it must be followed by all other courts in later cases, although it may be revised by a 'higher' court. When legislation is unclear, or when a judge is faced with a unique situation, then his decision is not merely the application of old rules but, in effect, the creation of a new law.

Many old laws have fallen into disuse but, since they have not actually been repealed, could be revived on some future occasion. Most of our politicians could be imprisoned for life if the old common law against sedition which makes it an offence to 'excite ill-will between different classes of Sovereign subjects . . . or to bring into hatred or contempt the Sovereign or the Government, the laws or constitution of the realm' were rigorously enforced.

Self-assessment question

3 (i) Find an example of a pressure group or campaign that seeks to change the law or have an existing law enforced more energetically.

  (ii) What tactics does it use to obtain its aims?

  (iii) What do you think are the motives of the people involved?

  (iv) Do they represent the positive wishes of the majority of the population?

Their law to keep their order

'Hang the Ripper' screamed the placards and the demonstrators outside the court as the arrested man made his first court appearance. Male, female, the old and the very young – all seemed to be gripped by the same hysteria.

This is the emotional hanging lobby at work; people who believe that revenge is the only justice. They are quite ordinary people who arrive, baying for blood, everytime someone is arrested for a particularly horrible murder, especially when women and children are the victims.

The official hanging lobby, the judges who regret they can only give life sentences, the top policemen who believe that the threat of violence will stop violence, the politicians who believe they are born with the right to give life and to take it away, will bide their time, and when they are assured of the maximum popular support they will introduce a new hanging bill.

They try to pretend that hanging will deter people from murdering, but most murders take place regardless of the penalty. Since hanging was abolished in Britain the proportion of murders has not increased. Hanging is no more than a vicious and barbaric form of retribution. A hundred years ago men and women could be hanged for stealing. It never deterred them. They stole because for most there was little other means of survival.

The law and order lobby is not concerned with that fact. Nor are they concerned with the growing number of thefts, break-ins or rapes. If they were they would look to the causes of crime, to growing unemployment, poverty, frustration with life, particularly family life, and poor education, and they would do something about these things to set people's lives on a better course.

But they're not interested in doing anything about the causes. In fact they are part of the cause of these problems themselves. Law and order is for them a political slogan, by which they mean *their right to use their law to keep us in their order*.

The police and the judges will be pleased that they have caught the alleged Ripper. If he is found guilty he will be locked up for the rest of his life. Even socialists cannot argue that a man who apparently uncontrollably murders women should be allowed to go free. But we should remember, prison doesn't look to the root of the problem of why people murder. It provides a simple solution which gets the problem out of the way. And the fear of violence still exists.

The law and order brigade and the hanging lobby are not in the least interested in the fact that many women are terrified to go out alone at night. They will just use that fear for their own ends.

Explain this conclusion

Comment on the validity of these two paragraphs

Womens Voice February 1981

Who is a criminal?

Those whom the State regards as criminals are not always considered badly by the public. History is full of bandits who turned into folk heroes: Robin Hood, Rob Roy, Dick Turpin, Ned Kelly, Jesse James, etc. Outlaws may be seen by their people as fighters against injustice and so be helped and supported.

From the statistics available on crime it appears that the typical criminal is:

Male   About five times as many males are found guilty of serious crimes than females.

Young   The peak age for being arrested is between fourteen and seventeen years. People under twenty-one commit about half of all serious offences.

Urban   Crime is more common in towns than in rural areas.

Working class   The sons of manual workers are convicted of criminal offences four times more frequently than those of professional persons.

A survey of eighteen-year-old males has shown that while only 15 per cent had been *convicted* of a criminal offence:

over 75 per cent admitted that, at some time or other, they had committed a crime which carries a possible prison sentence;

89 per cent had kept something they had found;

53 per cent had stolen something from a shop;

25 per cent had stolen something from work;

15 per cent had got something by threatening others;

14 per cent had stolen a motor-bike or cycle.

The crime rate

Newspaper headlines often tell us that the crime rate is rising. But what does this mean? The police keep records of crimes that are:

(i)   Reported to them or which they discover themselves ('known crimes').

(ii)   'Cleared-up': someone is charged with an offence, even if he is later acquitted in court.

The dark area of crime

It is likely that official figures greatly underestimate the actual amount of crime that occurs. The police find out about most crimes because they are reported by the victims or witnesses. An official survey in the USA showed that there were three times as many burglaries and rapes as were actually reported. A similar proportion of crimes probably remain 'unknown' in Britain because:

(i)   The people involved may not realize that a crime has been committed (for example common assaults).

(ii)   The crime is known only to those who commit it (for example drivers speeding).

(iii)   Those involved disagree with the law (for example drug offences).

(iv)   The crime may be known only to friends or relatives who wish to protect the offender (for example violence by parents against children).

(v)   The victim may be frightened of retaliation from the offender.

(vi)   The victim may be sympathetic to the offender and wish to protect him.

(vii)   It may be embarrassing to report the crime (for example sexual offences).

(viii)   It may be inconvenient or too much bother to report the crime and testify in court (for example most trivial offences).

(ix)   The victim has no confidence that the police will deal with the crime to his satisfaction (for example recover his stolen property). You are more likely to report a theft if this is a condition of your insurance cover.

(x)   Police investigations may uncover offences committed by the victim.

More crimes will be reported (and therefore the crime rate will rise) if:

The police have good relations with the public and are regarded as efficient at solving crimes.

The public become less tolerant towards certain kinds of law-breaking. The media may play a part in making people sensitive to particular 'problems' (for example soccer hooliganism).

The police have a degree of discretion over how they enforce the law. Obviously they have no alternative but to prosecute if they have evidence that a serious offence has been committed. At the same time:

(i)   The police may decide not to charge people they find committing trivial offences. If they did in every case they would clog up the already overburdened courts.

(ii)   The police must often use their discretion to decide whether an offence has actually been committed (for example breach of the peace, obstruction, threatening or abusive language. Studies have shown that the attitude of a person towards the police (polite and respectful or hostile and insolent) can decide whether or not they get arrested.

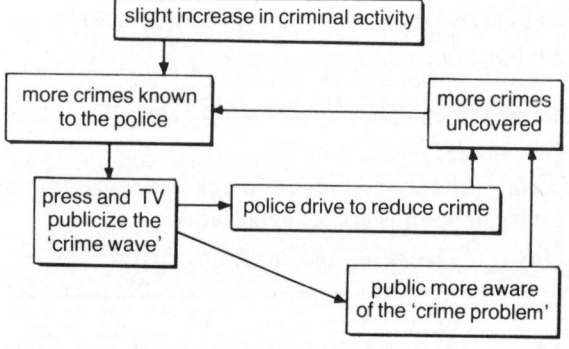

Figure 60

(iii)   Chief Constables have different views about which laws should be enforced rigorously. They may initiate local drives against specific crimes: after-hours drinking, pornography, speeding, etc. Which laws do you think should be enforced 'to the letter'? When should the police 'turn a blind eye'?

The police and the media

The police are a popular subject for TV series and films.

The great pay robbery: mean bosses filch £22 million from workers

Rogue bosses have pulled off the robbery of the century.

They got away with £22 million from the pay packets of their workers last year.

Only twelve of them were fined a total of £1250 by the courts.

The success of their Great Pay Robbery is revealed in a report today by the independent Low Pay Unit and the Workers Educational Association.

The bosses lined their own pockets by underpaying nearly 300,000 already low-paid employees – mostly women.

Each worker lost an average £67 a year. But for many the illegal underpayment of pay fixed by wages councils totalled £2 a week or more.

Simon Crine, of the Low Pay Unit, said yesterday: 'Nearly one in three employers who were inspected were underpaying.

'They filched £22 million from the wage packets of some of Britain's lowest-paid workers last year.

'In spite of the gravity of the problem, the Government has very quietly abandoned its special "blitz" tactics for catching rogue employers.

'This secret change of policy amounts to a charter for the law-breaking boss.'

The report says that the workers robbed in this way are already Britain's lowest-paid, with wages fixed at between £36 and £53 a week.

Roger Todd, *Daily Mirror* August 1980

Self-assessment question

5   Do you think that the media present an accurate picture of the work and performance of the police? Bear in mind that: dealing with crime is only about a quarter of all police work; violent crimes are only a tiny fraction of total crime; only about half of all crimes committed are cleared up.

It has been suggested that the law is biased in favour of the rich and powerful. Consider this:

Social security fraud

In 1978 the Department of Health and Social Security (DHSS) uncovered frauds totalling £2.5 million: less than 30 pence in every £1000 paid out was fraudulently claimed. Obviously not all frauds are discovered, and government estimates of the real level range from £50 million to over £200 million. The DHSS employs over 5000 specialist staff to investigate fraud, and offenders are usually prosecuted.

Tax fraud

In the tax-year 1978–9 the Inland Revenue unearthed illegal tax evasions amounting to £70 millions. It is estimated that £500 million is lost through 'inaccurate' tax returns by the self-employed and a further £1000 million by non-payment of VAT and corporation tax. The head of the Inland Revenue put the actual level of tax fraud at between £200 million and £300 million. The Inland Revenue employs about 250 specialist investigators. When breaches of the law are discovered, the concern is often to 'put things right' rather than prosecute.

Self-assessment questions

6   Are we all equal before the law, or is there one law for the rich and another for the poor?

7   How does the popular image of the social security 'scrounger' differ from that of the tax 'fiddler'?

Trouble with the law

Dave Evans

I am sixteen and last night I was watching television with my girl-friend Sue Jones at our house. We had no money, nowhere to go, and we were bored stupid. During an advert about road safety Sue dared me to take my brother's bike, a new 350 c.c., for a blast up the by-pass. I knew Phil would be staying the night at Yvonne's place and so wouldn't be needing it. Not that he'd let me borrow it anyway. Still, getting the bike wasn't a problem because he keeps a spare set of keys in his drawer.

The bike was going really well on the by-pass and when we turned back on to the High Street I probably got a bit over-confident. We were doing about fifty-five miles per hour when a daft woman walked off the pavement right in front of me. The swerve wasn't wide enough and the impact nearly had us over. I kept the bike upright though, and after dropping a gear we were OK. Once back home I laid the bike on its fairing as though it had overbalanced. Phil will kill me when he finds out what I've done.

Not long after I got to bed, mum and dad arrived back home. They were just in time to beat the police to the door. Listening from the landing I could hear that it was Phil they were looking for. I decided not to say anything and to see what would happen to Phil when dad took him down the cop shop. From the bedroom window I could see the police taking bits off the broken fairing and put them into a plastic bag.

Sue Jones

I am very worried. I dared Dave to take his brother's motor-bike. While going very fast we crashed into a woman on a crossing. The impact nearly threw us off. When Dave dropped me off at the end of the street, he made me promise not to tell anyone. I couldn't sleep last night and kept remembering the sound of the woman's body when the bike hit her.

Phil Evans

I am nineteen and last night I slept with Yvonne. Her parents were away visiting her sick granny. When I started going out with Yvonne about three months ago, I thought she was seventeen, but recently she admitted that she is only fifteen.

When I got home early this morning I found dad waiting up for me. The police had been round and dad had promised he would take me down to the station. Dad doesn't know why they want me, but he says they will be back soon and it would be better if I went down to the police station voluntarily. I'm not so sure. And on top of that I found my bike's fairing all smashed in.

Detective Constable Roberts

While on duty at about 8.45 p.m. last night I received a call about a hit and run incident in the High Street. The mobile unit assigned to investigate the accident reported that a motor-cycle had knocked down and killed an elderly woman on the pedestrian crossing opposite Marks and Spencers. The vehicle's registration number was noted by a witness who reported that the bike was travelling at high speed.

The computer gave the owner as a Philip William Evans. A patrol was assigned to pick him up for questioning. The suspect was not at home but his father, Mr Thomas Evans, promised to bring him to the station as soon as he returned. Mr Evans was not told of the offence and does not know that samples from a damaged fairing on the motor-cycle were taken for forensic examination.

Self-assessment questions

8   Have Dave, Sue, Phil and Yvonne committed any offences and, if so, what are they?

9   (i)   What are the maximum punishments for these offences?

    (ii)   What are the likely punishments under the circumstances of this case?

10 Under what circumstances can the police arrest you without a warrant?

11 Can the police make Phil go to the police station without arresting him?

12 What are the 'Judges' Rules' and how do they govern the questioning of suspects by the police?

13 Must you answer the questions that the police ask?

14 How soon must an arrested person be brought before a Magistrates' Court?

15 What is bail and why might it be refused to an arrested person?

16 Is it an offence not to admit to a crime and let someone else take the blame?

17   (i) Imagine that you are Detective Constable Roberts. What would you do to uncover who was responsible for the woman's death?

  (ii) How can you be sure that the accused person is really guilty?

  (iii) How can you improve your chances of obtaining a conviction in court?

The book *What Right Have You Got?* BBC Publications 1976) will help you to answer these questions.

Figure 62 *Inside the Magistrates' Court*

The law courts

The structure of the law courts is shown in Figure 61, and each court deals with different types of case.

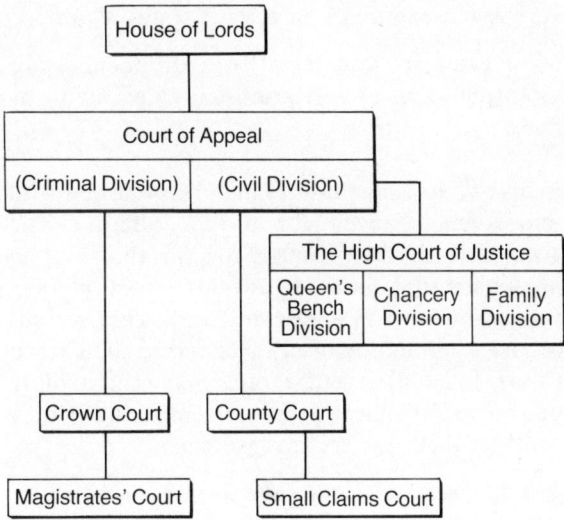

Figure 61 *The courts*

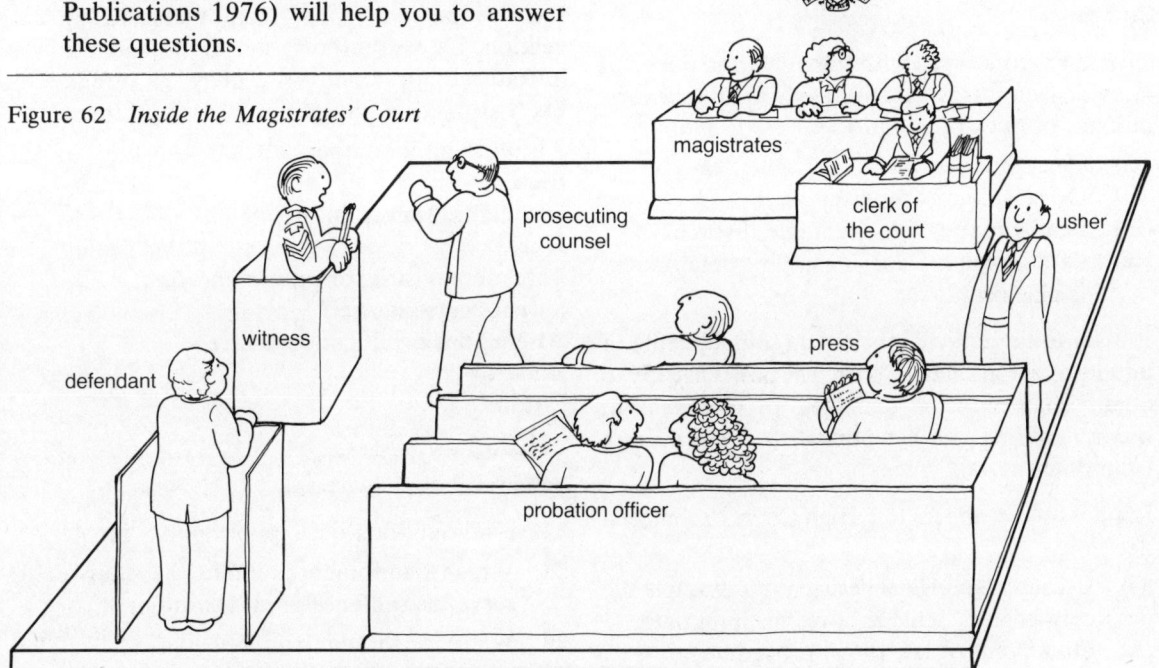

Criminal law

Criminal law is concerned with offences that are punished by the State.

Summary (minor) offences are always tried – with very few exceptions – in a Magistrates' Court.

Most cases are concerned with drunkenness or motoring offences and are usually dealt with by fines.

Indictable (serious) crimes may be punished with imprisonment, even for a first offence. The accused (defendant) usually has the choice of an immediate trial in the Magistrates' Court or going for trial *by jury* in a Crown Court. Very serious offences are automatically referred to the Crown Court. In addition, magistrates may send a guilty person to a Higher Court for sentencing if they consider their powers are insufficient.

The Magistrates' Courts try the vast majority of criminal cases. They also have a civil jurisdiction, dealing with applications for pub licences and disputes between husbands and wives (for example separation, maintenance).

Civil law

Civil law is concerned with the rights and duties of individuals towards each other. It embraces various sets of rules relating to:

  (i)   Contracts;
 (ii)   Ownership of property;
(iii)   Family matters (for example divorce);
 (iv)   Civil wrongs (for example defamation, negligence).

It is up to the individual citizen (complainant) to initiate a case in a Civil Court. The aim is usually to obtain compensation (damages) or to obtain an order requiring another person to do or abstain from doing certain things.

It is possible to appeal to a High Court to change a decision:

  (i)   Because the original decision (for example the conviction or sentence) was inappropriate.
 (ii)   On a point of law (legal procedure).

There are other specialized courts:

Coroner's Court – to deal with causes of death.

Juvenile Courts – to deal with young persons under seventeen years of age.

Administrative Tribunals – for rents, industrial injury compensation, claims for social security benefits, etc.

Self-assessment questions

18   What is *Legal Aid and Advice*?

19   Who is eligible to receive it? (Leaflets giving details are usually available at the Citizen's Advice Bureau.)

20   What are the rules of admissible evidence in court?

21   Arrange a visit to a Magistrates', Crown, or County Court.

Punishment

Before the nineteenth century, the only law-breakers who could expect imprisonment were debtors. Physical punishments such as flogging and the stocks were common, and over 200 crimes, such as pickpocketing, were punished by execution. Later transportation to the colonies was introduced for criminals. Today an offender is likely to receive one of the following sentences:

Absolute or conditional discharge
Binding over
Disqualification from driving
Fine
Care, supervision, or probation order
Suspended sentence
Attendance or detention centre
Borstal
Prison

Self-assessment questions

22   Find out what these punishments involve.

23   Which punishments require the offender to serve his sentence in an institution?

24   What are these institutions like?

What are the purposes of punishment?

Retribution
Society taking revenge for the crime 'an eye for an eye . . .'

Deterrence
To discourage people from committing the same crime again.

Prevention
To prevent the offender from committing more crimes, for example by detention.

Rehabilitation
To reform the law-breaker into an honest citizen.

The desired aim of the punishment will influence the form that it takes.

Self-assessment questions

25 What are the merits and demerits of:
    (i) Corporal punishment? (Abolished in 1948.)
    (ii) Capital punishment? (Abolished in 1965.)
26 For which types of crime might they be appropriate?
27 How effective are they as deterrents?

Civil liberties

The growth of computerized information systems and private security organizations, together with the introduction of special measures to deal with the situation in Northern Ireland, has led to concern over civil liberties. There have also been controversies over police powers to stop and search, the activities of the London-based Special Patrol Group, and the issuing of firearms. These matters must be seen against a background of increasingly stormy political confrontations and industrial conflicts, terrorism and violent crime.

Self-assessment questions

28 How do you explain these changes?
29 How far should the State's concern for law, order and security be allowed to infringe the legitimate and democratic rights of citizens?

Unlike countries such as the USA, Britain does not have a 'bill of rights' guaranteeing the freedoms to which citizens are entitled. However, Britain has accepted as binding the European Convention on Human Rights which includes the following:

(i)   Everyone's right to life shall be protected by law.
(ii)   No one shall be subjected to torture or to inhuman or degrading treatment or punishment.
(iii) Everyone has the right to liberty and security of person. No one shall be deprived of liberty save . . . in accordance with a procedure prescribed by law.
(iv)   Everyone who is arrested shall be informed promptly . . . of the reasons for his arrest and of any charge against him.
(v)   Everyone arrested or detained . . . shall be brought promptly before a judge . . . and shall be entitled to a trial within reasonable time or to release pending trial.
(vi)   Everyone is entitled to a fair and public hearing . . . by an independent and impartial tribunal.
(vii) Everyone has the right to:
       (a) Respect for his private and family life, his home and his correspondence.
       (b) Freedom of thought, conscience and religion.
       (c) Freedom of expression.
       (d) Freedom of peaceful assembly and to freedom of association with others, including the right to form and to join trade unions.
       (e) Free elections at reasonable intervals by secret ballot.
(viii) Every person is entitled to the peaceful enjoyment of his possessions.
(ix)   No person shall be denied the right to education.

The enjoyment of these rights is limited by certain restrictions 'necessary in a democratic society in the interests of national security, public safety, prevention of crime, protection of health and morals, and the rights and freedoms of others'. However, there should be no discrimination on any grounds such as sex, race, colour, language, religion, political or other opinion, national or social origin, property, birth, or other status.

Self-assessment questions

30 Do you think that these rights are respected at all times in Britain?

31 Do you think that we should be entitled to any additional rights (for example to work, to the highest attainable standards of physical and mental health, to guarantee access to information about decisions that affect our lives)?

32 Do you think that any of these rights is unreasonable?

14 Leisure and health

The aim of this section is to investigate changing patterns of leisure and its relationship with work, age, and drug-use. You will be encouraged to consider popular entertainment, holidays, socially accepted forms and harmful effects of drug-taking, and ways to improve your fitness and health.

Work and leisure

For some people 'work is its own reward': they obtain satisfaction and fulfilment from their occupation. Many others, however, only feel truly at ease and able to express their personality during their leisure time. They see work, not as an end in itself, but as a means towards something else: the money they earn not only pays for the necessities of life but also enables them to enjoy their free time.

The sociologist S. R. Parker has argued that the nature of a person's employment influences not only the degree of commitment to his employment, but also the way in which he spends his leisure time and what he expects from it. Parker suggests three different relationships of work and leisure:

Leisure as an extension of work

Some people allow their work to spill over into their leisure and a proportion of their free time will be taken up with things connected with work (for example the engineer reads technical journals at home or the teacher spends his Saturday mornings supervising the school football team). In so far as this behaviour is not motivated by the unwelcome intrusion of career pressures into leisure time, it reflects a positive commitment to this individual's occupation. He will probably see leisure as satisfying in a different way from work, but makes little distinction in his mind between these two spheres of his life.

Leisure as complementary to work

People who are indifferent to their occupation are not likely to have much to do with work-related matters during their spare time. Their central life interest tends to be their family and friends, and leisure is enjoyed because it is relaxing – a complete change from work.

Leisure as opposition to work

Workers in dangerous or unpleasant jobs (for example coal-miners, distant-water fishermen) want their free time to be a complete contrast. They see the purpose of their leisure as a compensation for the hardships of their employment: a period of recuperation from work that is physically or mentally damaging. They will try to emphasize the sharp distinction between work and leisure (for example different clothes). The contradictory attitude of some people is shown by the fact that they spend much of their leisure time in the company of their work mates talking about the jobs they hate.

The changing pattern of leisure

Self-assessment question

1 Contrast typical leisure activities during three periods of history: Tudor times; Victorian times; and the years between the world wars. How do these periods compare with the present day? Here are some notes to start you off.

Tudor times

The pre-industrial artisan probably had more free time than the modern employee. Popular amusements included:

fairs, plays, dancing
taverns
hunting and horse-racing
cruel entertainments such as cock-fighting and
   bull-baiting
rough and unruly games of football through the
   streets

Victorian times

The Industrial Revolution changed leisure patterns together with every other aspect of people's lives. The growth of towns led to the disappearance of open spaces and the worker who toiled for seventy hours, fifty-two weeks of the year, in a factory was often left too poor and exhausted to make much use of the leisure time that remained. During this period the railway, tram and bicycle greatly increased personal mobility and reductions in working hours (for example Ten Hours Act, 1847; Bank Holidays Act, 1871) allowed ordinary people a little more spare time.

All social classes met together in the sham splendour of the music hall, but generally they had little contact and their leisure activities were distinct and separate:

(i)   Working-class entertainment was typified by the cut-glass and mirrored gin palace and the rise of mass spectator sports, especially association football.

(ii) The respectable middle-class family enjoyed musical evenings, although in the 1880s the piano began to give way to the phonograph. For a week in the summer families took an annual holiday at one of the new seaside resorts.

(iii) The very rich 'leisure classes' went on a grand tour of the Continent and flocked to London for the summer season: several months of balls, receptions, croquet on the lawn, and being seen in fashionable places such as Royal Ascot and Henley Regatta.

Between the wars

Two technological developments revolutionized entertainment – the radio and the cinema (a fantasy-escape from the problems of the economic depression). The dance-hall continued to be immensely popular. On the eve of the Second World War, over half of the working population still did not receive a paid holiday, although the half-day Saturday was becoming common. While the middle-class enjoyed the new freedom provided by cheaper, mass-produced motor-cars, the working-class climbed aboard the 'charabanc' for a short excursion. A sign of the times was that William Butlin opened his first holiday camp at Skegness in 1937. This was also the period when cheap cosmetics were introduced and publicized in the mass-circulation newspapers that began to rely on advertising for their revenue.

Recent trends

Since the war, homes have generally become more comfortable with the gradual acquisition of durable consumer goods. The television set, in particular, has encouraged the shift towards home-centred entertainment and activities (symbolized by the off-licence, DIY and gardening).

Technology and changing social attitudes have combined to break the chains that tied women to the home and the never-ending drudgery of housework. The cooking range has given way to washing machines and vacuum cleaners. The development of 'convenience' foods, refrigerators and supermarkets – together with the trend to smaller families – has allowed women more leisure time.

The spread of car ownership has turned motoring into a major leisure activity (indeed, most families that drive out into the countryside never leave sight of their cars). At the same time, the development of group travel has significantly reduced the cost of going abroad for a holiday.

While there has been a steady decline in the numbers attending the cinema and football matches, actual participation in sport and recreation has

Table 26 *Participation in social and cultural activities: Britain, 1977 (during the four weeks prior to interview)*

Activity	Age 16 to 24		Age 45 to 59	
	Men	Women	Men	Women
	(percentage)		(percentage)	
Visit to a park	2	5	2	2
Outings (car, train, etc.)	5	3	3	2
Going to the cinema	28	27	5	5
Going to a pop concert	3	1	—	—
Going to the theatre/opera/ballet	3	6	4	7
Amateur music/drama	7	5	3	3
Going out for a meal/drink	83	79	70	58
Dancing	27	36	14	14
Visiting/entertaining relatives and friends	91	96	86	92
Social and voluntary work	6	5	9	11
Church going	1	2	2	2
Listening to records/tapes	90	88	59	59
Gardening	23	19	60	42
Games of skill	29	21	18	14
Needlework	2	45	2	54
DIY	41	19	55	24
Hobbies	17	4	11	3
Reading books	52	60	49	54
Bingo	4	8	7	14
Betting/pools	16	7	35	15

Source: General Household Survey 1977; Social Trends 1980

probably increased. There has been a great expansion in many leisure activities that were formerly the preserve of a rich minority: for example skiing, sailing, golf, squash.

Since the 1950s several distinctive youth styles have developed, all linked to patterns of leisure.

Television

Watching the television is the most popular leisure activity in Britain. One US survey has shown that more homes have a TV than indoor plumbing, and that by the time a person is sixteen he has spent more time watching television than he has spent in school. On average people spend about seven years of their life watching TV.

Self-assessment questions

2   (i) What are the main differences between the leisure patterns of men and women; and young people and older people?
  (ii) How do you explain them?
  (iii) Do these figures actually conceal differences by listing what are really distinct activities under the same heading (for example dancing)?

3 Design your own leisure survey to discover the activities of students in your class or college. If your college has a computer, it may be possible to programme it to correlate leisure activities with other factors (for example, age, sex, social class, job, income, tastes in music, fashion).

Self-assessment question

4 (i) Select a typical night's viewing and analyse the content of TV programmes according to the following scheme. Draw a table similar to Table 27 and shade in the period during which the programme is broadcast.

(ii) What pattern emerges?

(iii) What techniques do the TV companies employ to catch audiences early in the evening?

(iv) Would you like to see more programmes of a particular type?

Table 27

		5	6	7	8	9	10	11	12
						Time (p.m.)			
News/documentary/ current affairs	BBC 1								
	BBC 2								
	ITV								
	CHANNEL 4								
Serials	BBC 1								
	BBC 2								
	ITV								
	CHANNEL 4								
Series	BBC 1								
	BBC 2								
	ITV								
	CHANNEL 4								
Comedy	BBC 1								
	BBC 2								
	ITV								
	CHANNEL 4								
Children's programmes	BBC 1								
	BBC 2								
	ITV								
	CHANNEL 4								
Films and drama	BBC 1								
	BBC 2								
	ITV								
	CHANNEL 4								
Sport	BBC 1								
	BBC 2								
	ITV								
	CHANNEL 4								
Music	BBC 1								
	BBC 2								
	ITV								
	CHANNEL 4								
Education	BBC 1								
	BBC 2								
	ITV								
	CHANNEL 4								
Other programmes	BBC 1								
	BBC 2								
	ITV								
	CHANNEL 4								

Taking a gamble

Millions of people engage in some form of gambling – bingo, football pools, a flutter on the Grand National. Gambling is generally exciting. It is also about losing money: the speed with which it happens depends on luck, skill and the odds offered.

Self-assessment question

5 List as many forms of gamling as you can think of, and *rank* them according to the degree of skill that is required to win (for example playing a simple fruit machine requires no skill, card games usually a great deal).

The Royal Commission on Gambling, 1978, worked out the true odds of popular forms of betting. Table 28 refers to types of gambling where the punter bets against 'the house'. It shows the percentage of stake money that will be returned to the individual (with average luck and skill), who gambles over a long period of time.

Table 28

Form of gambling	Percentage of money returned as winnings, after tax
Casinos	97.5
Licensed cash bingo	95 (but only 80 if participation fees taken into account)
Off-course betting (greyhound and horse races)	81
Slot machines	70 (75 in licensed premises)
Public lotteries	50 (this is the maximum allowed by law – no minimum, so may be less)
Football pools	30

Football pools

What is the link between the rate at which cash is returned and the size of the potential prize? People are prepared to accept the low return from the

Figure 63 *Over the last few years there has been a marked decline in attendances at football matches and cinemas. However, both activities remain popular among young people*

pools because of the prospect of a dream win. But in order to win half a million pounds, it is necessary not only to successfully forecast the results of a certain combination of matches, but also to do so in a way that no other punters have done, since all those with maximum points share the first dividend.

Bingo

During the 1960s hundreds of cinemas were converted into bingo halls as the craze swept the country. Originally introduced into holiday camps as a way of keeping holiday-makers amused during wet weather, bingo established itself as a major entertainment for housewives. It is a safer gamble because you don't lose much money and glamorous prizes are offered. The rate of return on stake money is high: the proprietors make their profit from admission charges, refreshments and fruit machines. It is not only exciting, but a friendly social gathering.

Drugs

For many people leisure time is closely associated with the consumption of various kinds of drugs – during our breaks at work we drink coffee and smoke cigarettes, and in the evening we relax over a pint of beer. Next morning we take a few aspirins to ease our hangover.

Drugs are poisons. A large quantity of any drug will make you feel ill or even kill you, but used in relatively small amounts it may have a beneficial or pleasant effect. Why do people start using drugs? Why do people continue to use them despite their bad effects?

Drugs affect your body directly and indirectly. The immediate effects are usually on the blood, muscles and central nervous system. If used over a longer period of time they may have unpleasant and dangerous consequences. Not only can you permanently damage your body, but you may become addicted either physically or mentally.

After a time some drugs become a habit that you cannot do without. You may suffer withdrawal symptoms if the supply is suddenly stopped (anxiety, depression, illness, etc.).

Classification of drugs

Here is a rough guide to some different types of drugs classified according to their effects:

Stimulants
Caffeine (in tea and coffee)
Nicotine (in tobacco)
Amphetamines: Benzedrine
              Dexedrine;
              methedrine, etc.

Depressants
Sleeping pills
Tranquillizers: Valium; Librium.
Barbiturates: Mandrax;
              phenobarbitone;
              Nembutal;
              Amytal, etc.

Inebriants
Alcohol
Cannabis: marijuana (grass)
          hashish (pot)

Narcotics
Codeine
Opium
Morphine
Heroin
Cocaine (effect is a combination of stimulant and inebriant).

Psychedelics
LSD (acid)
Mescalin
Psilocybin (magic mushrooms)

Sniffers
Spirit glues
Methylated spirits
Cleaning fluids, aerosols, etc.

Table 29 *What's your poison?*

Drug	Legal use and supply	Condemned use	Common method of consumption; short term effects	Health hazards
Tobacco (nicotine)	The majority of people in Britain have smoked a cigarette during their lifetime. Widespread throughout the world. Sold in shops – two major manufacturers.	By children and in certain public places.	Inhaled: blood pressure rises and supply of oxygen to the brain reduced. Breathlessness, dizziness, stimulant.	Physical and psychological addiction. Cancer, bronchitis, ulcers, thrombosis. 100,000 tobacco-linked deaths per year in Britain.
Alcohol	Used by half the adult population in Britain. Widespread throughout the world. Tolerated use: social drinking and to relieve stress. Legal control: licensing laws; pubs and off-licences.	Public drunkenness, especially young people. Prohibition: USA 1919–33; some Moslem societies.	Ingested: relaxation, euphoria, impaired judgement and motor functions.	Addition: alcoholism. Brain and liver damage. 2,000 fatal road accidents a year in Britain. Absenteeism from work. Six per cent of men drink an amount which involves a risk of seriously damaging their health in the long term.
Barbiturates	Half a million regular users in Britain (usually middle-aged women). Doctors' prescriptions for tranquillizers and sleeping pills.	Young addicts injecting intravenously.	Ingested: capsule and tablet form. Slows heart and lowers blood pressure. Relaxation, relief of stress and anxiety.	Over 1000 suicides per year from overdose. Addictive: painful withdrawal symptoms (for example convulsions).
Amphetamines	100,000 regular users. Source: doctors' prescriptions (for example for slimmers). Given to 72 million troops during the Second World War; and to astronauts.	Black market: young people at parties, discos, etc.	Ingested (can be injected). Forces body to race at high speed for a long time; sense of well-being, sleeping difficulties, loss of appetite and later, depression.	Used in large amounts: anxiety, depression, hallucinations. Damage to liver, kidney, brain and blood vessels.

continued

Drug	Legal use and supply	Condemned use	Common method of consumption; short term effects	Health hazards
Cannabis	No legal use in Britain. 200 million users throughout the world – North Africa, India, South America. Obtained from Indian hemp plant: active ingredient called THC.	All in Britain but used by a minority of young people in Western societies. 25 million users in USA.	Small dose: sense of well-being, giggly and talkative. Heightened sensitivity to colour, sound, taste. Heavy dose: confusion, short term loss of memory, drowsiness. Reddening of eyes, increased heart rate. Inhaled (sometimes ingested).	No significant evidence. May lead to cigarette smoking, etc. Regular user needs smaller quantity to achieve same effect. Excessive use: possible brain damage.
LSD	Virtually none (some research/medical use). Synthetic chemical.	All (but used by a minority of middle-class youth in Western societies).	Ingested: capsules, tablets, paper squares, microdots, etc. Changes brain biochemistry: distorts/expands existing emotions (excitement, euphoria, anxiety, despair, etc.). Hallucinations, greater sensitivity to colour, etc.	Mental upheavals resulting from 'bad trips'. Possible accidents owing to distorted perceptions.
Opiates	Medical use for example morphine as pain killer. Headache tablets are very dilute form (Codeine). Registered heroin addicts can obtain supply by doctor's prescription.	Street addicts.	Injection (also inhaled by sniffing and smoking). Depressant: peaceful drowsiness. Tolerance develops. Larger doses may act as stimulant.	Addiction with severe withdrawal symptoms. Constipation, sexual impotence. Overdose, infection from unsterilized needles (hepatitis, tetanus). Adulterants. Life-style may lead to malnutrition, lowering resistance to disease.
Sniffers	Not illegal. Chemists and DIY shops	All.	Inhaled: intoxication, dizziness, nausea, headache, loss of appetite, coma. The effects of solvents occur and disappear very rapidly.	Tolerance but no addiction. Lung, liver, brain, blood damage. Accidental suffocation. Aerosols are extremely dangerous.

Do you really want to give up smoking?

If the answer is 'yes', it may help to identify the kind of smoker you are and the factors that motivate you to smoke.

Table 30

Do you smoke. . .	Factor	Alternative to smoking
to keep you from slowing down? to perk you up?	Stimulation.	Take moderate exercise. Drink tea or coffee. Breathing deeply may hold your desire to smoke in check.
because you enjoy the steps involved in lighting up, handling the cigarette and watching the smoke you exhale?	Handling.	Find alternative things to do with your hands (for example doodle, bite your nails). As a first step try switching to a pipe or an unlit cigarette.
because it is pleasurable? when you feel comfortable?	Relaxation.	Find some other satisfying activity (for example music, reading, TV, hobby).
when you feel angry? when you feel uncomfortable? when you feel depressed or worried?	Tension reduction.	Work out your frustration through physical activity (for example exercise). Try sweets instead, but beware of too many extra calories.
automatically, without being aware of it?	Habit.	Since you get no real satisfaction from smoking, giving up should be relatively easy. Watch out for 'trigger events' (for example having a cup of tea) that cause you to subconsciously reach for a cigarette. Throw away your cigarettes and matches.
because you get a craving for a cigarette when you haven't smoked for a while? because you find it unbearable when you run out of fags?	Psychological addiction.	Withdrawal symptoms are greatest here. The only way to give up is to stop in one go. If it is really painful, consult your doctor.

Giving up

Many smokers would like to stop but can't break the habit: they are addicted. The best advice is not to start: if you are not a smoker by the time you are twenty, the chances are that you never will be. But if you're already hooked, you will need a lot of will-power to kick the habit. It may help to remember that smokers are four times more likely to die from lung cancer than non-smokers and the earlier you started smoking, the greater the risks. If you stop today, it may take ten years before your body has cleaned itself up.

Self-assessment questions

6 Design an effective anti-smoking poster that can be displayed in your college.

7 Why do people start smoking?

Alcohol

About thirty-two million pints of beer are drunk in Britain every day: thirty gallons per year for every adult. Like tobacco, the drug alcohol is big business: over three-quarters of a million people are employed in the malting, brewing, distribution and sale of beer alone. Nine out of every ten pints of beer and lager are produced by the seven biggest brewers: Bass Charrington, Allied Breweries, Courage, Watney, Whitbread, Scottish & Newcastle and Guinness. All these companies sell beer under a variety of labels and, except Guinness, own thousands of public houses where their products are sold.

In order of increasing alchol content, the most popular alcoholic drinks are: beer and cider; wine; fortified wine (port, sherry, vermouth, etc.); spirits and liqueurs (whisky, gin, vodka, etc.). One shot of whisky is about as strong as half a pint of beer.

Alcohol slows down your metabolism (the complex chemical changes that occur in the body); it depresses the nervous system and weakens muscle control. A small amount of alcohol will help you relax and lose your inhibitions so that you may laugh more easily and say or do things that you really want. The drug will also make you feel sleepy, and impair your judgement, vision, balance and co-ordination. If you continue to drink beyond this stage, you may become aggressive or do things you later regret. The effects of drunkenness (alcohol poisoning) include loss of body control and memory, nausea and vomiting, headache and unconsciousness. These symptoms can continue for several hours in the form of a hangover. The use of large and regular amounts of alcohol can lead to addiction with severe withdrawal symptoms (trembling, anxiety) and to brain or liver damage.

Pubs

Most beer is drunk in pubs, which are used by ten million people each day. Pubs grew up after the Industrial Revolution as a warm, friendly and comfortable alternative to the drabness of workers' homes. They developed as centres for sports and social activities and convenient meeting places.

Self-assessment questions

8　(i)　How is beer made?

(ii)　What are its ingredients?

(iii)　What is the difference between tradiional (draught) and keg beer?

(iv)　Between beer and lager?

9　(i)　What is the image of the drinker portrayed in most alcohol advertising?

(ii)　How accurate is it?

(iii)　What are the most heavily advertised alcoholic drinks?

The Good Beer Guide published by CAMRA (Campaign for Real Ale) contains a great deal of interesting information on this subject.

Keeping fit

From around your mid-twenties your body mechanism will start slowing down and the earlier you start countering this the better. The physical activity that you are capable of in short bursts is a good deal above the level of your normal activity. Regular exercise can stretch your capacity and build up a reserve of energy for coping with extra strain. It will improve your health and help to prevent you getting fat.

Exercise can help to develop your:

(i)　Endurance by stretching the capacity of your heart and lungs.

(ii)　Suppleness by stretching your joints and also improve your co-ordination.

(iii)　Strength by building up your muscles.

Self-assessment question

10　Rate these exercises (out of five) according to how suitable they are for improving your endurance, suppleness and strength.

(i)　*Walking*　(must be really strenuous: leisurely walking is a useless exercise)

(ii)　*Cycling*　(stay alert for dangers from motor vehicles)

(iii)　*Swimming*　(don't swim when there is

no one about. Be careful in the sea)
  (iv) *Jogging* (can be boring)
   (v) *Keep-fit exercises* (try the Royal Canadian Air Force system)
  (vi) *Yoga* (local education authorities often run classes)
 (vii) *Sports* (for example football, squash. Must be strenuous and played regularly)
(viii) *Dancing* (fun too)

How long will you live?

This table is only a rough guide to how long you can expect to live, taking into account aspects of your lifestyle and personality. The estimates of how much these factors will lengthen or shorten your life are only approximations, but the risks and good habits are real enough.

If you are aged between 16 and 25, your life expectancy is about 71 years.

Cumulative totals	
personal life expectancy	*years lost/ not gained*

* If you are female, add 3 years.
* If your intelligence is above average, add 2 years.

Smoking
* If you smoke more than 40 cigarettes a day, deduct 12 years.
* If you smoke 20–40 cigarettes, deduct 7 years.
* If you smoke less than 20 cigarettes, deduct 2 years.

Food
* If you stop eating before you are full, add 1 year.
* If you are overweight, deduct 2 years.
* If you eat a lot of fruit and vegetables, add 1 year.
* If you eat a lot of animal fats, deduct 1 year.

Drink
* If you drink 2 pints of beer a day, add 3 years.
* If you don't drink as much as 2 pints a day add 1 year.
* If you drink more than 4 pints a day, deduct 8 years.

Exercise
* If you drive or ride to work, deduct 1 year.
* If you cycle or walk to work, add 1 year.
* If you take at least 15 minutes of vigorous exercise at least twice a week, add 3 years.

Sleep
* If you sleep in once a week, add 1 year.
* If you relax before you go to bed, add 1 year.
* If you sleep more than ten hours or less than five each night, deduct 3 years.

Home
* If you live in a town, deduct 1 year.
* If you live in the countryside, add 1 year.

Family history
* Add 1 year for any grandparent (or great-grandparent) in your family who has lived to be 80.
* Add ½ year for any relative who has lived to be 70.
* Deduct 4 years for any relative who died of a heart attack, stroke, or arteriosclerosis before the age of 50.

Cumulative	totals
personal life	*years lost/*
expectancy	*not gained*

Job
* If you are a professional, add 1½ years.
* If you are a skilled technician, add 1 year.
* If you are a semi-skilled worker, deduct 4 years.
* If you are a labourer, deduct 4 years.
* If you have a desk job, deduct 2 years.
* If you are not a labourer but your job involves a fair amount of physical exercise, add 2 years.
* If your job involves piecework, deadlines, or some kind of payment by results, deduct 2 years.
* If you normally work overtime at least once a week, deduct 1 year.

Stress
* If you regard yourself as ambitious or competitive, deduct 2 years.
* If you are impatient or things or people make you angry, deduct 2 years.
* If you are married and living with your partner, add 1 year.
* If you have one or two close friends in whom you can confide everything, add 1 year.
* If you have recently experienced a major disturbance in your life (for example death in the family, changed job, moved to new home, serious injury, new baby), deduct 2 years.
* If you have recently experienced an emotional upset (for example trouble with your boss, break-up with your girl-friend), deduct ½ year.

Self-assessment question

11 What changes should you make to your life-style in order to increase your chances of survival?

15 World conflict

The aim of this section is to help you to understand some of the political and social changes that are occurring in the world. You will be encouraged to consider the problems of economic under-development and the danger of nuclear war.

Conflicts around the world

The press, radio and TV present a picture of the world as being in a constant state of tension and conflict. Allowing for the fact that news reporting is a highly selective business, the media image does reflect reality.

The Second World War claimed fifteen million military and over thirty-six million civilian deaths. Every year since 1945 there has been a 'small' war somewhere, and between 1955 and 1980 over 120 armed conflicts in sixty-five countries have claimed twenty-five million lives. While the situation has frequently been complicated by the direct or indirect intervention of the major powers, these conflicts have taken two distinct forms:

(i) *Conventional wars* between neighbouring states.
(ii) *Liberation struggles* within a country fought between government forces and internal 'insurgents' using guerrilla tactics.

Add to this the fact that, across the planet, there are more dictatorships than elected governments and that military coups are the most common means by which rulers come to power.

An unstable world torn by wars, revolutions and the arms race; political rivalries between and within nations fuelled by economic difficulties – are we locked into a nightmare action-replay of the conditions that produced this century's previous world wars?

On an international level, these conflicts have two major dimensions:

(i) Between the *Western bloc* led by the USA and the *Eastern bloc* led by the USSR.
(ii) Between the rich, white, industrialized nations of the northern hemisphere and the poor, coloured, under-developed nations of the southern hemisphere.

Why do these conflicts occur? A number of explanations have been suggested: religion, race, class, imperialism, colonialism, communism and several other '-isms'. The reality is often a complex combination of several factors and the most obvious cause may conceal deeper, underlying issues. Liam de Paor begins his book *Divided Ulster* by saying: 'In Northern Ireland Catholics are Blacks who happen to have white skins. . . .' This is an over-simplification but it is better than to see the conflict '. . . in terms of religion. Catholics and Protestants are not quarrelling with one another . . . because of matters of theology or faith. There is no burning urge on either side to convert the other to the one true faith. . . . The Northern Ireland problem is a colonial problem, and the "racial" distinction . . . between the colonists and the natives is expressed in terms of religion.'

Self-assessment questions

1 (i) Analyse the coverage of international affairs in the press.
   (ii) Which newspaper provides the most information?
   (iii) What kind of issues are dealt with?
   (iv) How does press coverage compare with TV news programmes?

Latin America

1973 President Allende of Chile, the first Marxist to win an election in a Western country, overthrown by a military coup backed by the CIA and US multi-national companies. All political and trade union activity banned; strict censorship imposed; and widespread violations of human rights.

1976 In Argentina a military junta seized power amid increasing disorder and economic crisis. Over the next three years 30,000 people disappeared as a result of political kidnapping and murder, mainly by right-wing groups.

1979 After seventeen years of guerrilla war, Nicaragua's President Somoza was forced to flee the country. The victorious left-wing 'Sandinistas' nationalized much of industry, restored civil rights, replaced the army with a people's militia, and conducted a successful literacy campaign.

1980 Civil war in El Salvador. The ruling junta was aided by the USA but guerrillas increased their control of rural areas.

1981 Concern in Nicaragua about counter-revolution by exiled members of Somoza's National Guard supported by the USA. Opposition protested over the postponement of elections.

1982 Mexico's 80 billion dollar debts threatened an international banking crisis. Many underdeveloped countries were forced to 'reschedule' their debts and adopt austerity measures.

Partly to distract attention from Argentina's growing labour unrest, and after unsuccessful negotiations over a long-standing claim for sovereignty, General Galtieri invaded the Falkland Islands. In June a British Task Force successfully recovered the dependency.

Northern Ireland

1969 Agitation for civil rights by the Catholic minority led to a violent response from Protestants and the intervention of British troops.

1972 Direct rule from London introduced.

1974 An attempt at power-sharing between representatives of the two communities failed in the face of Protestant opposition.

1981 Hunger strikes by Republican prisoners failed to win 'political status'.

1983 Terrorism and sectarian violence continues.

Poland

1970, 1976 and **1980** The introduction of higher food prices led to waves of unrest spreading from the Baltic port of Gdansk. Violent demonstrations and factory occupations forced the Government to make concessions. They permitted independent trade unions: 'Solidarity'.

1981 As demands for higher wages and shorter hours developed into protests against the economic and political management of the country martial law was imposed and all trade union activity outlawed. Sporadic disturbances have continued.

Southern Africa

1972 Guerrilla war began in Zimbabwe. The white minority had rebelled seven years earlier when Britain made independence conditional on progress towards African majority rule.

1974 After years of costly wars in its African colonies, an army revolt sparked off a revolution in Portugal. The new government immediately granted independence for Mozambique and Angola.

1976 In Namibia SWAPO began an armed struggle for independence from South Africa. Meanwhile in Soweto police crushed riots by black youths, leaving over 400 dead.

1980 After a conference in London, elections were held in Zimbabwe. Robert Mugabe's party won and the country became legally independent. Factional differences between former guerrillas have continued.

1981 An increase in guerrilla attacks in South Africa by the African National Congress. Opposition grows to 'apartheid' – white supremacy based on the principle of separate development of racial groups – but the mass of discriminatory laws, detention without trial, banning of African political organizations, and the forced removal of Africans from some areas continues. So do long-distance raids by South African forces on guerrilla bases in neighbouring territories.

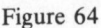

Figure 64

Afghanistan

78 A military coup installed a revolutionary government whose position was weakened by factional disputes and internal purges. The new regime was soon fighting traditionalist Moslem tribesmen whose opposition was aggravated by the brash implementation of reforms.

82 The regime relies heavily on Soviet military aid. 100,000 Russians are in the country to help keep order. Fighting continues.

Iran

1979 The Shah's dictatorship overthrown and Ayatollah Khomeini returned from exile to lead the Islamic revolution.

1980 A border dispute with Iraq blew up into a full-scale war, but drags on in stalemate. Also fighting with Kurdish rebels as ethnic minorities press their demands for regional independence.

1981 Thousands of political executions, mostly of left-wing militants.

South-east Asia

1975 Vietnam reunified for the first time in twenty-two years after eleven years of war. The South Vietnam regime and the USA had been defeated by North Vietnam and insurgent guerrilla forces. Victory also for the Kymer Rouge rebels in Kampuchea.

1976 The death of Mao Tse-Tung, leader of China since the revolution of 1948. His successors have adopted more conservative policies and improved relations with the West.

1978 Exodus of about 300,000 Vietnamese refugees, mostly ethnic Chinese: the 'boat people'.

1979 Civil war in Kampuchea between the forces of Pol Pot (supported by China) and Samrin (backed by Vietnam). Vietnamese intervention in the conflict provoked a punitive attack by China on Northern Vietnam. Heng Samrin set up a new government, promised to restore freedom, and claimed Pol Pot was responsible for three million deaths by murder, famine, and disease. Resistance to his rule continues in the countryside.

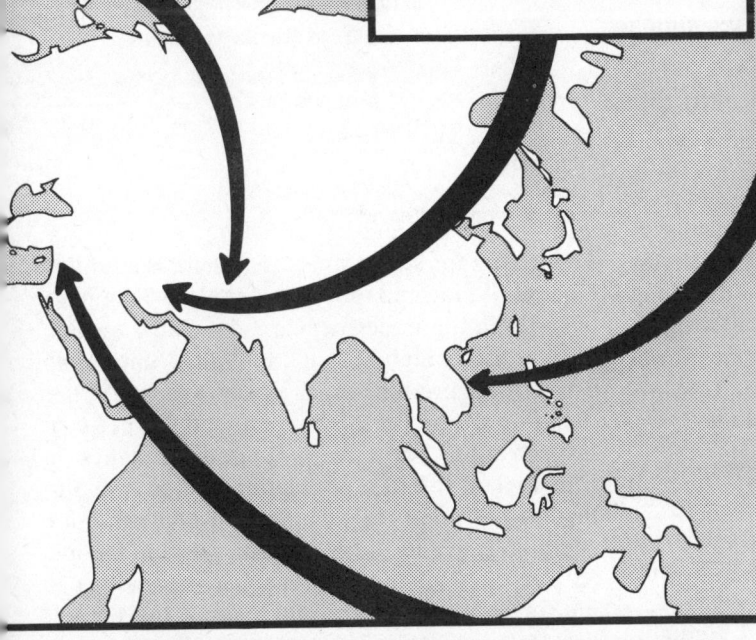

Middle East

After 1945 Many Jewish refugees arrived in British-controlled Palestine. A United Nations resolution called for partition into two states: one Arab and one Jewish. The Arabs rejected this solution. When fighting between the two groups died down in 1949, Israel controlled three-quarters of Palestine. The rest was incorporated into adjoining states and many Arabs became refugees. As a result of wars with Arab states in 1956, 1967 and 1973, Israel also occupied the Jordan West Bank, Gaza Strip, and Sinai. The Palestine Liberation Organization (PLO) was founded to fight for a Palestinian homeland.

1975 Civil war in Lebanon between right-wing Christians and left-wing Moslems. Beirut had become the headquarters of the PLO, and Southern Lebanon was occupied briefly by Israel in retaliation for PLO cross-border raids. Intervention by Syria put a temporary stop to the fighting.

1979 President Sadat of Egypt concluded a peace treaty with Israel that secured Israeli withdrawal from Sinai. This agreement was denounced as a sell-out of Palestinian aspirations by other Arab states. In 1981 Sadat was assassinated by Moslem fundamentalists.

1982 Fighting flares up again in Lebanon. Israel occupies Beirut, defeats the PLO, and supports Lebanese Christian forces – such as those of Major Haddad, responsible for massacres in Palestinian refugee camps.

2   (i)   Identify the world's 'trouble spots'.
(ii)   What do you think are the causes of conflict?
(iii)   What forces are on each side?
(iv)   Who do you support and why?

Development and under-development

On a personal level this inequality is reflected in our quality of life. The average inhabitant of the North consumes thirty times as much as a person in the poor world. The sixteen million babies who are born in the rich world each year have four times as much impact on world resources as the 109 million babies born in the South.

It has been estimated that an adult's healthy diet will contain at least 2350 kilo-calories and 70 grams of protein per day. If you fall permanently below this level, as do more than 500 million poor people in Asia, Africa and Latin America, you won't automatically drop dead, but you will suffer from malnutrition. We are accustomed to seeing horrific pictures of people dying from starvation on the TV, but there are tens of millions of children who have irreversible brain damage caused by protein deficiency during gestation and infancy.

If you are a poor person in the Third World, you are more likely to:

(i)   Die soon after birth: infantile mortality rates are similar to Europe before the Industrial Revolution.

(ii)   Be less physically developed and mentally alert.

(iii)   Be less resistant to parasitic and infectious diseases. People who eat a monotonous diet are likely to be deficient in some protein, vitamin, or mineral and so suffer from a disease like kwashiorkor, marasmus, goitre, pellagra and beriberi. Add to this the strength-sapping effects of malaria, bilharzia and yellow fever.

(iv)   Be one of the 70 million who are so severely undernourished that they are using up their bodily reserves of protein and literally starving.

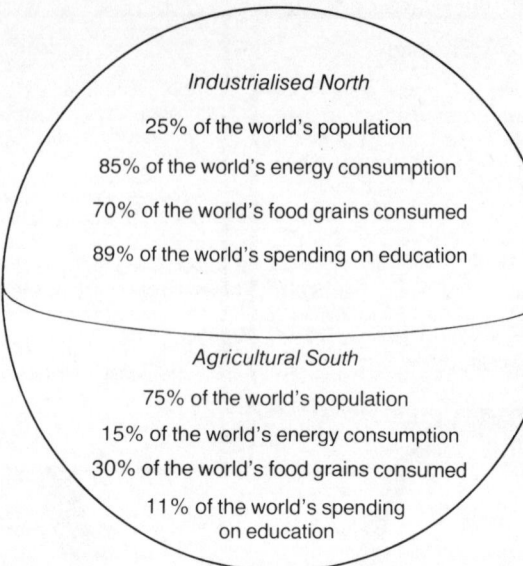

Industrialised North

25% of the world's population

85% of the world's energy consumption

70% of the world's food grains consumed

89% of the world's spending on education

Agricultural South

75% of the world's population

15% of the world's energy consumption

30% of the world's food grains consumed

11% of the world's spending on education

Figure 65

Why do people starve?

The reason for starvation is that there is a limited amount of food and too many people around, particularly in the under-developed countries where birth rates are highest – right? *Wrong*! Since 1945 world food production has been growing *faster* than population (at 2.8 per cent and 2.0 per cent respectively). There were periodic famines in China when it had a population of 500 millions, but now it manages to feed 800 millions quite adequately. The 13.5 million Dutch people (density: 326 inhabitants per square kilometre) do not suffer from malnutrition: many of the 5.5 million Bolivians do (density: five people per square kilometre).

The birth rates in the under-developed countries are higher than in the developed world, being similar to those in Europe 150 years ago during the Industrial Revolution. The reasons are the same:

(i)   High infantile mortality (children have a 50 per cent chance of surviving to their fifth birthday).

(ii)   Children can contribute to the family income at an early age.

(iii)   Outside the centrally-planned countries, there are no old age pensions, health insurance or social security. The family is the only support in times of need, so the bigger the better.

Ambitious birth-control programmes in the Third World will continue to fail as long as poverty and insecurity persist. But if:

Living standards rise → health improves → death rates fall → birth rates fall.

There will be a time-lag in the short run, while parents get used to the fact that their children will survive, during which rapid population growth occurs.

So why do people starve? The reasons are:

The poor don't have enough land
Although 80 per cent of the population of Asia and 95 per cent in parts of Africa live in the countryside, a large proportion have no land or the land is insufficient to grow enough food to feed their families adequately. In South America the richest 17 per cent of landowners control 90 per cent of all the land, while the poorest third of the rural population have to share only 1 per cent of the total crop land. The large landholdings produce the least food: the labour-intensive and lovingly tended small plots of Colombia produce fourteen times as much food per acre as the vast estates (latifundia). It is not that the poor are lazy or backward: they just don't have anything to work on.

The poor don't have enough money
Averages are misleading. The average Brazilian may consume 2620 kilo-calories per day, but this figure conceals the fact that the poor in North East Brazil get only 1240 while the rich of Rio de Janeiro stuff themselves with 4290. The rich continue to eat during periods of shortage, when high food prices are boosted by smuggling, hoarding and the black market.

Planned scarcity
The governments of the advanced capitalist countries encourage a policy of systematic non-production, hoarding, and even destruction of food when it is necessary to maintain price levels.

During the late 1960s and early 1970s, four major cereal producers took one-third of their grain out of production.

Cash-crop economies
Many under-developed countries have been turned into suppliers of raw materials and foodstuffs for the industrial nations. Instead of producing food to eat themselves, crops are grown – often on huge plantations – for export. These cash crops may be non-edible (cotton, rubber, sisal) or edible but of no food value (tea, coffee). Even when they are edible (sugar, bananas, peanuts), they are never consumed by the growers. The under-developed countries have virtually no choice about this situation: they must earn foreign currency to pay for their imports. Except for the OPEC countries (Organization of Petroleum Exporting Countries), under-developed economies have very little muscle in the world market and prices for their products have fallen in relation to manufactured goods. Over a period of time a country may need to produce twice as much to buy the same tractor. And if Brazil, Central African Republic, Colombia, Costa Rica, Ecuador, Ethiopia, Guatemala, Uganda, etc. all try to increase their coffee production to earn more, they will only succeed in causing a glut and driving down the price.

Wars and natural disasters
We often read or hear of spectacular famines following wars, droughts, floods and earthquakes. Under-developed countries are usually located in areas that are prone to natural disasters, but it is not these events that cause the starvation. It is rather that under-developed countries have economies and social systems that cannot handle extra burdens. The USA and USSR can deal with a typhoon or volcanic eruption without the disastrous consequences that would arise in Africa, Latin America or Asia.

But aren't things getting better?

Certainly there have been improvements, but under-developed countries are actually getting worse off compared to the advanced nations.

Table 31

		Population	Income per capita (US dollars)		
			1975	1985 (estimate)	Increase
Under-developed countries	poorest	1200 million	150	180	20 per cent
	better off	900 million	950	1350	42 per cent
Developed countries		700 million	5500	8100	47 per cent

What about new technology?

The Green Revolution is the name given to the spread of new crops, especially grains and rice, with the potential of much higher yields. However, they are less resistant to disease than the old varieties and so need heavy doses of fertilizer, herbicides, pesticides and fungicides; improved irrigation; and a whole range of mechanical implements (tractors, high pressure sprayers, dryers, etc.).

The Green Revolution has encouraged the cultivation of cash-crop rather than subsistence crops and has impoverished those small farmers who cannot afford to buy the new machinery, etc. Their plots have been absorbed into the large landholdings and they have either become landless labourers or migrated to the towns in search of work. The population of Lima in Peru, for instance, has exploded from 0.6 million in 1940 to 3.5 million in 1975.

In many under-developed countries new technology has been associated with large international companies (called 'agribusiness' in the USA). Attracted by low wages and tax concessions, they have obtained much of the best land and use energy-intensive methods to grow entirely for export.

A major reason for the protein shortage in the South is the nature of *our* diet in the North. We insist on getting most of our protein in the form of meat, eggs and dairy products. To do this the North outbids the South for any available grain surplus and then feeds it to our livestock. This is a very inefficient way of obtaining protein as it takes over 10 kg of vegetable protein to produce half a kilogram of meat protein. Add to this the fact that more fertilizer is used on golf courses and lawns in the rich countries than on agriculture in under-developed countries. Our cats and dogs are better fed than millions of Third World children.

It has been argued that a major cause of the civil rights campaign in the USA was that during the 1950s black people saw for the first time the sort of life-style that whites enjoyed and began to demand the same. In the 1980s it will be possible to transmit television programmes to any part of the world via satellite. When gathered round their village TV, what will poor people of the Third World think when they are told that a chocolate bar 'could mean the end of hunger between meals'?

What about aid?

The United Nations has set the industrialized nations the target of devoting 0.7 per cent of the GNP to foreign aid. Britain has achieved about half this amount, equivalent to about 25 pence per week for each of us. About two-thirds of this aid is 'tied' to the purchase of British goods and services. Much of the rest goes to paying the wages of British experts and consultants who provide 'technical co-operation' to the under-developed countries.

The offer to give or the threat to withdraw aid is often used by the rich nations as a weapon of foreign policy. An official responsible for the administration of US aid once commented: 'A lot of criticism of foreign aid is because the critic thought the object was to get economic growth, and this was not the objective at all.' As President Kennedy explained: 'Foreign aid is a method by which the US maintains a position of influence and power around the world, and sustains a good many countries which would definitely collapse, or pass into the Communist bloc.'

Under-developed countries do not receive aid on equal terms: in 1977 India got $1.60 per person and Israel $226. Neither are the sums substantial: Jamaica earns fifteen times more from its exports than it receives in all forms of aid. Much of this money then flows back to the rich North in the form of repayments on earlier loans. The poor nations have needed to borrow heavily: they invest about 15 per cent of their GNP, much more than the rich countries.

Self-assessment questions

3 Make a list of everything you have eaten during the last twenty-four hours. Be as specific as possible (that is, did you put sugar in your tea? Were your chips cooked in vegetable or ground nut oil?).

4 Try to work out what processed food-stuffs contain (for example, breakfast cereals are mainly maize/wheatbran/rice and sugar; a chocolate bar may contain milk, cocoa, raisins, and nuts). The ingredients are often listed on the packet, in descending order of quantity.

5 Find out where these products are likely to come from (the country of origin is printed on the label of many tinned foods). Which items are imported? Britain imports about half its food requirements. Do they come from developed or under-developed areas?

6 Imagine you are the president of an under-developed country. What would you do to develop your country? What are the major problems you are likely to encounter? How could these be overcome?

7 What practical things can you do to help? You are not responsible for world hunger and so don't have any reason to feel guilty about it. But you live in a relatively affluent society that benefits from relations with the Third World.

8 Discuss with your class ways in which you can actually *do* something directly to help. Try to come up with something more original than a conscience-easing donation to Oxfam or War on Want (although *organizing* a collection is better than nothing). How can you make sure that the 'right people' benefit?

The arms race

It has been estimated that it would cost about £10 billion a year to provide everyone in the world with adequate food, water, health, education and housing. That is a lot of money: about as much as the world spends on arms every two weeks.

Since the development of the 'Cold War' during the 1950s, world conflict has happened against a background of antagonism between the two economic and political superpowers: the USA and USSR. During the early 1970s tension relaxed during a period of 'detente' with moves towards the limitation of the arms race. More recently relations have deteriorated and the basis of peaceful coexistence has appeared more fragile.

Self-assessment question

9 (i) What is the reason for the rivalry between the West and the East?
(ii) Does either side want to dominate the world?
(iii) If so, why?

The search for ever more deadly weapons almost defies logic. The nuclear competitors have stockpiled the equivalent of 20 tons of TNT (trinitrotoluene) for every person on earth: enough explosives to kill every single person 50,000 times over. Even the precarious nuclear balance between America and Russia is threatened by constant development of new weapons systems.

What would nuclear war be like?

Nearly twenty years ago the BBC banned a film called *The War Game* which showed the consequences of a nuclear attack on Britain because it was likely to cause undue alarm to the population. The prospects certainly are alarming.

Commenting upon the effects of even a limited nuclear strike on this country, Lord Zuckerman (the Government's chief scientific adviser 1964–71) said: 'It is still inevitable that were military installations rather than cities to become the objectives of nuclear attack, millions, even tens of millions of civilians would be killed, whatever the proportion of missile sites, airfields, armament plants, ports and so on that would be destroyed.'

We cannot say for sure, but a full-scale attack would probably result in 20–35 million casualties, depending on our degree of preparation. What are your chances of survival? To estimate these you will need to know:

  (i)   The enemy's probable targeting strategy.

  (ii) The likely size of warheads used.

 (iii) The immediate effects of a nuclear explosion: light-flash, blast, fire-storms.

 (iv) The delayed effects: radiation fall-out.

The vocabulary of nuclear war

Strategic weapons
Inter-continental missiles of immense destructive power which may be submarine-launched or sited in silos behind the Urals or in the US mid-west.

Theatre weapons
Long, medium and short range bombs and missiles which may be carried on aircraft or submarines, permanently sited, or moved around on mobile launch platforms.

Tactical weapons
Small, battlefield nuclear devices: land-mines and artillery shells. Also the neutron bomb.

Conventional weapons
Non-nuclear weapons such as nerve gas bombs.

Mutual assured destruction (MAD)
A strategy that sees nuclear weapons as a deterrent to aggression because neither side could expect to 'win' a nuclear war. If one side launched a pre-emptive 'first strike', the other would still have enough undamaged missiles left to destroy the enemy's cities.

Limited nuclear war
A strategy that envisages a short war using theatre weapons, probably with Europe as the battleground. Here strategic weapons are held in reserve for a 'second strike' if the conflict cannot be resolved within a few days.

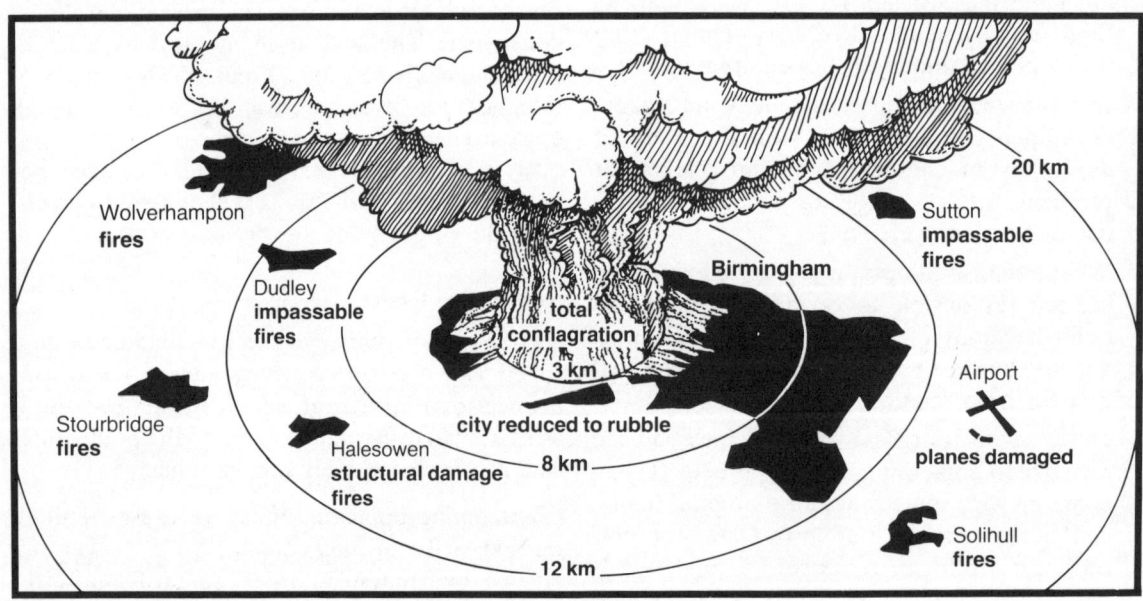

Figure 66   *The likely effect of a one-megaton bomb dropped on the centre of Birmingham*

Preparing for a nuclear attack

The Government has contingency plans for a possible Russian nuclear attack on Britain. Official expectations are that the target would be a single city with lower yield weapons aimed at military and other bases. The city attacked is unlikely to be London because the capital contains the government leaders who must be preserved so that they can make the decision to surrender. In 1945 the Americans did not use their atom bomb on Tokyo because they needed the Japanese Government intact in order to end the war. It is more probable that Birmingham or Manchester would be on the receiving end of a nuclear strike of between one and twenty megatons. Those who survived the initial attack would still have to deal with fall-out radiation; millions of dead and wounded; refugees from the desolated regions; and the dislocation of food, energy, and raw material supplies.

In 1980 the Government took the decision to spend £6000 millions on the Trident missile as a replacement for the Polaris system. Among other possible uses, this sum could have provided shelters for the one million households most at risk. America, Russia, Sweden and Switzerland have plans to evacuate whole cities or ensure that the population is adequately protected by purpose-built shelters. In Britain, on the other hand, a few days before a possible attack people will be issued with a booklet that explains how to make a do-it-yourself shelter from planks, sandbags and furniture (see Figure 67).

If you lack confidence in the ability of your home-made shelter to withstand the holocaust, you may invest in a luxury model for the price of a modest detached house. Underground bunkers already exist for senior politicians, civil servants and local officials who will form a post-war military government to deal with the inevitable civil disturbances. It is uncertain what they will rule because most of the workplaces and crops above ground will have been destroyed or contaminated. The Cambridge County Council post-attack plan seems to envisage a situation similar to a feudal society when it states: 'Large numbers of people

Figure 67   *Building your own shelter: use tables if they are large enough and surround them with heavy furniture filled with sand or earth, etc.*

may have to be assembled and allocated to tasks normally undertaken by machines: field cultivation and harvesting.'

Any nation that possesses nuclear weapons must be prepared to use them and to receive them.

Self-assessment questions

10   Are the risks 'acceptable'?

11   Are you prepared to endorse nuclear retaliation against 'innocent' members of the enemy's population (for example children, the aged)?

12   Are surrender and occupation preferable to massive destruction?

13   Is there an alternative to the arms race as a means of achieving peaceful coexistence?

14   What can *you* do about it anyway?

Scenario for 1990

What new developments are likely during the next ten years? It has become popular among political scientists to write scenarios for the future (a scenario is the script for a drama). We have produced our own vision of the future based on possible world developments. If you think that it seems improbable, just compare it with the 'unlikely' events that occurred during the 1970s. While none of our predictions for the 1990s is totally implausible, they are still only possible directions in which the world drama might unfold.

The Peking Conference of Oppressed Nations declares

We are united in our aim to redistribute wealth away from the plundering super-powers of West and East in favour of the poor and weak

A Russian-backed coup d'état to overthrow the Chinese leadership ends in chaos and China occupies Mongolia

As unemployment grows to 30 per cent, the USA and EEC impose a total ban on imports from Japan. Datsun cars and Sanyo TVs are burned in the streets. As foreign trade collapses, Japan is unable to pay for its massive food imports. With bread riots in Tokyo, Japan looks with envy towards the food surplus of Australia

Cuban volunteers spearhead the African guerrilla army forces that capture Johannesburg. White settlers fight a rear-guard action around Cape Town. Millions of European refugees return to Britain and Holland

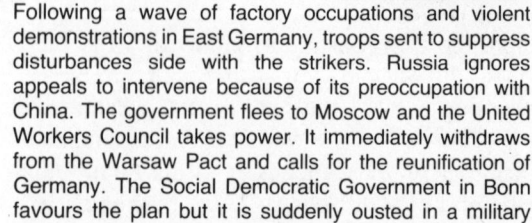

Following a wave of factory occupations and violent demonstrations in East Germany, troops sent to suppress disturbances side with the strikers. Russia ignores appeals to intervene because of its preoccupation with China. The government flees to Moscow and the United Workers Council takes power. It immediately withdraws from the Warsaw Pact and calls for the reunification of Germany. The Social Democratic Government in Bonn favours the plan but it is suddenly ousted in a military take-over by West German generals

Northern Ireland is near to civil war after an upsurge of communal violence. The Anglo-Irish all-party talks chaired by US President Patrick O'Connelly end in deadlock. United Nations forces are flown in to separate warring factions and replace British troops. The army of the Irish Republic invades Armagh and Fermanagh to protect Catholics. Then the British Prime Minister receives an ultimatum from the 'Knights of King William'

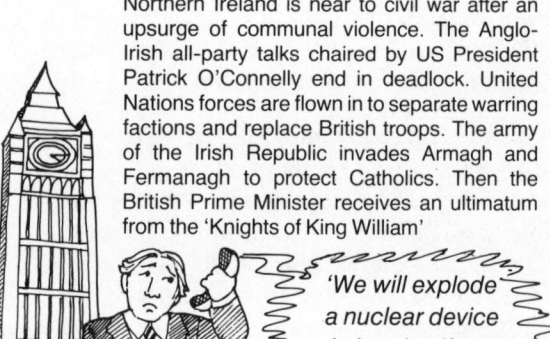

'We will explode a nuclear device in London if you betray the protestant cause!'

Fuel rationing has been imposed in the industrial nations since the energy crisis worsened. The United Islamic Arab Federation declares a total boycott on oil sales to the West until they receive compensation for past exploitation of their lands by multi-national corporations. Israeli commandos seize the main oil fields and hold them against sabotage until relieved by a US Task Force. Russia and China unite to threaten nuclear war unless America withdraws within twenty four hours

The world holds its breath

Figure 68

Self-assessment questions

15 Write a number of your own scenarios that outline the possible development of conflict on a world scale for the next decade. These must be based on realistic assumptions about areas of tension.

16 Consider the most 'optimistic' and the most 'pessimistic' outcomes for each of the following:
  (i) Rising expectations of the poor South.
  (ii) Food shortage.
  (iii) The development of the world economy.
  (iv) The depletion of oil reserves.
  (v) Political revolution.
  (vi) Escalation of the arms race and the spread of nuclear weapons.

16 The future

The aim of this section is to review some of the changes that may occur during your lifetime. You will be encouraged to consider both the uncertainties associated with prediction and a few of the problems that we may face before the end of the century.

Forecasting the future

Prediction is an unreliable and tricky business, usually associated with astrological zodiacs and crystal balls. Nevertheless, since you may be around for another fifty years or more, it is important to have an idea of what to expect in the future as a basis for making decisions. Forecasts come in all shapes and sizes:

(i) Fewer workers will be needed in the future because more jobs will be done by robots.

(ii) Aliens from outer space will land on our planet and exterminate all human life.

(iii) By the year 2000 the world's population will be over 7000 million.

(iv) A British football team will win the next World Cup.

(v) There will be a war between America and Russia by the end of the century.

(vi) You will catch cold if you don't wear your vest.

Many predictions merely reflect our hopes and fears; some are likely – although by no means inevitable – on the basis of past social or technical developments; and others are reliable assumptions founded on sound scientific work. You should be able to distinguish between wild guesses and realistic forecasts obtained by projecting present trends into the future. However, this process of extrapolation is fraught with difficulties. During the latter part of the last century, London faced severe problems arising from the use of increasing numbers of horses for transport. It was predicted that if this trend continued the capital would eventually become clogged into immobility under a pile of manure. Fortunately the development of the internal combustion engine forestalled this disaster.

Self-assessment question

1 How does *probability theory* help you to estimate the likelihood of something happening?

Another kind of forecast involves a change in our existing behaviour or attitudes, and can only happen if enough people work together to make it happen. It will soon be technically possible to eliminate the drudgery of work, but whether this happens depends upon political and social changes. The act of making a prediction may actually influence an outcome: the forecast that there will be a shortage of a particular product often results in panic-buying. On the other hand, predictions that the blue whale and tiger will soon become extinct may stimulate action to protect endangered species. When is a forecast likely to make the predicted outcome more or less probable?

People who make forecasts are often left with egg on their faces when a contrary outcome actually occurs. But don't be deterred: a lot of famous people have been wrong in the past.

'I see no reason to believe that these machines [railway locomotives] will ever force themselves into general use.'
The Duke of Wellington

'We of the older generation will not live to see the revolution.'
Vladimir Lenin

'I am of the opinion that generations will pass before man lands on the moon and, should he eventually succeed, there is little chance that he would return to earth to tell of his experiences.'
Sir Harold Spencer Jones, Astronomer Royal, 1957

'I have always consistently opposed high tension and alternating current systems of electric lighting, not only on account of danger, but also of unreliability and unsuitability for any general electric distribution system.'
Thomas Edison

'The bomb will never go off and I speak as an expert in explosives.'
Adviser to the President of the USA about the atomic bomb, 1945

Transport and communications

As it becomes relatively easier to transmit information, there will be less reason to transport ourselves around the planet. It will be possible, for instance, to sit at home and order goods from the supermarket using a direct computer link. The store's computer will debit your account at the bank and instruct the automated warehouse to dispatch your goods.

It will be common for homes to contain a communication and information centre (comprising computer keyboard, TV console, camera, microphone, video-recorder and hard-copy print-out) linked to a central electronic data bank. There will even be small, portable computer terminals with flat-screen visual display units that plug into any telephone line and allow you to talk, via satellite, to distant computers anywhere in the world.

Newspapers will disappear when we can get any type of news or book merely by dialling the right channel. The information will flash on the screen and, if you want a full colour copy to file or read elsewhere, you can obtain a written print-out. Microfiche is already taking over from books for storage: it is now possible to keep a whole library in a single filing cabinet. The next stage is micro-chip-based word storage. This new communication revolution, which will have as much impact as the introduction of radio and TV, is still in its early stages. Nevertheless teletext (Ceefax and Oracle in Britain) is already transmitting a limited amount of information over the television channels and the more comprehensive viewdata system (Prestel) makes use of telephone lines.

A more sinister side to these developments is that the technology for George Orwell's 1984 is being created. The Government has the means to process and manipulate citizens within their own homes: all that is missing is the political will to set up a one-party state and a centralized processing system. Big Brother's propaganda could be pumped into every home through the same tele-computers that may be used to monitor the reactions of each citizen on every issue (and record the views of dissidents). Voice lie-detectors have been developed that enable anyone, such as your employer or the police, to check whether you are telling the truth. They operate over the telephone so you may not realize that you are being tested.

What does the State know about you?

A complex system of interlocking computers and data banks already exists to record information about you (see Figure 69).

A changing society

Our society is changing from one that produces goods to one that processes information. This means that it will become increasingly unnecessary to travel to work: it is already possible for those with executive jobs or professional skills to work at home rather than go to a central office building. Eventually it may even be possible for a brain

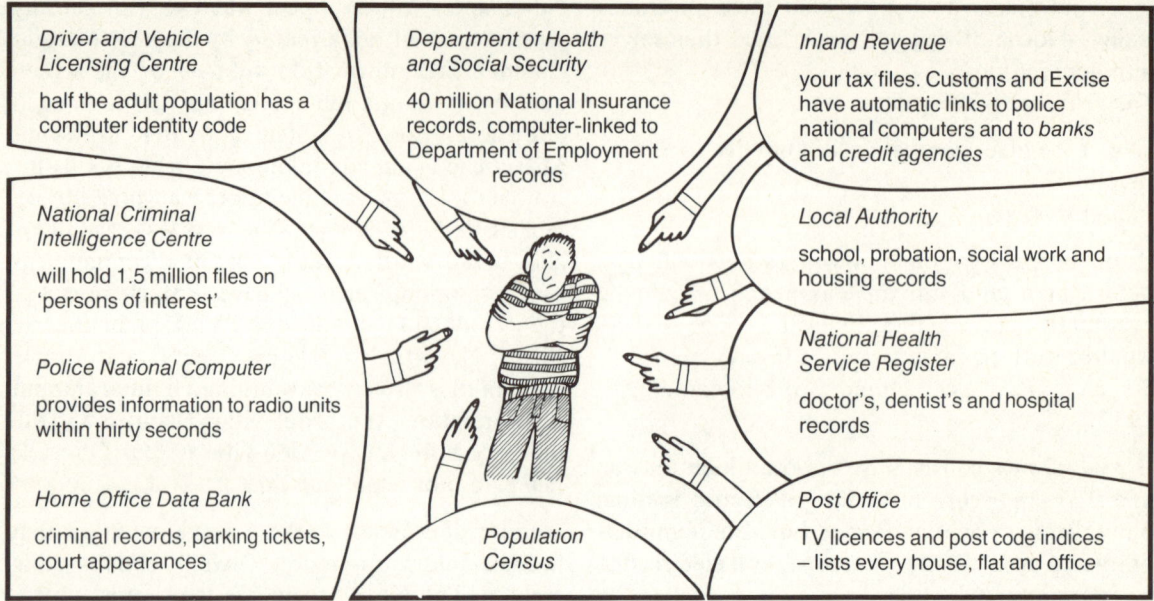

Driver and Vehicle
Licensing Centre

half the adult population has a
computer identity code

Department of Health
and Social Security

40 million National Insurance
records, computer-linked to
Department of Employment
records

Inland Revenue

your tax files. Customs and Excise
have automatic links to police
national computers and to *banks*
and *credit agencies*

National Criminal
Intelligence Centre

will hold 1.5 million files on
'persons of interest'

Police National Computer

provides information to radio units
within thirty seconds

Home Office Data Bank

criminal records, parking tickets,
court appearances

Local Authority

school, probation, social work and
housing records

National Health
Service Register

doctor's, dentist's and hospital
records

Population
Census

Post Office

TV licences and post code indices
– lists every house, flat and office

Figure 69

surgeon to operate on patients all over the world through remote-controlled artificial hands, like those used in nuclear energy plants. People will have far greater freedom to choose where they live, and settle in previously uninhabited areas. On the other hand, people may choose to live in self-sufficient mobile homes, moving round from one beauty spot to another.

Will we all enjoy the benefits of these developments, or are information systems likely to be so expensive that only companies and the rich will have access to them? What about those who cannot afford to pay their electricity bill, let alone buy a computerized TV? What about the old and inadequately educated who will obstinately continue to live in the day before yesterday? What will happen to the old city centres when the information handlers move away to the Scottish Highlands or Cornwall?

Even if there is a great reduction in travel for work, there is likely to be an increase in transportation for leisure. Here are a few developments that we may see:

(i) Electric cars: quiet and less polluting.

(ii) Moving pavements: feasible in busy urban areas.

(iii) Hover trains: magnetic levitation lifts the train two centimetres above the track. It is propelled by a linear induction motor: no friction or vibration.

(iv) Automatic taxis: computer-controlled vehicles running on monorails that could be operated by coins or credit cards.

(v) Sailing ships: a return to wind power as fuel costs rise.

(vi) Air ships: with new materials and improved designs – a come-back for freight transport.

(vii) Pedal power: a person on a bicycle has the highest efficiency rating among all moving animals and machines. In terms of energy consumed in moving a certain distance as a function of body weight, it is more efficient than walking, and it beats express trains and race horses. Swedish engineers have even developed an all-purpose vehicle (a combination of tricycle and wheelbarrow) that can carry heavy loads.

Population

The world population explosion has resulted from a reduction of the death rate rather than an increase in the birth rate.

The number of people in the world is going to reach seven billion in the next thirty years and there is absolutely nothing that anybody can do to stop it. Even the most spectacular, sustained and successful family planning programme imaginable could only slow down an even more dramatic rise in numbers during the twenty-first century.

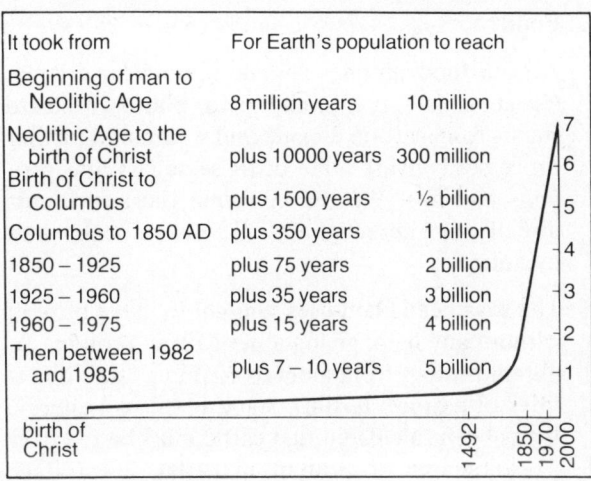

It took from		For Earth's population to reach
Beginning of man to Neolithic Age	8 million years	10 million
Neolithic Age to the birth of Christ	plus 10000 years	300 million
Birth of Christ to Columbus	plus 1500 years	½ billion
Columbus to 1850 AD	plus 350 years	1 billion
1850 – 1925	plus 75 years	2 billion
1925 – 1960	plus 35 years	3 billion
1960 – 1975	plus 15 years	4 billion
Then between 1982 and 1985	plus 7 – 10 years	5 billion

Figure 70   *Population versus time*
Source: S. Hartley, *Population: Quantity vs Quality* p.5 (Prentice-Hall 1972)

Self-assessment questions

2   (i)   What is the 'optimum' world population: one, four, seven or ten billions?
   (ii)   If we rule out the inhumane 'solution' of simply allowing the death rate to rise, how might this optimum level be achieved?

3   What might be the consequences if population growth is not brought under control?

4   By the year 2000 there will be fifteen urban areas with populations of 14 millions or more, most of them in the Third World. The largest, Mexico City, will have 31 million inhabitants. What problems are likely to arise in these large urban concentrations?

Cities will go on growing, of course, like dinosaurs – for the same reasons, and with the same results. I can even see the time when only the uneducated and criminal elements are left in the cities; the wars of 2001 may be internal military operations against the decaying concrete jungles. Watching the TV news, I wonder if the preliminary skirmishes may not already have started.

Arthur C. Clarke, *Report on Planet Three and Other Speculations* (Corgi 1972)

5   What will the communities of the future be like?

6   Will some new form of communal living unit replace the traditional family home?

7   Will the trend away from high-rise developments continue?

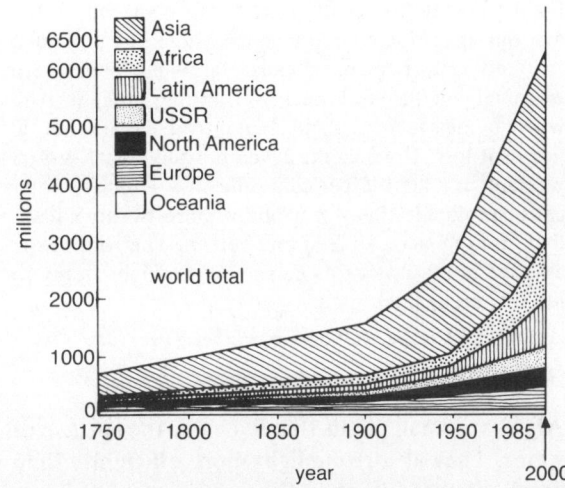

Figure 71   *World population, 1750–2000*
Source: *Population and Labour* (ILO 1973)

8   (i)   Design the kind of living space where you would like to reside by the end of the century (assume that cost is not a problem).
   (ii)   In what ways do you think your home in 2001 will differ from this ideal design?

Food

All our food supplies depend upon solar energy. Green plants use sunlight to photosynthesize sugars from carbon dioxide and water, and further processes convert some of these sugars into proteins and fats. We can consume these nutrients directly, or indirectly, after they have been eaten by animals.

The soya bean plant uses sunlight to make protein without any help, giving a net gain in protein. To obtain protein from animals requires large quantities of pasture, fertilizers and fossil fuel energy. It has been calculated that cattle must be fed over 21 kilograms of protein in order to produce 1 kilogram of beef protein for human consumption. The protein conversion ratio for pork is 8.3, for poultry 5.5, for cow's milk 4.4, for eggs 4.3 and less than 4 for fish. In theory it would be less wasteful if we ate more plants and less meat.

By the twenty-first century, agriculture will be on the way out. It's a ridiculous process: a whole acre is needed to feed one person, because growing plants are extremely inefficient devices for trapping sunlight. And when animals feed on plants, that introduces another 90 per cent loss. If we could develop a biological system working at a mere 5 per cent efficiency – today's solar cells can double that – it would require twenty square feet, not one acre, to feed one person. The roof of the average house intercepts more than enough energy to feed its occupants!

Arthur C. Clarke, *Report on Planet Three and Other Speculations*

Algae are small plants that live near the surface of water. They absorb sunlight more efficiently than more complex plants and grow very quickly. They can be cultivated under controlled conditions and even fertilized with organic waste. If people didn't like the taste, the algae could be fed to pigs or cattle.

Marine farming may be an alternative to marine hunting: it has already been applied successfully to mussels, oysters and lobsters.

Food production is the last major industry to yield to modern technology. The chemical industry is presently investigating the production of proteins from petroleum by microbiological conversion: a similar process to the use of yeast micro-organisms to make alcohol from sugar. It would take only a small proportion of petroleum output to provide enough high-quality proteins to feed the whole of the world's population.

The development of factory farming methods and convenience foods has already led to certain changes in our diet:

(i) Less roughage (fibre) is contained in highly processed foods, such as modern white bread, compared with traditional foods. This has been linked with a greater rate of diseases affecting the digestive system (for example piles, constipation).

(ii) More sugar. We now eat, on average, almost one kilogram of sugar per week each; half of it contained in manufactured foods that we buy (sweets, cakes, biscuits, soft drinks, tinned foods). More sugar means more tooth decay.

(iii) More additives: colouring, flavouring, stabilizers, preservatives, emulsifiers. It is cheaper to make cakes appear buttery and full of eggs by adding small amounts of artificial substitutes than to use real butter and eggs. The long term effects of these chemicals are virtually unknown but sodium nitrate, for instance, present in nearly all processed meat, fish and cheese, forms potential cancer causing agents called nitrosamines. The breast milk of many American mothers would be banned if sold as food because its level of additives from the mother's diet exceeds the permitted amounts.

Self-assessment question

9   (i) Consider your own diet and the menu in the college canteen.
    (ii) What proportion of fresh and unprocessed food does it contain?
    (iii) How could it be improved?

Growing your own food

During the Second World War nearly 1.5 million allotments produced about one-tenth of the food grown in this country. Is there any waste land in your area that could be used for growing food? Food is likely to become more expensive in the future and even a small vegetable patch could supplement your diet (and you would have control over what goes into the food before you eat it).

Material resources

During the early 1970s, a number of studies were published that attempted to predict how long the world's material resources might last. It is difficult to compare their conclusions because each study was based on different assumptions about the future rate of use of resources and the prospects of discovering new reserves. Table 32 lists these assumptions.

Table 32   *The expected year when reserves will be exhausted (according to various assumptions)*

Assumptions about future rate of use	Remains steady at 1965 level		Continues to rise exponentially
Discovery of new reserves	No new reserves discovered after 1965		New reserves are discovered to boost the 1965 reserves by five times
Fossil fuels			
Coal	2880	2076	2115
Petroleum	2000	1985	2015
Natural Gas	1990	1987	2014
Nuclear fuel			
Uranium	1988	—	—
Iron and iron-alloy metals			
Iron	2360	2050	2138
Manganese	2135	2020	—
Nickel	2105	2000	—
Tungsten	2010	2000	2037
Other industrial metals			
Copper	2005	1991	2013
Lead	1985	1982	2029
Zinc	1986	1984	2015
Tin	1992	1982	2026
Aluminium	2130	2003	2020
Precious metals			
Gold	1986	1982	1994
Platinum	1987	1982	—

'There are no substantial limits in sight either in raw materials or in energy that alterations in the price structure, product substitution, anticipated gains in technology and pollution control cannot be expected to solve.'
Frank Notestein

'Virtually no one will argue that material growth on this planet can go on for ever. With almost unlimited nuclear power, recycling resources and mining the most remote reserves the result is still an end to growth before the year 2100 AD.'

Denis Meadows

Self-assessment questions

10   Are the assumptions on which the figures in Table 32 are based reasonable?

11   What has been the pattern of resource use during the 1970s?

12   What major discoveries have occurred since 1965?

13   Are supplies of lead and tin, for instance, virtually exhausted?

14   What are these materials used for?

15   What will life be like without them?

16   How can we make these resources last longer?

Mining more

Our idea of what constitutes a reserve changes over time. During the 1930s it was only economic to mine copper ores containing at least 2 per cent metal, but today ores with about 0.75 per cent copper content are being mined. As metals become increasingly scarce, their market price will rise and it will be commercially worthwhile to extract the less accessible reserves that are presently too expensive. There will be no shortage of minerals as long as we are prepared to pay a high enough price. It is even theoretically possible to exploit extra-terrestrial resources on neighbouring planets and passing asteroids.

Recycling more

Steel, copper, aluminium and lead are already recycled on a large scale. This is relatively easy with large items such as ships, aircraft and railway locomotives. It becomes more difficult and expensive for smaller items of scrap: beer cans and bottle-tops that have become widely dispersed.

The tin content of standard fruit and vegetable cans contaminates the steel and renders it almost useless for recycling with present technology.

Self-assessment question

17   Would it be feasible to store these materials until new techniques are developed?

We dump a million cars a year in Britain, but only about a quarter of this scrap is properly recycled. The practice of recycling *components* as well as materials is already well developed, but it could be extended further if all car manufacturers would agree to use standardized parts that could be inter-changed easily between different makes and models. Bottle banks (strategically placed skips) have been introduced to encourage the recycling of glass. However, more energy is consumed when melting down old bottles and then casting them again into new shapes than to merely sterilize and re-use them. It would be simple to standardize glass bottles and to arrange a deposit system. In Britain we throw away 6000 million glass jars and bottles each year, most of them designed for only one trip. The average milk bottle makes twenty-five trips to households during its life.

Substitution

Alternative materials that are more abundant may be substituted for scarce resources. Lead plumbing is already giving way to plastic pipes and copper telephone cables could be replaced with optical fibres made of glass.

Using less

This could mean that we have to make do with fewer goods, or that we modify products to last longer and waste fewer resources. Nearly 40 per cent of the world's lead production is added to petrol as a cheap way to increase the octane rating, yet it is possible to design cars that operate on non-leaded fuel.

Durable goods should be designed so that they do not break down or wear out as quickly. Until the 1960s the average car lasted for fifteen years but its life is now less than ten years. Greater protection from rust could help cars to last twice as long. Long-lasting light bulbs, mass produced for industrial use, have been suppressed for the domestic market – thus wasting tungsten and rare gases.

Advertising is designed to stimulate demand: we are encouraged to want the latest model or the newest gadget. Useful items such as clothes are often discarded simply because they are no longer 'in fashion'. Moreover, the development of self-service shopping has resulted in an emphasis on packaging as a means of selling the product (for example plastic bubble-packs). Does toothpaste need to be sold in a box and a paper bag as well as a metal tube?

We are accustomed to the convenience of throw-away cans, cartons and wrappers. It is not surprising that packaging now constitutes about half of all waste. In addition to using resources, packaging increases the price of the product. Plastic bags cost twice as much to make from ethylene gas as paper bags from recycled pulp. Is it worth paying an extra ten pence or more for the convenience of an aerosol can rather than applying the substance by brush, rag or hand?

Self-assessment questions

18 What facilities exist in your area for recycling domestic and industrial waste? The separation of waste is one of the most expensive stages of recycling.

19 What provisions exist for householders and firms to separate materials for salvage (that is, metals, rags, glass, paper)?
We each dump, on average, about one kilogram of rubbish per day.

20 What policy does your local authority have for reclaiming waste?

21 What alternative uses can you think of for the materials that you throw away (for example, organic waste for garden compost)?

22 What substitutes are available for rare materials that are in common use?

23 How could manufacturers improve the design of consumer goods to ensure that they last longer?

24 What savings can we make in our use of materials?

25 Would using less involve a reduction in our standard of living?

26 In the USA the packaging industry consumes 75 per cent of all glass production, 40 per cent of paper, 29 per cent of plastic, 14 per cent of aluminium and 8 per cent of steel. What disposable items could be eliminated in Britain and how?

27 How could you persuade your local supermarket to co-operate in a scheme to conserve scarce resources?

Energy resources

Since the Industrial Revolution we have been burning fossil fuels at a massive rate: our technology has been supported by *depletable* resources. During the first seventy-five years of this century, world energy consumption increased ten-fold. We are slowly realizing that our major source of energy will eventually be exhausted and that our economy must adapt to alternative fuels.

Petroleum, which constitutes over half of the capitalist world's primary energy, will reach its peak level of production by the end of the century and then start to decline. It is possible to manufacture synthetic oil from coal, and there are extensive reserves contained in deposits of tar sands and shale oil (although their exploitation involves considerable capital and environmental costs: open cast mining, separation of bituminous content, waste disposal). Depending upon future discoveries and policies for the conservation of existing reserves, petroleum may either run out during your life-time or else last for another 500 years. However, we may be certain that the era of cheap oil is over.

The most controversial alternative to oil is nuclear power. Twenty-five grams of uranium can provide as much energy as 90 tonnes of coal or 400 litres of oil. However, the *thermal reactor* only extracts a small proportion of the potential energy available from the controlled fission of uranium. This process involves bombarding atoms of uranium 235 (a scarce isotope) with neutrons so that they split and send off flying particles to collide with other uranium atoms and thus start a chain reaction. It is possible to obtain greater efficiency from *fast breeder reactors* which burn plutonium (a by-product of thermal reactors) and convert the relatively common uranium 238 into a usable fuel. Hopes are placed on the development of breeder reactors fuelled by thorium which is about five times more abundant than uranium. Nevertheless, severe problems remain unsolved:

(i)   The possibility of accidents, especially in cooling the reaction and storing materials.
(ii) The disposal of radio-active waste.
(iii) The diffusion of radio-activity into the environment.
(iv) The economic costs: a massive input of energy is required before any electricity can be produced.
(v)   The threat to civil liberties resulting from the security measures required to protect nuclear materials from sabotage or theft.
(vi) The spread of nuclear weapons manufactured with plutonium from thermal reactors.

Physicists have long dreamed of harnessing *fusion energy* by causing the nuclei of very light atoms, such as hydrogen, to collide so violently that their major parts stick together. This reaction requires a temperature of 100 million degrees centigrade which no material container can hold: experiments are being carried out with magnetic fields and lasers. Although this process may provide virtually unlimited energy, it is not likely to become a practical possibility before the twenty-first century.

Fortunately abundant supplies of *renewable* energy are available now. These sources are generally replenished at a constant rate by natural processes. The problem remains how to harness these forces.

Solar energy

If we could tap only one per cent of the energy that constantly reaches us from the sun, we could supply all our needs indefinitely. Sunlight may be used directly to heat water (using a sort of central heating radiator in reverse) or employed to generate electricity with photovoltaic cells. Over half of the sun's energy is absorbed by the atmosphere or reflected back into space. However, an orbiting satellite could act as a suntrap to catch light energy (at a rate of 1.3 kilowatts per square metre of surface area) and beam it down to earth as microwaves. The ground stations could transform these radiation microwaves into electricity.

Water power

Rivers have been used for centuries to power water-mills and, more recently, hydro-electric plants. The massive power of the sea with its tides and currents has been virtually ignored. Plans have been drawn up for a barrage across the Severn Estuary and the French have already built a small station on the river Rance which has proved workable and cheap to run. Wave power is less advanced but it is possible to construct a system of hinged rafts or submerged vanes that would capture the up-and-down motion of wave energy and use it to generate electric current.

Geothermal

In several countries power stations are fuelled by steam from natural springs. Over half of Iceland's space heating is directly provided by natural sources of hot water. There are also numerous 'dry hot-spots' beneath the earth's crust. It is possible to drill down to them, then inject water into the heat-well and extract it through pipes.

Waste

The poorest areas of the world already obtain a large proportion of their energy from burning firewood and dried dung. In Britain there is growing interest in production of combustible gas (for example methane) in small fermentation plants fed by kitchen waste, pig slurry and sewage.

Conservation

The future will certainly see a greater variety of energy sources than exist today. One alternative, however, is to make far more efficient use of our reserves of fossil fuels.

Most of the coal and much of the oil and gas that is consumed in Britain is burned to produce electricity. About two-thirds of this primary energy is lost in the process of generation and distribution. Electricity is a very convenient form of energy but its range of uses is limited. Will the future be an all-electric world?

About two-thirds of the heat that we use to warm our homes may be escaping through the roof, walls and windows. How can we insulate houses to conserve energy?

250 million Americans use more fuel for transport than 1300 million Chinese and Indians do for all purposes. The main reasons for this is the wastefulness of the private car: the internal combustion engine produces twice as much heat energy as motion. The efficiency of different forms of passenger transport has been calculated in Table 33.

Self-assessment question

28 (i) What are the problems and possibilities associated with each form of energy?
  (ii) Suggest the most appropriate uses for each one (for example uranium thermal reactors – generation of electricity).

Pollution

Litter, air, water and noise pollution appear to be an inevitable feature of modern living. Industrial operations have been releasing massive quantities of harmful chemicals into the atmosphere for two centuries. Add to this the more recent contribution of the internal combustion engine. It has been estimated that every year British cars emit into the air:

(i)   Six million tonnes of carbon dioxide.
(ii) 300,000 tonnes of unburned hydrocarbons.
(iii) 200,000 tonnes of oxides of nitrogen.
(iv) 20,000 tonnes of sulphur dioxide.
(v)   Huge amounts of tiny, cancer-producing particles of lead, rubber and asbestos.

On Earth the problem had been with cars. The disadvantages involved in pulling lots of black sticky slime from out of the ground where it had been safely hidden out of harm's way, turning it into tar to cover the land with, smoke to fill the air with and pouring the rest into the sea, all seemed to outweigh the advantages of being able to get more quickly from one place to another – particularly when the place you arrived at had probably become, as a result of this, very similar to the place you had left, i.e. covered with tar, full of smoke and short of fish.

Douglas Adams, *The Restaurant at the End of the Universe* (Pan 1980)

The four-fold increase in agricultural productivity in Britain during the past thirty years has been made possible by a much greater growth in the use of fertilizers and pesticides. These chemicals run

---

Table 33

Method	Speed (m.p.h.)	Seat capacity	Assumed occupancy (percentage)	Efficiency: British thermal units per passenger mile
Fast train	100	360	55	980
Bus	50	43	58	1000
747 jet	500	360	55	5900
Motor-car	67	4	50	4100
			(driver only:	8100)

off farmland and infiltrate every niche of the ecosystem, especially water supplies. Over two hundred insect pests throughout the world are already immune to DDT (a complex chemical mixture), and even greater applications of these chemicals will be required in the future because they become less effective at doing the jobs they were designed to do.

Food itself is becoming polluted. Antibiotics are used to prevent the spread of diseases among densely concentrated populations of poultry, pigs and cattle. These substances build up in the tissues of animals, thus reducing our resistance to disease-carrying bacteria which may develop immunity to some of our most useful medical drugs. The higher up the food chain the animal is – and humans are at the top – the more likely it is to accumulate all the contaminants of plants and animals lower down.

Sea water is threatened too: by accidental oil spillage from tankers and by deliberate dumping of untreated sewage, industrial waste products and mildly radio-active coolant water from nuclear reactors.

Law makers are beginning to adopt the principle that polluters must pay for the damage that they cause. A chemical plant, for instance, could be compelled either to install its own water pollution control system or else pay to the local water authority the full cost for treatment of liquid wastes. If the firm could afford neither alternative, it would simply have to close down. In Sweden chemical companies are already required to convince the government that there will be no environmental damage before being permitted to introduce a new process.

However, even the most reasonable of principles can be grossly distorted for narrow political ends. A university researcher, who had been repeatedly refused a grant to investigate pollution in his area caused by a well-known brick company, appealed to the Minister of the Environment. The minister refused the grant on the grounds that 'the polluter must pay' and, therefore, he was not justified in assigning government funds to the project. How-

ever, he was not prepared to force the offending brickworks to finance any such research either.

Self-assessment questions

29 Is pollution likely to become better or worse in the future?

30 Who are the major polluters in your area?

31 How can they be made to stop?

Work and leisure

Self-assessment questions

32 What will be the consequences of new technology?

33 What existing skills and occupations are likely to be replaced by automated systems?

34 What new trades and industries will arise in the future?

We generally assume that there will be more leisure time in the future. Probably you will spend your spare time repairing the household robot once you have finished the overtime required to finance the repayments on the telecomputer and hover-car.

No new animals have been domesticated since Neolithic times. Dolphins are already being trained to help us exploit the sea's resources. Perhaps the combination of genetic engineering and psychological training techniques will result in a new breed of ape that will work for us as a household servant.

How will we spend our leisure time in the future? In active and creative activities such as gardening, crafts and music making? Or in pastimes requiring little thought: spectator sports, TV, drug-taking, etc.?

We will certainly need to change our attitude to work. In both the developed and under-developed world there are millions of people without jobs. At the same time there is plenty of work that needs to be done: growing more food: building new homes;

improving our environment; caring for the elderly, sick and disabled.

Self-assessment questions

35 How can we end this wastage of human skills and energy?

36 Why do people dislike 'work' while undertaking more difficult and exhausting tasks as 'recreation'?

What next?

The most imaginative visions of the future have come from science fiction writers. Their past predictions have generally proved both as precisely accurate and as wildly off-target as those of any other group: scientists, politicians, teachers, etc. At its best, science fiction achieves an ingenious blend of fantasy and scientific knowledge, reflecting contemporary issues long before the general public is aware of them. But prediction is of little value on its own: we all have a part to play in *making* the future as well.

Decisions are being taken today that will shape tomorrow's world. For instance, the decision to spend £155 millions on research into nuclear power compared with only £4 millions on all other energy sources, makes it far more likely that Britain will have a nuclear future.

Self-assessment questions

37 What other important decisions are being taken by governments, planners, industrialists, workers, consumers, young people?

38 What effects will these decisions have during the next ten years?

39 Are they likely to produce a future that you want to live in?

40 What are you going to do about it?

Further reading

Section 1

Asimov, I., *Asimov's Guide to Science* (Penguin 1975)
Bronowski, J., *The Ascent of Man* (BBC Publications 1973)
Leakey, R. E., *Origins* (Macdonald & Jane's 1977)

Section 2

Berger, J., *Ways of Seeing* (BBC and Penguin 1972)
Postman, N., and Weingartner, C., *Teaching as a Subversive Activity* (Penguin 1971)
Rogers, J., *Foreign Places, Foreign Faces* (Connexions Series, Penguin 1970)

Section 3

Barnes-Gutteridge, W., *Psychology* (Hamlyn 1974)
Buzan, T., *Use your Head* (BBC Publications 1974)
Harris, T. A., *I'm OK – You're OK* (Pan 1973)
Payne, J., *All in the Mind* (Standpoints Series, Oxford University Press 1976)
Sagan, C., *Dragons of Eden: speculations on the evolution of human intelligence* (Hodder & Stoughton 1978)
Skurnik, L. S., and George F., *Psychology for Everyman* (Pelican 1964)

Section 4

Davies, M. J., and King, B. J., *Discovering Society: a first course in sociology* (National Extension College 1979)

Section 5

Adams, C., and Laurikietis, R., *The Gender Trap: a closer look at sex roles* (Virago 1976)
Conger, J., *Adolescence: generation under pressure* (Harper & Row, Life Cycle Series 1975)
Gillott, J., *For Better, For Worse* (Connexions Series, Penguin 1971)
Groombridge, J., *His and Hers* (Connexions Series, Penguin 1971)

Hansen, S., and Jensen, J., *The Little Red School Book* (Stage 1, 1971)
Jones, A., Marsh, J., and Watts, A. G., *Male and Female* (Careers Research and Advisory Centre 1974)

Section 6

Tolfree, W. R., *Money: the facts of life* (Martin Books 1980)
The Way the Money Goes (BBC Publications 1978)

Section 7

Agricola, G., *De Re Metallica* (New York Dover Publications 1950). Translated from the Latin edition of 1556. Useful for its detailed illustrations of sixteenth-century machinery.
Bono, E. De., *Eureka!* (Thames & Hudson 1974)
Burke, J., *Connections* (Macmillan 1978)
Derry, T. K., and Williams, T. I., *A Short History of Technology* (Oxford University Press 1960)
Encyclopaedia Britannica, Macropaedia Volume 18: article by R. A. Buchanan, *Technology, History of* (Encyclopaedia Britannica International Ltd 1976)
Greaves, W. F., and Carpenter, J. H., *A Short History of Mechanical Engineering* (Longmans 1978)
Hodges, H., *Technology in the Ancient World* (Allen Lane 1970)
Lilley, S., *Men, Machines and History* (Lawrence & Wishart 1965)

Section 8

Coote, R. J., *Britain Since 1700* (Longman 1968)
British Social History Series (BBC Television 1974)
The New Technology (Counter Information Services 1980)

Section 9

Benyon, H., *Working for Ford* (Penguin 1973)
Emery, F. E., and Thorsrud, E., *Democracy at Work* (BBC Publications 1976)
Hird, C., *Your Employers' Profits* (Pluto Press 1975)

Kinnersly, P., *The Hazards of Work* (Pluto Press 1974
Terkel, S., *Working* (Penguin 1977)
Ward, C., *Work* (Connexions Series, Penguin 1972)

Section 10

Johnson, E., *Industrial Action* (Arrow 1976)
O'Higgins, P., *Workers' Rights* (Arrow 1976)
Topham, A. J., *Organized Worker* (Arrow 1975)
Twitchin, J., and Matthews, T., *Trade Union Studies, Book 1* (BBC Publications 1975)

Section 11

Donaldson, P., *Illustrated Economics* (BBC Publications 1976)
Schumacher, E. F., *Small is Beautiful: a study of economics as if people mattered* (Sphere 1974)

Section 12

Davies, M. J., and King, B. J., *Discovering Society, Volume 2, Unit 14* and *Volume 3, Unit 15* (National Extension College 1978)
Thompson, J. L., *Studying Society* (Hutchinson 1978)

Section 13

Civil Liberty: The NCCL guide to your rights (Penguin 1978)
Greenoak, F., *What Right Have You Got?, Parts 1 and 2* (BBC Publications 1976 and 1977)
Hodge, H., *Legal Rights* (Arrow 1976)
Roshier, R. J., and Cootes, R. J., *Crime and Punishment* (Longman 1976)

Section 14

The Good Beer Guide (Campaign for Real Ale 1981)
Young, J., *The Drug Takers* (Pelican 1980)

Section 15

Cox, J., *On the Warpath* (Oxford University Press 1976)
The Europa Year Book: A world survey (Europa Publications 1983)
George, S., *How the Other Half Dies* (Pelican 1977)
Kidron, M., and Segal, R., *The State of the World Arts* (Pluto Press/Pan 1981)
New Internationalist (a magazine published monthly)
Protect and Survive (HMSO 1980)
Thompson, E. P., *Protest and Survive* (Spokesman pamphlet 1980)
The War Game (a film directed by Peter Watkins, available from CND, Eastbourne House, Bullards Place, London E2 0PT)

Section 16

Allsop, K., *Fit to Live in?* (Connexions Series, Penguin 1970)
Calder, N., *Living Tomorrow* (Connexions Series, Penguin 1970)
George, F., *Science Fact* (Topaz Books 1977)
Gribbin, J., *Future Worlds* (Abacus 1979)
The Little Green Book – an owner's manual to the planet (Green Alliance 1979)
Merrill, R., and Gage, T., *Energy Primer: solar, water, and biofuels* (Dell Publishing Co. Inc. 1978)
The Nuclear Disaster (Counter Information Services 1980)

Index

Hutchinson TECtexts
– objectively the best!! –

Engineering Drawing and Communication
First Level
P. Collier and R. Wilson

09 133591 4   192 pages

Physical Science
First Level
A. D. Carroll, J. E. Duggan and R. Etchells

'... as with the others (in this series), the book is well and copiously illustrated, attractively printed and lucidly written ... a worthwhile addition to the shelf of any lecturer involved in the TEC courses – as well as being a useful student text.'
NATFHE Journal

09 133581 7   288 pages

Workshop Processes and Materials
First Level
P. Collier and B. Parkinson

09 140491 6   208 pages

Electronics
Second Level
G. Billups and M. T. Sampson

09 133331 8   192 pages

Engineering Drawing
Second Level
P. Collier and R. Wilson

09 146611 3   240 pages

Engineering Science
Second Level
D. Tipler, A. D. Carroll and R. Etchells

09 138371 4   256 pages

Mathematics
Second Level
G. W. Allan and A. Hill

09 138101 0   310 pages

Site Surveying and Levelling
Second Level
J. Pettet

09 143621 4   128 pages

Electronics
Third Level
G. Billups and M. T. Sampson

09 140341 3   176 pages

Communication Skills
P. Panton

This book covers the broad learning objectives which the student has to achieve in order to satisfy the communication requirements of all levels of TEC programmes. The book contains many self-assessment exercises, thereby making it particularly suitable for technicians and managers who have passed beyond the stage of formal study, but who may still want to improve their ability to communicate.

09 141281 1   120 pages

TEC Microelectronics Books

These books comprise a series of microelectronics/microprocessors published by Hutchinson in association with the Technician Education Council. These titles have been written and designed for use with units associated with Technician Education Council programmes.

The series itself evolved through an initiative from the Department of Industry and the National Enterprise Board to encourage the use and development of microprocessor technology. An important aspect of such a development programme was seen as being the education and training of personnel for both the research, development and manufacture of microelectronics material and equipment, and the application of these in other industries.

In 1979 a project was established by the Technician Education Council for the development of technician education programme units and associated textbooks, this project being funded by the Department of Industry and managed on their behalf by the National Computing Centre Ltd.

The seven titles to be published by Hutchinson are the 'fruits' of the TEC project. Each title has been written and approved by TEC itself – the first time that the Council has co-published such books with an outside publisher.

Five of the titles are for units to be introduced into the A2 (Electronics and Communication Engineering) programme in autumn 1982. These are units for technicians and technician engineers concerned with the design, manufacture and servicing aspects incorporating microelectronic devices.

Microelectronic Systems Level I (U79/602)
Microelectronic Systems Level II (U79/603)
Microelectronic Systems Level III (U79/604)
Microprocessor-based Systems Level IV (U80/674)
Microprocessor-based Systems Level V (U80/675)

The two remaining titles are for those technicians (for example, in the A5 Mechanical and Production sector) who require general understanding of the range of applications of microelectronic devices and their potential.

Microprocessor Appreciation Level III (U79/639)
Microprocessor Principles Level IV (U79/640)